Agile Artificial Intelligence in Pharo

Implementing Neural Networks, Genetic Algorithms, and Neuroevolution

Alexandre Bergel

Apress®

Agile Artificial Intelligence in Pharo: Implementing Neural Networks, Genetic Algorithms, and Neuroevolution

Alexandre Bergel
Santiago, Chile

ISBN-13 (pbk): 978-1-4842-5383-0   ISBN-13 (electronic): 978-1-4842-5384-7
https://doi.org/10.1007/978-1-4842-5384-7

Managing Director, Apress Media LLC: Welmoed Spahr
Acquisitions Editor: Steve Anglin
Development Editor: Matthew Moodie
Coordinating Editor: Mark Powers

Cover designed by eStudioCalamar

Cover image designed by Freepik (www.freepik.com)

Distributed to the book trade worldwide by Apress Media, LLC, 1 New York Plaza, New York, NY 10004, U.S.A. Phone 1-800-SPRINGER, fax (201) 348-4505, e-mail orders-ny@springer-sbm.com, or visit www.springeronline.com. Apress Media, LLC is a California LLC and the sole member (owner) is Springer Science + Business Media Finance Inc (SSBM Finance Inc). SSBM Finance Inc is a **Delaware** corporation.

For information on translations, please e-mail editorial@apress.com; for reprint, paperback, or audio rights, please email bookpermissions@springernature.com.

Apress titles may be purchased in bulk for academic, corporate, or promotional use. eBook versions and licenses are also available for most titles. For more information, reference our Print and eBook Bulk Sales web page at http://www.apress.com/bulk-sales.

Any source code or other supplementary material referenced by the author in this book is available to readers on GitHub via the book's product page, located at www.apress.com/9781484253830. For more detailed information, please visit http://www.apress.com/source-code.

Printed on acid-free paper

Table of Contents

About the Author

Alexandre Bergel, Ph.D., is a professor (associate) at the Department of Computer Science (DCC), at the University of Chile and is a member of the Intelligent Software Construction laboratory (ISCLab). His research interests include software engineering, software performance, software visualization, programming environment, and machine learning. He is interested in improving the way we build and maintain software. His current hypotheses are validated using rigorous empirical methodologies. To make his research artifacts useful not only to stack papers, he co-founded Object Profile.

About the Technical Reviewer

 **Jason Whitehorn** is an experienced entrepreneur and software developer and has helped many companies automate and enhance their business solutions through data synchronization, SaaS architecture, and machine learning. Jason obtained his Bachelor of Science in Computer Science from Arkansas State University, but he traces his passion for development back many years before then, having first taught himself to program BASIC on his family's computer while in middle school.

When he's not mentoring and helping his team at work, writing, or pursuing one of his many side-projects, Jason enjoys spending time with his wife and four children and living in the Tulsa, Oklahoma region. More information about Jason can be found on his website: `https://jason.whitehorn.us`.

Acknowledgments

Agile Artificial Intelligence in Pharo is the result of a long and collective effort made by the ESUG community and beyond. The writing and the necessary research of the book was sponsored by Lam Research and ESUG. Thank you! You made the book happen!

Many people helped get the book in shape. In no particular order, we are deeply grateful to CH Huang, Chris Thorgrimsson, Milton Mamani, Jhonny Cerezo, Oleks Zaytsev, Stéphane Ducasse, Torsten Bergmann, Serge Stinckwich, Alexandre Rousseau, Sean P. DeNigris, Julián Grigera, Cesar Rabak, Yvan Guemkam, John Borden, Sudhakar Krishnamachari, Leandro Caniglia, mldavis99, darth-cheney, Andy S., Jon Paynter, Esteban Lorenzano, Juan-Pablo Silva, Francisco Ary Martins, Norbert Fortelny, forty, Sebastián Zapata, and Renato Cerro.

Publishing a book involves some legal aspects that need to be carefully considered. We thank Fernanda Carvajal Gezan and Rosa Leal, from the University of Chile.

We also thank the Apress team for trusting in the project and thank Jason Whitehorn, who tech-reviewed the book.

Introduction

Artificial Intelligence (AI) is radically changing the way we use computers to solve problems. For example, by exploiting previous experience, which may be expressed in terms of examples, a machine can identify patterns in a given situation and try to identify the same patterns in a slightly different situation. This is essentially the way AI is used nowadays. The field of AI is moving quickly, and unfortunately, it is often difficult to understand.

The objective of the *Agile Artificial Intelligence in Pharo* book is to provide a practical foundation for a set of expressive artificial intelligence algorithms using the Pharo programming language. The book makes two large contributions over existing related books. The first contribution is to bring agility in the way some techniques related to artificial intelligence are designed, implemented, and evaluated. The book provides material in an incremental fashion, beginning with a little perception and ending with a full implementation of two algorithms for neuroevolution.

The second contribution is about making these techniques accessible to programmers by detailing their implementation without overwhelming the reader with mathematical material. There is often a significant gap between reading mathematical formulas and producing executable source code from those formulas, unfortunately. The book is meant to be accessible to a large audience by focusing on executable source code.

Overall, this book details and illustrates some easy-to-use recipes to solve actual problems. Furthermore, it highlights some technical details of these recipes using the Pharo programming language. *Agile Artificial Intelligence in Pharo* is not a book about how to use an existing API provided by external libraries. Instead, this book guides you to build your own API for artificial intelligence.

Book Overview

Agile Artificial Intelligence in Pharo is divided into three parts, each targeting a specific topic within the field of artificial intelligence—neural networks, genetic algorithms, and neuroevolution.

The first part of the book is about *neural networks*. A neural network is a computational metaphor simulating the interaction occurring between biological neurons. The chapter begins with the implementation of a single neuron and shows its limitations in terms of what it can achieve. Neural networks are then presented to solve more complex problems. Various examples involving relatively simple data classification tasks are presented.

The second part of the book covers *genetic algorithms* (GAs). The GA is a computational metaphor simulating the evolution occurring in biological species. GAs provide a way to solve problems without knowing the structure and shape of the solution in advance. GAs simulate the way biological species evolve over time. For two candidate solutions, as soon as the machine is able to say which one is closer to the solution, then GAs may be considered to solve the problem. Numerous examples are provided in this second part of the book, including an implementation of zoomorphic creatures, which is a simulation of artificial life. We define a zoomorphic creature as an artificial organism able to evolve in order to move itself through obstacles.

The third part of the book covers the field of *neuroevolution*, which is a combination of genetic algorithms and neural networks. The evolution of neural networks is called neuroevolution. Instead of *training a* neural network, as in classical deep learning (Part 1 of the book), neuroevolution begins with extremely simple networks and incrementally adds complexity to them. Evolution makes those networks able to solve particular tasks. This third part uses a Mario Bros-like game, which is used to build an artificial player using neuroevolution.

Installing Pharo

Pharo works on the three common platforms, Mac OSX, Windows, and Linux. The web page at https://pharo.org/download gives a very detailed instruction set and some links to download Pharo. Pharo is easy to install. Just a matter of a few clicks.

The content of the book is known to work up until Pharo 9. The code provided in the book does not heavily rely on the Pharo runtime. So the code provided in this book should be easy to adapt to future versions of Pharo or to another dialect of Smalltalk.

Accompanying Source Code

Agile Artificial Intelligence in Pharo is a book about programming. It provides and details a sizable amount of source code. Most of the code in the book is self-contained. This means that no external libraries are used besides the Pharo core and the Roassal visualization engine. Roassal is used to visually explore data and build a user interface. Readers may prefer to transcribe the code into Pharo or use our dedicated Git repository at https://github.com/Apress/agile-ai-in-pharo.

A script that begins with ellipses (i.e., ...) means that you need to append the script to the last one seen before.

The code provided in this book is known to run on Pharo 8 and 9. To load the code, you simply need to open a playground and execute the following code:

```
Metacello new
        baseline: 'AgileArtificialIntelligence';
        repository: 'github://Apress/agile-ai-in-pharo/src';
        load.
```

The GitHub repository contains the scripts folder, which contains all the scripts and code snippets provided in the book.

The book focuses on Pharo; however, at the cost of a few small adaptations, all the provided code will run on an alternative Smalltalk implementation (e.g., VisualWorks).

Who Should Read This Book?

This book is designed to be read by a wide audience of programmers. As such, there is no need to have prior knowledge of neural networks, genetic algorithms, or neuroevolution. There is even no need to have a strong mathematical background. We made sure that there is no such prerequisite for most of the chapters. Some chapters require mild mathematical knowledge. However, these chapters are self-contained and skipping them will not negatively affect your overall understanding.

The book exposes some sophisticated AI techniques through the lenses of Pharo. Readers will acquire the theoretical and practical tools to be used in Pharo. Note that people willing to learn Pharo through AI are encouraged to complement it with additional sources of information.

The book is not made for people who want to learn about AI techniques without heavily investing in a programming activity. Instead, *Agile Artificial Intelligence in Pharo* is made for programmers who are either familiar with Pharo or are willing to be.

The Pharo Experience

The code provided in this book uses the Pharo programming environment. Programming in Pharo is a fantastic and emotional experience. Literally. Pharo gives meaning to Agile programming that cannot be experienced in another programming language, or at least, not to the same degree. We will try to convey this wonderful experience to the readers.

Pharo has a very simple syntax, which means that code should be understandable as soon as you have some programming knowledge. Chapter 2 briefly introduces the Pharo programming language and its environment in case you want to be familiar with it.

Why did we pick Pharo for this book? Pharo is a beautiful programming language with a sophisticated environment. It also provides a new way of communication between a human and a machine. By offering a live programming environment and a language with minimal syntax, programmers may express their thoughts in an incremental and open fashion. Although a number of similar programming environments exist (e.g., Scratch and Squeak), Pharo is designed to be used in an industrial software development setting.

Pharo syntax is concise, simple, unambiguous, and requires very little explanation to be fully understood. If you do not know Pharo, we encourage you to become familiar with the basics of its syntax and programming environment. Chapter 2 should help in that respect. The debugger, inspector, and playground are unrivaled compared to other programming languages and environments. Using these tools really brings an unmatchable feeling when programming.

Additional Reading

Agile Artificial Intelligence in Pharo provides a gentle introduction to Pharo in Chapter 2. However, the presentation of Pharo is shallow and not complete. Readers who do not know Pharo and but have experience in programming may find the chapter to be enough. Readers who want to deepen their knowledge may want to look for additional sources of learning. Here are some good readings on Pharo:

- `http://pharo.org` is the official website about Pharo.

- `https://mooc.pharo.org` is probably the most popular way to learn Pharo. It provides many short videos covering various aspects of Pharo.

- `http://books.pharo.org` offers many valuable books and booklets on Pharo.

- `http://agilevisualization.com` describes the Roassal visualization engine, which also contains a gentle introduction to Pharo.

Visualization is omnipresent in *Agile Artificial Intelligence in Pharo*. Roassal is used in many chapters and the reader is welcome to read *Agile Visualization* to become familiar with this wonderful visualization toolkit.

PART I

Neural Networks

CHAPTER 1

The Perceptron Model

All major animal groups have brains made of neurons. A *neuron* is a specialized cell that transmits electrochemical stimulation using an axon to other neurons. A neuron receives this nerve impulse via a *dendrite*. Since the early age of computers, scientists have tried to produce a computational model of a neuron. The perceptron was one of the first models to mimic the behavior of a neuron.

This chapter plays two essential roles in the book. First, it presents the *perceptron*, a fundamental model on which neural networks are based. Second, it also provides a gentle introduction to the Pharo programming language. The chapter builds a simple perceptron model in Pharo.

1.1 Perceptron as a Kind of Neuron

A perceptron is a kind of artificial neuron that models the behavior of a biological neuron. A perceptron is a machine that produces an output for a provided set of input values. Figure 1-1 gives a visual representation of a perceptron.

A perceptron accepts one, two, or more numerical values as inputs. It produces a numerical value as output (the result of a simple equation that we will see shortly). A perceptron operates on numbers, which means that the inputs and the output are numerical values (e.g., integers or floating point values).

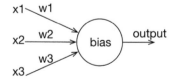

Figure 1-1. *Representing the perceptron*

© Alexandre Bergel 2020
A. Bergel, *Agile Artificial Intelligence in Pharo*, https://doi.org/10.1007/978-1-4842-5384-7_1

Figure 1-1 depicts a perceptron. A perceptron is usually represented as a circle with some inputs and one output. Inputs are represented as incoming arrows located on the left of the central circle and the output as an outgoing arrow on the right of it. The perceptron in Figure 1-1 has three inputs, noted x1, x2, and x3.

Not all inputs have the same importance for the perceptron. For example, an input may be more important than other inputs. Relevance of an input is expressed using a weight (also a numerical value) associated with that input. In Figure 1-1, the input x1 is associated with the weight w1, x2 with the weight w2, and x3 with w3. Different relevancies of some inputs allow the network to model a specialized behavior. For example, for an image-recognition task, pixels located at the border of the picture usually have less relevance than the pixels located in the middle. Weights associated with the inputs corresponding to the border pixels will therefore be rather close to zero. In addition to the weighted input value, a perceptron requires a *bias*, a numerical value acting as a threshold. We denote the bias as b.

A perceptron receives a stimulus as input and responds to that stimulus by producing an output value. The output obeys a very simple rule: if the sum of the weighted inputs is above a particular given value, then the perceptron fires 1; otherwise, it fires 0. Programmatically, we first compute the sum of the weighted inputs and the bias. If this sum is strictly above 0, then the perceptron produces 1; otherwise, it produces 0.

Formally, based on the perceptron given in Figure 1-1, we write z = x1 * w1 + x2 * w2 + x3 * w3 + b. In the general case, we write $z = \Sigma_i \ x_i \ * \ w_i \ + \ b$. The variable i ranges over all the inputs of the perceptron. If z > 0, then the perceptron produces 1 or if z ≤ 0, it produces 0.

In the next section, we will implement a perceptron model that is both extensible and maintainable. You may wonder what the big deal is. After all, the perceptron model may be implemented in a few lines of code. However, implementing the perceptron functionality is just a fraction of the job. Creating a perceptron model that is testable, well tested, and extensible is the real value of this chapter. Soon will see how to train a network of artificial neurons, and it is important to build this network framework on a solid base.

1.2 Implementing the Perceptron

In this section, we will put our hands to work and implement the perceptron model in the Pharo programming language. We will produce an object-oriented implementation of the model. We will implement a class called Neuron in a package called NeuralNetwork. The class will have a method called feed, which will be used to compute two values—z and the perceptron output.

This code will be contained in a package. To create a new package, you first need to open a *system browser* by selecting the corresponding entry in the Pharo menu. The system browser is an essential tool in Pharo. It allows us to read and write code. Most of the programming activity in Pharo typically happens in a system browser.

Figure 1-2 shows a system browser, which is composed of five different parts. The top part is composed of four lists. The left-most list gives the available and ready-to-be-used packages. In Figure 1-2, the names Announcement, AST-Core and Alien are examples of packages. The Announcement package is selected in the figure.

The second list gives the classes that belong to the selected package. Many classes are part of the Announcement package, including the classes called Announcement, AnnouncementSet, and Announcer.

The third list shows the method categories of the selected class. Method categories sort methods into logical groups to clarify their purpose and make them easier to find. Think of them as a kind of package for methods. Since no class is selected in the figure, no method category is listed.

The right-most list shows the methods of the selected class, filtered by the selected method category if any. Since no class is selected, no methods are listed. The bottom part of a system browser displays source code, which is one of the following:

Selection	Code Displayed
Method	Selected method source code
Class	Selected class definition
None	New class template

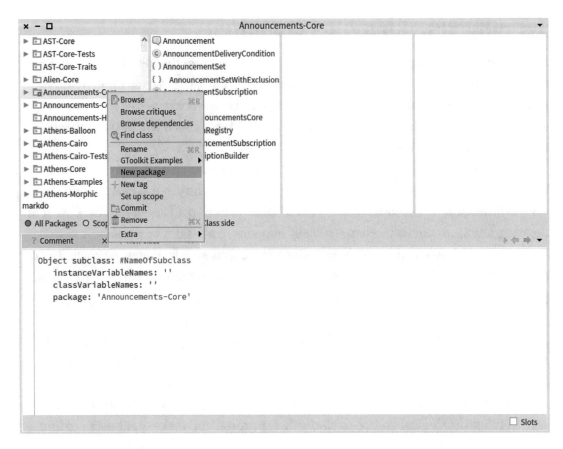

Figure 1-2. *The Pharo system browser*

Right-click the left-most top list to create a new package, named NeuralNetwork. This package will contain most of the code we will write in this first part of the book.

Select the package NeuralNetwork you just created and modify the template in the bottom pane as follows:

```
Object subclass: #Neuron
        instanceVariableNames: 'weights bias'
        classVariableNames: ''
        package: 'NeuralNetwork'
```

You then need to compile the code by "accepting" the source code. Right-click the text pane and select the Accept option. The Neuron class defines two instance variables—weights and bias. Note that we do not need to have variables for the inputs and output values. These values will be provided as message arguments and returned values. We need to add some methods to define the logic of this perceptron. In particular, we need to compute the intermediate z and the output values. Let's first focus on the `weights` variable. We will define two methods to write a value in that variable and another one to read from it.

You may wonder why we define a class called `Neuron` and not `Perceptron`. In the next chapter, we will extend the `Neuron` class by turning it into an open abstraction for an artificial neuron. This `Neuron` class is therefore a placeholder for improvements we will make in the subsequent chapters. In this chapter we consider a perceptron, but in the coming chapter we will move toward an abstract neuron implementation. The name `Neuron` is therefore better suited.

Here is the code of the `weights:` method defined in the `Neuron` class:

```
Neuron>>weights: someWeightsAsNumbers
    "Set the weights of the neuron.
    Takes a collection of numbers as argument."
    weights := someWeightsAsNumbers
```

To define this method, you need to select the `Neuron` class in the class panel (second top list panel). Then, write the code given *without* `Neuron>>`, which is often prepended in documentation to indicate the class that should host the method. It is not needed in the browser because the class is selected in the top pane. Figure 1-3 illustrates this. Next, you should accept the code (again by right-clicking the `Accept` menu item). In Pharo jargon, accepting a method has the effect of actually compiling it (i.e., using the Pharo compiler to translate the Pharo source code into some bytecodes understandable by the Pharo virtual machine). Once it's compiled, a method may be executed. The code defines the method named called `weights:` which accepts one argument, provided as a variable named `someWeightsAsNumbers`.

The `weights := someWeightsAsNumbers` expression assigns the value `someWeightsAsNumbers` to the variable `weights`.

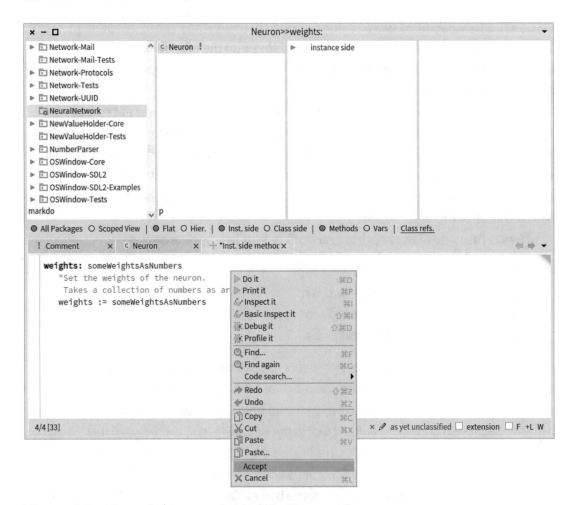

Figure 1-3. *The* weights: *method of the Neuron class*

Your system browser should now look like Figure 1-3. The weights: method writes a value to the variable weights. Its sibling method that returns the weight is

```
Neuron>>weights
    "Return the weights of the neuron."
    ^ weights
```

The ^ character returns the value of an expression, in this case the value of the variable weights.

Similarly, you need to define methods to assign a value to the bias variable and to read its content. The method bias: is defined as follows:

```
Neuron>>bias: aNumber
    "Set the bias of the neuron"
    bias := aNumber
```

Reading the variable bias is provided by the following:

```
Neuron>>bias
    "Return the bias of the neuron"
    ^ bias
```

So far, we have defined the Neuron class, which contains two variables (weights and bias), and four methods (weights:, weights, bias:, and bias). We now need to define the logic of this perceptron by applying a set of input values and obtaining the output value. Let's add a feed: method that does exactly this small computation:

```
Neuron>>feed: inputs
    | z |
    z := (inputs with: weights collect: [ :x :w | x * w ]) sum + bias.
    ^ z > 0 ifTrue: [ 1 ] ifFalse: [ 0 ].
```

The feed: method simply translates the mathematical perceptron activation formula previously discussed into the Pharo programming language. The expression inputs with: weights collect: [:x :w | x * w] transforms the inputs and weights collections using the supplied function. Consider the following example:

```
#(1 2 3) with: #(10 20 30) collect: [ :a :b | a + b ]
```

The expression #(1 2 3) is an array made of three numbers—1, 2, and 3. The expression evaluates to #(11 22 33). Syntactically, the expression means that the literal value #(1 2 3) receives a message called with:collect: with two arguments, the literal array #(10 20 30) and the block [:a :b | a + b]. You can verify the value of that expression by opening a playground (accessible from the Tools top menu). A playground is a kind of command terminal for Pharo (e.g., xterm in the UNIX world). Figure 1-4 illustrates the evaluation of the expression (evaluated either by choosing Print It from the right-click menu or using the adequate shortcut—Cmd+p on OSX or Alt+p on other operating systems).

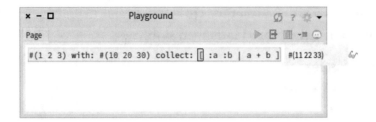

Figure 1-4. *The playground*

We can now play a little bit with the perceptron and evaluate the following code in the playground we just opened:

```
p := Neuron new.
p weights: #(1 2).
p bias: -2.
p feed: #(5 2)
```

This piece of code evaluates to 1 (since (5*1 + 2*2)-2 equals to 7, which is greater than 0), as shown in Figure 1-5.

Figure 1-5. *Evaluating the perceptron*

1.3 Testing the Code

Now it is time to talk about testing. Testing is an essential activity whenever we write code using Agile methodologies. Testing is about raising the confidence that the code we write does what it is supposed to do.

Although this book is not about writing large software artifacts, we *do* write source code. And making sure that this code can be tested in an automatic fashion significantly improves the quality of our work. More importantly, most code is read far more often than it is written. Testing helps us produce maintainable and adaptable code. Throughout this book, we will improve our code base. It is very important to make sure that our improvements do not break existing functionalities.

For example, we previously defined a perceptron and informally tested it in a playground. This informal test costs us a few keystrokes and a little bit of time. What if we could repeat this test each time we modified our definition of perceptron? This is exactly what *unit testing* is all about.

We will now leave the playground for a while and return to the system browser to define a class called `PerceptronTest`:

```
TestCase subclass: #PerceptronTest
    instanceVariableNames: ''
    classVariableNames: ''
    package: 'NeuralNetwork'
```

The `TestCase` class belongs to the built-in Pharo code base. Subclassing it is the first step to creating a unit test. Many perceptrons will be created by the tests we define. We can define the method as follows:

```
PerceptronTest>>newNeuron
    "Return a new neuron"
    ^ Neuron new
```

Tests can now be added to `PerceptronTest`. Define the following method:

```
PerceptronTest>>testSmallExample
    | p result |
    p := self newNeuron.
    p weights: #(1 2).
    p bias: -2.
    result := p feed: #(5 2).
    self assert: result equals: 1.
```

The `testSmallExample` method tests that the code snippet we previously gave returns the value 1. You can run the test by clicking the gray circle located next to the method name. The gray circle turns green to indicate that the test passes (see Figure 1-6).

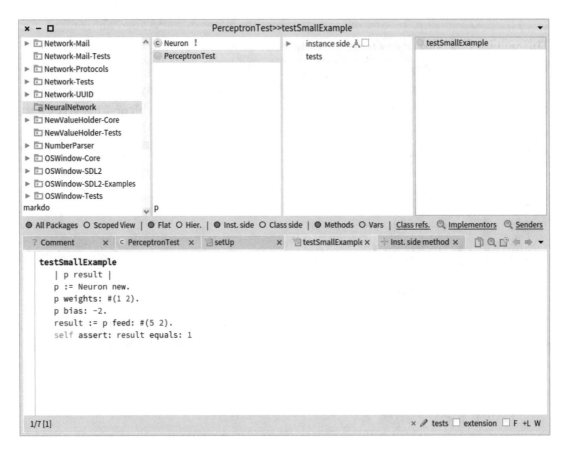

Figure 1-6. *Testing the perceptron*

A green test means that no assertion failed and no error was raised during the test execution. The testSmallExample method sends the assert:equals: message, which tests whether the first argument equals the second argument.

EXERCISE: So far, you have only shallowly tested this perceptron. You can improve these tests in two ways:

- Expand testSmallExample by feeding the perceptron p with different values (e.g., -2 and 2 gives 0 as a result).

- Test the perceptron with different weights and biases.

In general, it is a very good practice to write a thorough suite of tests, even for a small component such as this Neuron class.

1.4 Formulating Logical Expressions

A canonical example of using a perceptron is to express boolean logical gates. The idea is to have a perceptron with two inputs (each being a boolean value), and the result of the modeled logical gate as output.

A little bit of arithmetic indicates that a perceptron with the weights #(1 1) and the bias -1.5 formulates the AND logical gate. Recall that #(1 1) is an array of size 2 that contains the number 1 twice. The AND gate is a basic digital logic gate, and it is an idealized device for implementing the AND boolean function. The AND gate may be represented as the following table:

A	B	A AND B
0	0	0
0	1	0
1	0	0
1	1	1

We could therefore verify this with a new test method:

```
PerceptronTest>>testAND
    | p |
    p := self newNeuron.
    p weights: #(1 1).
    p bias: -1.5.

    self assert: (p feed: #(0 0)) equals: 0.
    self assert: (p feed: #(0 1)) equals: 0.
    self assert: (p feed: #(1 0)) equals: 0.
    self assert: (p feed: #(1 1)) equals: 1.
```

Similarly, a perceptron can formulate the OR logical gate:

A	B	A OR B
0	0	0
0	1	1
1	0	1
1	1	1

Consider the following test:

```
PerceptronTest>>testOR
    | p |
    p := self newNeuron.
    p weights: #(1 1).
    p bias: -0.5.

    self assert: (p feed: #(0 0)) equals: 0.
    self assert: (p feed: #(0 1)) equals: 1.
    self assert: (p feed: #(1 0)) equals: 1.
    self assert: (p feed: #(1 1)) equals: 1.
```

Negating the weights and bias results in the negated logical gate:

```
PerceptronTest>>testNOR
    | p |
    p := self newNeuron.
    p weights: #(-1 -1).
    p bias: 0.5.

    self assert: (p feed: #(0 0)) equals: 1.
    self assert: (p feed: #(0 1)) equals: 0.
    self assert: (p feed: #(1 0)) equals: 0.
    self assert: (p feed: #(1 1)) equals: 0.
```

So far we have built perceptrons with two inputs. The number of input values has to be the same as the number of weights. Therefore, if only one weight is provided, only one input is required. Consider the NOT logical gate, as follows:

```
PerceptronTest>>testNOT
    | p |
    p := self newNeuron.
    p weights: #(-1).
    p bias: 0.5.

    self assert: (p feed: #(1)) equals: 0.
    self assert: (p feed: #(0)) equals: 1.
```

1.5 Handling Errors

In testNOT, we defined a perceptron with only one weight. The array provided when calling feed: *must* have only one entry. But what would happen if we had two entries instead of one? An error would occur, as we are wrongly using the (small) API we have defined.

You should also test this behavior to make sure errors are properly generated. Define the following test:

```
PerceptronTest>>testWrongFeeding
    | p |
    p := self newNeuron.
    p weights: #(-1).
    p bias: 0.5.

    self should: [ p feed: #(1 1) ] raise: Error
```

The testWrongFeeding test passes only if the expression pfeed: #(1 1) raises an error, which it does.

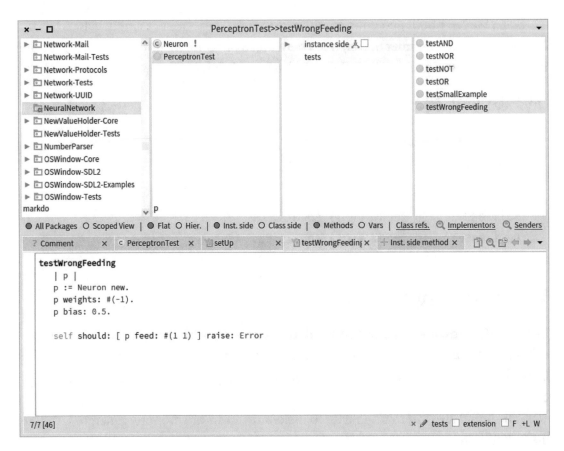

Figure 1-7. *Running the tests*

Until now, we have defined the Neuron class with five methods, and the unit test PerceptronTest with six test methods. You can run these tests by pressing the circle next to the unit test name, PerceptronTest (see Figure 1-7).

It is important to emphasize that rigorously testing your code, which also involves verifying that errors are properly handled, is important when you're implementing a neural network from scratch. Facing errors due to mismatched input sizes and weights is unfortunately too frequent to be lax on that front.

1.6 Combining Perceptrons

Until now, we defined the AND, NOR, NOT, and OR logical gates. Logical gates become interesting when combined. A digital comparator circuit is a combination of two NOT gates with two AND gates and one NOR gate. The overall combination is useful for comparing two values, A and B. There are three possible outcomes:

- A is greater than B

- A is equal to B

- A is less than B

We can therefore model our circuit with two inputs and three outputs. The following table summarizes the circuit:

A	B	A < B	A = B	A > B
0	0	0	1	0
0	1	1	0	0
1	0	0	0	1
1	1	0	1	0

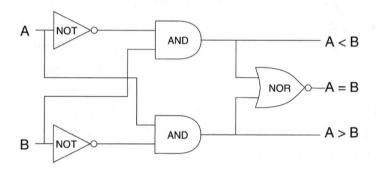

Figure 1-8. *Digital comparator circuit*

Figure 1-8 illustrates the circuit. Three different logical gates are necessary: AND, NOT, and NOR. We need to make the connection between these gates. As we previously did, some tests will drive this effort. The digitalComparator: method, defined in our unit test for convenience, models the digital comparator circuit:

```
PerceptronTest>>digitalComparator: inputs
    "Return an array of three elements"
    | not and nor a b aGb aEb aLb notA notB |
    a := inputs first.
    b := inputs second.
```

```
and := self newNeuron weights: #(1 1); bias: -1.5.
not := self newNeuron weights: #(-1); bias: 0.5.
nor := self newNeuron weights: #(-1 -1); bias: 0.5.
notA := not feed: { a }.
notB := not feed: { b }.

aLb := and feed: { notA . b }.
aGb := and feed: { a . notB }.
aEb := nor feed: { aGb . aLb }.
^ { aGb . aEb . aLb }
```

The method accepts a set of inputs as its argument. We begin by extracting the first and second elements of these inputs and assigning them to the temporary variables, a and b.

Next, we create our three logical gates as perceptrons and wire them together using the variables notA, notB, aGb (a greater than b), aLb (a less than b), and aEb (a equals b).

We then compute notA and notB. Here, we use an alternative syntax to define an array. The { A } expression creates an array with the object referenced by A. The elements of this array syntax will be evaluated at runtime, unlike the #(...) notation, which is evaluated at compile time. Therefore, for "literal" objects like numbers, always use #(...) (e.g., #(1 -1)). To create an array that contains the results of expressions, always use {...}. Note that technically we can also write numbers using the {...} syntax (e.g., {1 . -1}), but this is rarely done due to the performance penalty of runtime evaluation without any advantage. It is important to keep these two notations in mind, as we will use them heavily throughout the book.

The digitalComparator: method returns the result of the circuit evaluation as an array. We can test it using the following test method:

```
PerceptronTest>>testDigitalComparator
    self assert: (self digitalComparator: #(0 0)) equals: #(0 1 0).
    self assert: (self digitalComparator: #(0 1)) equals: #(0 0 1).
    self assert: (self digitalComparator: #(1 0)) equals: #(1 0 0).
    self assert: (self digitalComparator: #(1 1)) equals: #(0 1 0).
```

The digital comparator circuit example shows how perceptrons may be "manually" combined. The overall behavior is divided into parts, each referenced with a variable. These variables must then be combined to express the logical flow (e.g., the variable notA must be computed before computing an output).

1.7 Training a Perceptron

So far, we have used perceptron with a particular set of weights and bias. For example, we defined the AND logical gate with the value 1 for its two weights and a bias of -1.5. Consider the following exercise: manually compute the weights and bias to model the NAND logical gate (e.g., we recall that table for NAND is #(#(0 0 1)#(0 1 1)#(1 0 1) #(1 1 0)). Doing so requires a moment to compute some simple arithmetic. Imagine a perceptron taking thousands of inputs. Identifying adequate values for the weights and bias cannot be realistically done by hand. This is exactly what training a perceptron is about—finding adequate weights and bias to make the perceptron behave to solve a particular problem.

Learning typically involves a set of input examples with some known outputs. The learning process assesses how good the artificial neuron is against the desired output. In particular, as defined by Frank Rosenblatt in the late 1950s, each weight of the perceptron is modified by an amount that is proportional to (i) the product of the input and (ii) the difference between the real output and the desired output. Learning in neural networks means adjusting the weights and the bias in order to make the output close to the set of training examples.

The way a perceptron learns simply follows these rules

$$w_i(t + 1) = w_i(t) + (d - z) * x_i * \alpha$$

$$b(t + 1) = b(t) + (d - z) * \alpha$$

in which

- i is the weight index

- $w_i(t)$ is the weight i at a given time t

- b(t) is the bias at a given time t

- d is the desired value

- z is the actual output of the perceptron

- x_i corresponds to the provided input at index i

- α is the learning rate, typically, a small positive value, close to 0

We have $w_i(0)$ equal to a random number, usually within a narrow range centered on 0. The previous two equations given can be translated into the following pseudocode:

```
diff = desiredOutput - realOutput
alpha = 0.1
For all N:
    weightN = weightN + (alpha * inputN * diff)
bias = bias + (alpha * diff)
```

This pseudocode can be written in Pharo with the `train:desiredOutput:` method. But before that, we need to slightly adjust the definition of the Neuron class by adding the `learningRate` instance variable. The definition is as follows:

```
Object subclass: #Neuron
    instanceVariableNames: 'weights bias learningRate'
    classVariableNames: ''
    package: 'NeuralNetwork'
```

We can also provide the necessary methods to modify the `learningRate` variable:

```
Neuron>>learningRate: aNumber
    "Set the learning rate of the neuron"
    learningRate := aNumber
```

To obtain the value of the variable, use the following:

```
Neuron>>learningRate
    "Return the learning rate of the neuron"
    ^ learningRate
```

The variable can be initialized in the constructor, as follows:

```
Neuron>>initialize
    super initialize.
    learningRate := 0.1
```

We can now define the `train:desiredOutput:` method to make a perceptron learn.

```
Neuron>>train: inputs desiredOutput: desiredOutput
    | theError output newWeight |
    output := self feed: inputs.
    theError := desiredOutput - output.
    inputs
        withIndexDo: [ :anInput :index |
            newWeight := (weights at: index) + (learningRate * theError *
            anInput).
            weights at: index put: newWeight ].
    bias := bias + (learningRate * theError)
```

Before adjusting the weights and bias, we need to know how well the perceptron evaluates the set of inputs. We therefore need to evaluate the perceptron with the `inputs` argument, which is a collection of numerical values. The result is assigned to the `output` variable. The `theError` variable represents the difference between the desired output and the actual output. We also need to decide how fast the perceptron is supposed to learn. The `learningRate` value ranges between `0.0` and `1.0`. This example arbitrarily uses the value of `0.1`.

Let's see how to use the training in practice. Consider the perceptron p in the following example:

```
p := Neuron new.
p weights: #(-1 -1).
p bias: 2.
p feed: #(0 1).
```

You can evaluate this code in a playground. We have `pfeed: #(0 1)` equal to 1. What if we wish the perceptron to output 0 for the input `#(0 1)`? We would need to train p. As we said, this training will adjust the weights and the bias. Let's try the following:

```
p := Neuron new.
p weights: #(-1 -1).
p bias: 2.
p train: #(0 1) desiredOutput: 0.
p feed: #(0 1).
```

Evaluating this expression still outputs 1. Huh?! Were we not supposed to train our perceptron? A perceptron learns slowly. We therefore need to train the perceptron a few times on the desired output. We can repeatedly train the perceptron as follows:

```
p := Neuron new.
p weights: #(-1 -1).
p bias: 2.
10 timesRepeat: [ p train: #(0 1) desiredOutput: 0 ].
p feed: #(0 1).
```

Evaluating the code produces 0, which is what we were hoping for (see Figure 1-9). The perceptron has learned!

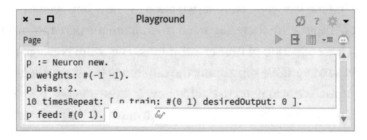

Figure 1-9. *Teaching a perceptron*

We can now train a perceptron to learn how to express the logical gates. Consider the following testTrainingOR:

```
PerceptronTest>>testTrainingOR
    | p |
    p := self newNeuron.
    p weights: #(-1 -1).
    p bias: 2.

    40 timesRepeat: [
        p train: #(0 0) desiredOutput: 0.
        p train: #(0 1) desiredOutput: 1.
        p train: #(1 0) desiredOutput: 1.
        p train: #(1 1) desiredOutput: 1.
    ].
```

```
self assert: (p feed: #(0 0)) equals: 0.
self assert: (p feed: #(0 1)) equals: 1.
self assert: (p feed: #(1 0)) equals: 1.
self assert: (p feed: #(1 1)) equals: 1.
```

The testTrainingOR method first creates a perceptron with some arbitrary weights and bias. We successfully train it with the four possible combinations of the OR logical gate. After the training, we verify whether the perceptron has properly learned.

In testTrainingOR, we train the perceptron 40 times on the complete set of examples. Training a perceptron (or a large neural network) with the complete set of examples is called an *epoch*. So, in this example, we train p with 40 epochs. The epoch is the unit of training.

Similarly, we can define a test that trains a perceptron to model the NOT logical gate:

```
PerceptronTest>>testTrainingNOT
    | p |
    p := self newNeuron.
    p weights: #(-1).
    p bias: 2.

    40 timesRepeat: [
        p train: #(0) desiredOutput: 1.
        p train: #(1) desiredOutput: 0.
    ].

    self assert: (p feed: #(0)) equals: 1.
    self assert: (p feed: #(1)) equals: 0.
```

EXERCISE:

- What is the necessary minimum number of epochs to train p? Try to reduce the number of epochs and run the test to see if it still passes.

- We have shown how to train a perceptron to learn the OR logical gate. Write methods called testTrainingNOR and testTrainingAND for the other gates we have seen.

- How does the value of the learningRate impact the minimum number of epochs for the training?

1.8 Drawing Graphs

Drawing graphs is often necessary to monitor progress made by the network. We will use the Roassal visualization engine to visualize such evolution. Roassal offers the Grapher API, which is dedicated to drawing graphs. You can load Roassal by executing the following in a playground:

```
Metacello new
    baseline: 'Roassal2';
    repository: 'github://ObjectProfile/Roassal2/src';
    load.
```

The coming section uses Roassal. Make sure you have it loaded, or part of the following code will not work or even compile. More information about Roassal may be found on http://AgileVisualization.com and detailed loading instructions may be found on https://github.com/ObjectProfile/Roassal2.

Here is an example of drawing a simple graph (see Figure 1-10):

```
g := RTGrapher new.
d := RTData new.
d connectColor: Color blue.
d points: (1 to: 100).
d y: [ :x | (x / 3.14) sin ].
g add: d.
g
```

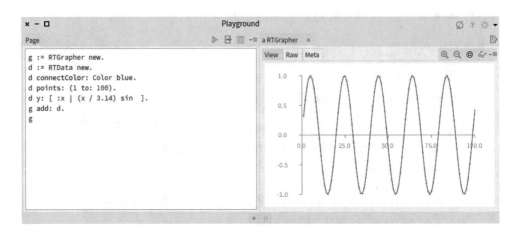

Figure 1-10. *Example of a graph*

We will make intense use of graphs throughout the book. More information about drawing graphs can be found in the examples of Roassal.

1.9 Predicting and 2D Points

We will now see a new application of the perceptron, which can be used to classify data and make some predictions. We will pick a simple classification problem. Consider the following:

- A space composed of red and blue points

- A straight line divides the red points from the blue points

Consider the following interaction between two (real) people, a teacher and a student. The goal of the teacher is to let the student infer where the straight separation line is between the blue and the red points. First, the teacher can give an arbitrary number of examples. Each example is given to the student as a location and a color. After a few examples, the student can guess the color of a random location. Intuitively, the more examples the teacher gives to the student, the more likely the student can correctly predict the color of a location.

Some questions arise:

- Can we teach a perceptron to correctly assign the color of a point?

- How many example points do we need to train the perceptron to make a good prediction?

Let's pick a linear function, such as $f(x) = -2x - 3$. A given point (x, y) is colored in red if $y > f(x)$; otherwise, it is blue. Consider the following script:

```
somePoints := OrderedCollection new.
500 timesRepeat: [
    somePoints add: {(50 atRandom - 25) . (50 atRandom - 25)}
].

f := [ :x | (-2 * x) - 3 ].

"We use the Roassal Grapher engine to plot our points"
g := RTGrapher new.
d := RTData new.
d dotShape
```

```
        color: [ :p | (p second > (f value: p first))
                      ifTrue: [ Color red trans ]
                      ifFalse: [ Color blue trans ] ].
d points: somePoints.
d x: #first.
d y: #second.
g add: d.
g
```

Inspecting this code snippet produces a graph with 500 colored dots (see Figure 1-11).

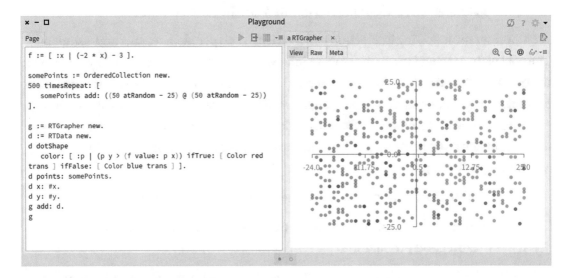

Figure 1-11. *Classifying dots along a line*

The script begins by defining a set of 500 points, ranging within a squared area of 50 (from -25 to +25). The 50 atRandom expression returns a random number between 1 and 50. The expression {(50 atRandom- 25). (50 atRandom- 25)} creates an array with two random values in it. Each point is represented as an array of two numbers. Our 500 points are kept in a collection, which is an instance of the class OrderedCollection.

We assign to the variable f a block representing our function f(x), written in the Pharo syntax. A block may be evaluated with the value: message. For example, we have f value: 3 that returns -9 and f value: -2 that returns 1.

The remainder of the script uses Grapher to plot the points. A point p is red if
psecond is greater than f value: p first; otherwise, it's blue. The expression Color
red trans evaluates to a transparent red color.

We can add the line defined by f to the graph. Consider the small revision (see
Figure 1-12):

```
somePoints := OrderedCollection new.
500 timesRepeat: [
    somePoints add: {(50 atRandom - 25) . (50 atRandom - 25)}
].

f := [ :x | (-2 * x) - 3 ].


g := RTGrapher new.
d := RTData new.
d dotShape
    color: [ :p | (p second > (f value: p first))
                    ifTrue: [ Color red trans ]
                    ifFalse: [ Color blue trans ] ].
d points: somePoints.
d x: #first.
d y: #second.
g add: d.

"Added code below"
d2 := RTData new.
d2 noDot.
d2 connectColor: Color red.
d2 points: (-15 to: 15 by: 0.1).
d2 y: f.
d2 x: #yourself.
g add: d2.
g
```

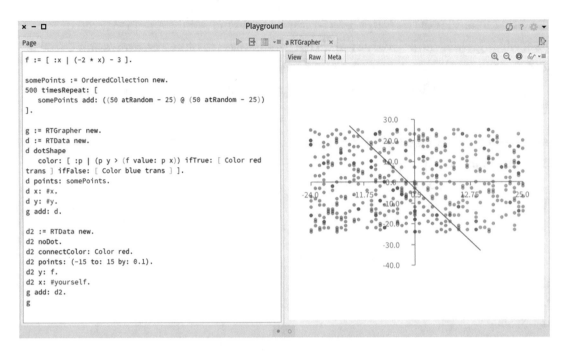

Figure 1-12. *Adding a separation line*

We will now add a perceptron to the script and see how well it guesses on which side of the line a point falls. Consider the following script (see Figure 1-13):

```
f := [ :x | (-2 * x) - 3 ].
p := Neuron new.
p weights: { 1 . 2 }.
p bias: -1.
r := Random new seed: 42.

"We are training the perceptron"
500 timesRepeat: [
    anX := (r nextInt: 50) - 25.
    anY := (r nextInt: 50) - 25.
    designedOutput := (f value: anX) >= anY
                            ifTrue: [ 1 ] ifFalse: [ 0 ].
    p train: { anX . anY } desiredOutput: designedOutput
].
```

```
"Test points"
testPoints := OrderedCollection new.
2000 timesRepeat: [
    testPoints add: { ((r nextInt: 50) - 25) . ((r nextInt: 50) - 25) }
].

g := RTGrapher new.
d := RTData new.
d dotShape
    color: [ :point | (p feed: point) > 0.5
                    ifTrue: [ Color red trans ]
                    ifFalse: [ Color blue trans ] ].
d points: testPoints.
d x: #first.
d y: #second.
g add: d.

d2 := RTData new.
d2 noDot.
d2 connectColor: Color red.
d2 points: (-15 to: 15 by: 0.1).
d2 y: f.
d2 x: #yourself.
g add: d2.
g
```

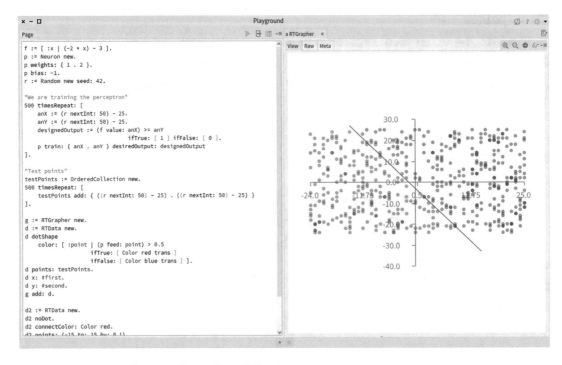

Figure 1-13. *Predicting the color of the dot*

Figure 1-13 gives the result of the prediction. We can see that some red dots are not properly classified. Some red dots are located on the right side of the line. In general, the precision is good since most of the dots are placed on the correct side.

As in the previous script, the script begins with the definition of the block function f. It then creates a perceptron with some arbitrary weights and bias. Subsequently, a random number generator is created. In the previous scripts, to obtain a random value between 1 and 50, we simply wrote `50 atRandom`. Using a random number generator, we need to write the following:

```
r := Random new seed: 42.
r nextInt: 50.
```

Why is this? First of all, being able to generate random numbers is necessary in all stochastic approaches, including neural networks. Although randomness is very important, we usually do not want to let such a random value create situations that cannot be reproduced. Imagine that our code behaves erratically, likely due to a random value. How can we track down the anomaly in our code? If we have truly random numbers, it means that executing the same piece of code twice may produce (even slightly) different behaviors. It may therefore be complicated to properly test. Instead, we will use a random generator with a known seed to produce a known sequence of random numbers. Consider this expression:

```
(1 to: 5) collect: [ :i| 50 atRandom]
```

Each time you evaluate this expression, you will obtain a *new* sequence of five random numbers. Using a generator, you have the following:

```
r := Random new seed: 42.
(1 to: 5) collect: [:i | r nextInt: 50]
```

Evaluating this small script several times always produces the same sequence. This is the key to having reproducible and deterministic behavior. In the remainder of the book, we will frequently use random number generators.

Our script then trains a perceptron with 500 points. Next, we create 2,000 test points, which will be displayed on the screen using Grapher. We wrote the condition (p feed: point)> 0.5 to color a point as red. We could instead have (p feed: point)= 1, but in an upcoming chapter we will replace the perceptron with another kind of artificial neuron, which will not exactly produce the value 1.

We see that the area of blue and red points is very close to the straight line. This means that our perceptron is able to classify points with a relatively good accuracy.

What if we reduce the number of trainings of our perceptron? You can try this by changing the value 500 to, let's say, 100. What is the result? The perceptron does not classify points as accurately. In general, the more training a perceptron has, the more accurate it will be (however, this is not always true with neural networks, as we will see later on).

EXERCISE: Reduce the number of times the perceptron is trained. Verify that lowering the value below 500 leads to some errors by the perceptron, illustrated as a mismatch between the red line and the area of colored points.

1.10 Measuring the Precision

We have seen that the accuracy of a perceptron in classifying points is very dependent on the number of times we train it. How much training do we need to have acceptable precision? Keeping track of the precision and training is essential to see how good our system is at classification.

Evaluate the following script in a playground:

```
learningCurve := OrderedCollection new.
f := [ :x | (-2 * x) - 3 ].
0 to: 2000 by: 10 do: [ :nbOfTrained |
    r := Random new seed: 42.
    p := Neuron new.
    p weights: #(1 2).
    p bias: -1.

    nbOfTrained timesRepeat: [
        anX := (r nextInt: 50) - 25.
        anY := (r nextInt: 50) - 25.
        trainedOutput := (f value: anX) >= anY ifTrue: [1] ifFalse: [0].
        p train: (Array with: anX with: anY) desiredOutput:
            trainedOutput ].

    nbOfGood := 0.
    nbOfTries := 1000.
    nbOfTries timesRepeat: [
        anX := (r nextInt: 50) - 25.
        anY := (r nextInt: 50)- 25.
        realOutput := (f value: anX) >= anY ifTrue: [1] ifFalse: [0].
        ((p feed: { anX . anY }) - realOutput) abs < 0.2
            ifTrue: [ nbOfGood := nbOfGood + 1 ].
    ].
    learningCurve add: { nbOfTrained . (nbOfGood / nbOfTries) }.
].

g := RTGrapher new.
d := RTData new.
d noDot.
d connectColor: Color blue.
d points: learningCurve.
d x: #first.
d y: #second.
```

```
g add: d.
g axisY title: 'Precision'.
g axisX noDecimal; title: 'Training iteration'.
g
```

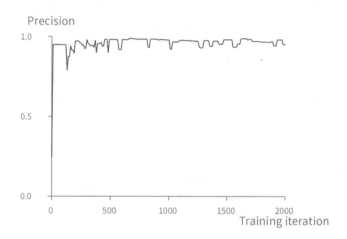

Figure 1-14. *Precision of the dot classification task*

The script produces a curve with the precision on the y axis and the number of trainings on the x axis (see Figure 1-14). We see that the perceptron started with a rather poor performance, around 0.25. However, it quickly steps up to reach a precision close to 1.0. After a few epochs, our perceptron can guess the color of a dot with good precision.

1.11 Historical Perspective

Warren S. McCulloch and Walter Pitts were the first to express a computation in terms of artificial neurons. They did so in 1943, in their seminal article, "A Logical Calculus of the Ideas Immanent in Nervous Activity." This paper had a significant impact on the field of artificial intelligence. It is interesting to read about the knowledge we had about biological neurons at that time. The perceptron model presented in this chapter originated from this seminal paper.

1.12 Exercises

- We have seen how the perceptron can be used to implement some logical gates. In particular, we have seen how AND, OR, and NOT can be implemented. What about the XOR gate? Can you train a perceptron to learn XOR behavior? (As a reminder, we have 0 XOR 0 = 0, 0 XOR 1 = 1, 1 XOR 0 = 1, and 1 XOR 1 = 0.)

- We have seen how five perceptrons may be combined to form a digital comparator. Do you think you can train the combination of these five perceptrons as a whole to learn the behavior of the digital comparator?

1.13 What Have We Seen in This Chapter?

This chapter covered the following topics:

- *Providing the concept of a perceptron.* We defined a perceptron, an essential abstraction that we will build upon in upcoming chapters.

- *A step-by-step guide to programming with Pharo.* While we implemented the perceptron, we sketched out how programming happens in Pharo. This chapter is by no means an introduction to Pharo. Instead, it is an example of how to use the Pharo programming environment. In particular, we saw how to write code using the system browser and how to run code using the playground. These two tools are fundamental and deserve to be well understood.

- *Implementing a perceptron.* We implemented and tested the perceptron. Testing is important, as it is a way to formalize the behavior we wish for the perceptron.

- *Making a perceptron learn.* We saw a rudimentary way to make a perceptron learn. It is rather simple, but, as you will see in future chapters, the very same technique can bring us very far.

1.14 Further Reading About Pharo

Pharo is a wonderful programming language and a live, dynamic programming environment. This first chapter has given you a taste of programming with Pharo. However, it is highly recommended that you seek further material in order to feel truly comfortable with Pharo and learn what makes it powerful. In particular, the *Pharo by Example* book is an excellent introduction to learn and master Pharo. The website `http://books.pharo.org` contains a free copy of the book as well as many others. Check it out!

CHAPTER 2

The Artificial Neuron

In the previous chapter, we saw how a perceptron operates and how a simple learning algorithm can be implemented. However, the perceptron has some serious limitations, which will motivate us to formulate a more robust artificial neuron, called the sigmoid neuron.

This chapter uses Roassal to plot values. As seen in the previous chapter, you can load Roassal into Pharo by executing the following script in a playground:

```
Metacello new
        baseline: 'Roassal2';
        repository: 'github://ObjectProfile/Roassal2/src';
        load.
```

A complete description of Roassal may be found in the book *Agile Visualization* (http://agilevisualization.com).

2.1 Limit of the Perceptron

A perceptron works well as an independent small machine. We learned that we can compose a few perceptrons to express a complex behavior such as the digital comparator. We also learned that a single perceptron can learn a simple behavior. However, there are two main restrictions with combining perceptrons:

- *Only 0 or 1 as output*: The fact that a perceptron can have only two different output values, 0 or 1, seriously limits the kind of problem it can solve. In particular, when some perceptrons are chained, using binary values significantly reduces the space we live in. Not everything can be reduced to a set of 0s and 1s without leading to an explosion of perceptrons.

© Alexandre Bergel 2020
A. Bergel, *Agile Artificial Intelligence in Pharo*, https://doi.org/10.1007/978-1-4842-5384-7_2

- *A chain of perceptrons cannot learn*: We have seen how to combine perceptrons, and how a single perceptron can learn. But, can a combination of perceptrons also learn? The answer is no. This is another consequence of having only two output values. An essential property of most common learning algorithms is the ability to express a smooth learning curve, which cannot be expressed using two different values. How can we tell if a perceptron is learning well, poorly, or not at all with only two different output values?

We have written that $z = w.x + b$, for which w is a vector of weights, b a vector of bias, and x the input vector. We said that the output of the perceptron is 1 if $z > 0$ and 0 otherwise. One important problem with the formulation of the perceptron is that a small variation of z can produce a large variation of the output—the output can go from 0 to 1, or from 1 to 0.

Algorithms that are commonly employed in neural networks require a very important property: a small variation of z *must* produce a small variation of the output. The perceptron does not fulfill this need, since a small variation of z can produce a large variation of the output.

2.2 Activation Function

Before discussing a better way to improve the learning, it is important to decouple the perceptron logic. Let's introduce a function called σ that takes as a parameter the $z = w.x + b$ value. The perceptron behavior can therefore be written as $\sigma(z) = 1$ if $z > 0$, else $\sigma(z) = 0$.

By adding the σ function, we are separating the computation of $w.x + b$ from the conditional. We call σ the *activation function*. It describes the activation of the perceptron (i.e., when it fires 1) according to the value of z.

The activation function used by the perceptron is called the *step function* and may be graphically represented, as shown in Figure 2-1.

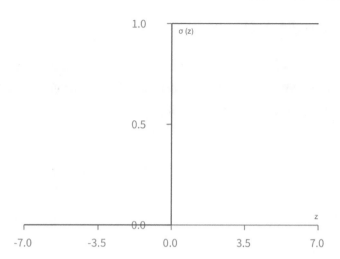

Figure 2-1. *The step function*

Figure 2-1 is the result of executing this script:

```
g := RTGrapher new.
d := RTData new.
d connectColor: Color blue.
d noDot.
d points: (-7.0 to: 7.0 by: 0.01).
d x: #yourself.
d y: [ :x | x > 0 ifTrue: [ 1 ] ifFalse: [ 0 ] ].
g add: d.
g
```

You may recognize the step function provided to the y: instruction. Note that the function provided to y: refers to the input as x while z is provided to σ. This is an inoffensive renaming.

Consider a value of z = 0. We therefore have σ(z) = 0. If we add 0.00001, a small value, to z, we get σ(z) = 1. A small value added to z produces a large change in σ(z), which goes from 0 to 1. The fact that a small change in z produces a big change in σ(z) is a serious problem: a chain of perceptron is not able to learn.

The step function is characterized for having a vertical step, which produces two angles in its curve. These angles make the step function non-derivable, which is quite a problem, as we will shortly see.

2.3 The Sigmoid Neuron

We will express a new kind of artificial neuron, called the *sigmoid neuron*. The increment in this case is to use a new activation function, called the *sigmoid function*. Consider the function $\sigma(z) = \dfrac{1}{1+e^{-z}}$, plotted in Figure 2-2.

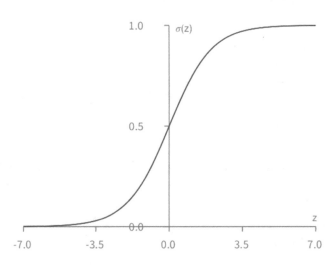

Figure 2-2. *The sigmoid function*

Figure 2-2 is the result of executing the script:

```
g := RTGrapher new.
d := RTData new.
d connectColor: Color blue.
d noDot.
d points: (-7.0 to: 7.0 by: 0.01).
d x: #yourself.
d y: [ :x | 1 / (1 + (x negated exp)) ].
g add: d.
g
```

This sigmoid function has several advantages:

- It is differentiable everywhere on the curve, or in other words, it has no vertical lines, and even better, no angle. We can easily draw a straight line for any value z that indicates the slope of $\sigma(z)$. When plotted, $\sigma(z)$ is very smooth by having no angle, which is a very good property.

- Its derivative has some interesting properties, as we will see later.

- The sigmoid function behaves similarly to the step function for very small and very large z values.

- A small increment in z produces a small variation of $\sigma(z)$, and as we have previously said, this is important for learning.

We define a sigmoid neuron as a neuron having the sigmoid function as its activation function. The sigmoid neuron is widely accepted as a mathematical representation of a biological neuron behavior.

As we will later see, the training has to be slightly adjusted to take advantage of the fact that $\sigma(z)$ is derivable.

2.4 Implementing the Activation Functions

In the previous chapter, we defined the class called Neuron. We will improve this class to accept an activation function. First, let's introduce a small class hierarchy for the activation functions.

The abstract class called ActivationFunction may be defined as follows:

```
Object subclass: #ActivationFunction
        instanceVariableNames: ''
        classVariableNames: ''
        package: 'NeuralNetwork'
```

An activation function object has the responsibility of computing two things: (i) the activation value and (ii) the transfer derivative. This transfer derivative is an essential piece of the backpropagation learning algorithm. Implementation of the backpropagation algorithm is given in this chapter, while the theoretical background is covered in Chapter 5.

We define the following two abstract methods. The eval: method computes the activation value:

```
ActivationFunction>>eval: z
    ^ self subclassResponsibility
```

and the method derivative: computes the transfer derivative:

```
ActivationFunction>>derivative: output
    ^ self subclassResponsibility
```

The two methods we just defined are abstract methods, which means they are placeholders for subclasses of `ActivationFunction` that provide an adequate implementation of these methods.

We can now define the two activation functions, each being a subclass of `ActivationFunction`. The sigmoid function may be defined as follows:

```
ActivationFunction subclass: #SigmoidAF
        instanceVariableNames: ''
        classVariableNames: ''
        package: 'NeuralNetwork'
```

We first implement the `eval:` function:

```
SigmoidAF>>eval: z
        ^ 1 / (1 + z negated exp)
```

We then implement the `derivative:` method, which represents the mathematical derivative of `eval:`:

```
SigmoidAF>>derivative: output
        ^ output * (1 - output)
```

Without going into details, we have $\sigma(z)' = \sigma(z) * (1 - \sigma(z))$. We will come back to that point in Chapter 5.

Similarly, we can define the step function as follows:

```
ActivationFunction subclass: #StepAF
        instanceVariableNames: ''
        classVariableNames: ''
        package: 'NeuralNetwork'
```

We implement the `eval` as follows:

```
StepAF>>eval: z
        ^ (z > 0) ifTrue: [ 1 ] ifFalse: [ 0 ]
```

We also need to implement the `derivative:`. We will simply make this method return the following argument:

```
StepAF>>derivative: output
        ^ 1
```

The formulation of the `derivative:` of the step function does not match the mathematical truth, which is 0 with an undefined value for `z` = 0. However, returning 1 instead eases the implementation of the revised `Neuron`, as we will see in the next section.

2.5 Extending the Neuron with the Activation Functions

We can now generalize the way an artificial neuron can learn from examples. Assume an example value (`x, d`), in which `x` is example input and `d` is the example output. At the beginning, when providing the input `x` = (x_1, ..., x_i, ..., x_N) to a sigmoid neuron, the output is likely to be different than `d`, a number between 0 and 1. This is not surprising since the weights and bias are randomly chosen. This is exactly why we are training the neuron with that example, to have the neuron output `d` if `x` is provided.

The learning mechanism may be summarized with the following rules:

$$\delta = (d - z) * \sigma'(z)$$
$$w_i(t + 1) = w_i(t) + \delta * x_i * \alpha$$
$$b(t + 1) = b(t) + \delta * \alpha$$

in which:

- δ is the difference between the desired output and the actual output of the neuron

- `d` is the example output, which is the desired value

- `z` is the output of the perceptron

- σ is the activation function (either the step or sigmoid function)

- σ' is the derivative function of σ

- `i` is the weight index, which ranges from 1 to `N`, the number of weights contained in the neuron

- w_i(`t`) is the weight `i` at a given time `t`

- `b(t)` is the bias at a given time `t`

- x_i corresponds to the provided input at index `i`

- α is the learning rate, a small positive value close to 0

With little or no training, the neuron will output a value z, which is very different from d. As a consequence, δ will also be large. With an adequate number of trainings, the δ should get close to 0.

These equations will be explained in Chapter 5. For now, the most important aspect is that they can be translated into the following pseudocode:

```
diff = desiredOutput - realOutput
delta = diff * derivative(realOutput)
alpha = 0.1
For all N:
    weightN = weightN + (alpha * inputN * delta)
bias = bias + (alpha * diff)
```

We are assuming that the neuron has N inputs, and therefore N weights. We can now extend our definition of neuron to use an activation function. We can do so by adding a new instance variable called `activationFunction` to the Neuron class:

```
Object subclass: #Neuron
        instanceVariableNames: 'weights bias learningRate
            activationFunction'
        classVariableNames: ''
        package: 'NeuralNetwork'
```

The `learningRate` variable must be accessed from the outside:

```
Neuron>>learningRate: aLearningRateAsFloat
        "Set the learning rate of the neuron. The argument should be a
            small floating value. For example, 0.01"
        learningRate := aLearningRateAsFloat
```

```
Neuron>> learningRate
        "Return the learning rate of the neuron"
        ^ learningRate
```

Feeding has to be adapted:

```
Neuron>>feed: inputs
        | z |
        z := (inputs with: weights collect: [ :x :w | x * w ]) sum + bias.
        ^ activationFunction eval: z
```

We are now ready to implement the algorithm to train a sigmoid neuron. Here is the method:

```
Neuron>>train: inputs desiredOutput: desiredOutput
        | diff output delta |
        output := self feed: inputs.
        diff := desiredOutput - output.
        delta := diff * (activationFunction derivative: output).

        inputs withIndexDo: [ :anInput :index |
            weights at: index put: ((weights at: index) + (learningRate *
                delta * anInput)) ].

        bias := bias + (learningRate * delta)
```

The train:desiredOutput: method is very similar to what we have seen with the perceptron. We introduced a delta local variable, which represents the error multiplied by the transfer derivative. We use the transfer derivative to formulate a *gradient descent*. We will explore that topic in detail in Chapter 5.

We now need to initialize a neuron as being a sigmoid:

```
Neuron>>initialize
        super initialize.
        learningRate := 0.1.
        self sigmoid
```

We can also define the two utility methods:

```
Neuron>>sigmoid
        "Use the sigmoid activation function"
        activationFunction := SigmoidAF new
```

```
Neuron>>step
        "Use the step activation function"
        activationFunction := StepAF new
```

2.6 Adapting the Existing Tests

If you run PerceptronTest you will see that several test methods fail. The reason is that a neuron is initialized with a sigmoid activation function. We therefore need to adapt the PerceptronTest class to produce neurons with a step function. Luckily, we can simply redefine the newNeuron method:

```
PerceptronTest>>newNeuron
        "Return a new neuron with the step activation function"
        ^ Neuron new step
```

All the tests contained in PerceptronTest are now green when they run.

2.7 Testing the Sigmoid Neuron

Since the behavior of a sigmoid neuron is very similar to a perceptron, we will reuse some of the tests. Define the NeuronTest class as follows:

```
TestCase subclass: #NeuronTest
        instanceVariableNames: ''
        classVariableNames: ''
        package: 'NeuralNetwork'
```

We can then train a neuron to learn some logical gates. The following method is very similar to what we saw with the perceptron:

```
NeuronTest>>testTrainingAND
        | p |
        p := Neuron new.
        p weights: #(-1 -1).
        p bias: 2.

        5000
                timesRepeat: [
                        p train: #(0 0) desiredOutput: 0.
                        p train: #(0 1) desiredOutput: 0.
                        p train: #(1 0) desiredOutput: 0.
                        p train: #(1 1) desiredOutput: 1 ].
```

```
self assert: ((p feed: #(0 0)) closeTo: 0 precision: 0.1).
self assert: ((p feed: #(0 1)) closeTo: 0 precision: 0.1).
self assert: ((p feed: #(1 0)) closeTo: 0 precision: 0.1).
self assert: ((p feed: #(1 1)) closeTo: 1 precision: 0.1).
```

There are two differences:

- The number of epochs has significantly increased. The reason is that the sigmoid neuron learns more slowly than the perceptron.

- The result of feeding the neuron is compared using the `closeTo:precision:` call. Since the result of the `feed:` method is now a floating value and not an integer, we need to adapt our way of comparing these values. If you are still unsure about what is wrong with using == between floats, evaluate the expression `0.1 + 0.2 - 0.3`. It returns `5.551115123125783e-17` and not 0 as one would expect. The way that float values are encoded causes this apparently weird behavior.

Similarly we can train a sigmoid neuron to learn the OR behavior:

```
NeuronTest>>testTrainingOR
    | p |
    p := Neuron new.
    p weights: #(-1 -1).
    p bias: 2.

    5000
        timesRepeat: [
            p train: #(0 0) desiredOutput: 0.
            p train: #(0 1) desiredOutput: 1.
            p train: #(1 0) desiredOutput: 1.
            p train: #(1 1) desiredOutput: 1 ].

    self assert: ((p feed: #(0 0)) closeTo: 0 precision: 0.1).
    self assert: ((p feed: #(0 1)) closeTo: 1 precision: 0.1).
    self assert: ((p feed: #(1 0)) closeTo: 1 precision: 0.1).
    self assert: ((p feed: #(1 1)) closeTo: 1 precision: 0.1).
```

As you can see, using a sigmoid neuron does not mess up our tests. We simply need (i) to increase the number of epochs to which we train the neuron and (ii) be more careful when comparing floating values.

EXERCISE: We wrote an adapted version of the OR and AND logical gates for the sigmoid neuron. Adapt the other logical gates to use the sigmoid neuron.

2.8 Slower to Learn

This chapter started by pointing out a strong limitation of the perceptron. This has motivated us to formulate the sigmoid neuron. There is one drawback to the sigmoid neuron: it is slower at learning than the perceptron. We are making a bet, which is trading efficiency for flexibility. As you will see in the next chapter, the sigmoid neuron can be nicely combined.

We can easily compare the learning of the sigmoid neuron and the perceptron. Consider the following script:

```
learningCurveNeuron := OrderedCollection new.
0 to: 1000 do: [ :nbOfTrained |
    p := Neuron new.
    p weights: #(-1 -1).
    p bias: 2.

    nbOfTrained timesRepeat: [
            p train: #(0 0) desiredOutput: 0.
            p train: #(0 1) desiredOutput: 0.
            p train: #(1 0) desiredOutput: 0.
            p train: #(1 1) desiredOutput: 1 ].

    res := ((p feed: #(0 0)) - 0) abs +
           ((p feed: #(0 1)) - 0) abs +
           ((p feed: #(1 0)) - 0) abs +
           ((p feed: #(1 1)) - 1) abs.
    learningCurveNeuron add: res / 4.

].
```

```
learningCurvePerceptron := OrderedCollection new.
0 to: 1000 do: [ :nbOfTrained |
     p := Neuron new.
     p step.
     p weights: #(-1 -1).
     p bias: 2.

     nbOfTrained timesRepeat: [
             p train: #(0 0) desiredOutput: 0.
             p train: #(0 1) desiredOutput: 0.
             p train: #(1 0) desiredOutput: 0.
             p train: #(1 1) desiredOutput: 1 ].

     res := ((p feed: #(0 0)) - 0) abs +
            ((p feed: #(0 1)) - 0) abs +
            ((p feed: #(1 0)) - 0) abs +
            ((p feed: #(1 1)) - 1) abs.
     learningCurvePerceptron add: res / 4.

].

g := RTGrapher new.
d := RTData new.
d label: 'Sigmoid neuron'.
d noDot.
d connectColor: Color blue.
d points: learningCurveNeuron.
d y: #yourself.
g add: d.

d := RTData new.
d label: 'Perceptron'.
d noDot.
d connectColor: Color green.
d points: learningCurvePerceptron.
d y: #yourself.
g add: d.
```

```
g axisY title: 'Error'.
g axisX noDecimal; title: 'Epoch'.
g legend addText: 'Perceptron vs Sigmoid neuron'.
g
```

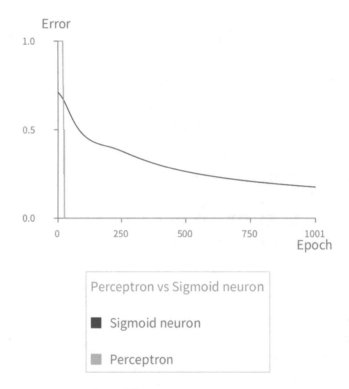

Figure 2-3. *Perceptron vs. sigmoid neuron*

The script produces the graph shown in Figure 2-3. No matter the learning rate defined, the perceptron is indeed much faster at learning than the sigmoid neuron.

The next chapter reveals the true power of sigmoid neuron, which will offset the fact that it is slower at learning.

2.9 What Have We Seen in This Chapter?

This chapter covered the following topics:

- *Briefly discussed the limitation of the perceptron.* The perceptron cannot learn when combined with other perceptrons. Although we have not discussed this aspect further, the next chapter we will develop this further.

- *Definition of the sigmoid neuron.* The sigmoid neuron is an improvement of the perceptron since it can be combined with other sigmoid neurons and this combination can learn. In the next chapter, we will cover the backpropagation algorithm, a central aspect when making a neural network learn.

- *Activation functions.* We have seen two activation functions, the step and sigmoid functions. Many other activation functions are around.

The next chapter is about composing sigmoid neurons to build artificial neural networks.

CHAPTER 3

Neural Networks

The previous chapter covered the design and implementation of an individual neuron. This chapter builds upon the effort initiated in previous chapters by connecting multiple neurons. We provide a complete implementation of a neural network and a backpropagation algorithm, which brings us to the core of the first part of the book.

3.1 General Architecture

An artificial neural network is a computing system inspired by the biological neural networks found in animal brains. An artificial neural network is a collection of connected artificial neurons. Each connection between artificial neurons can transmit a signal from one to another. The artificial neuron that receives the signal can process it, and then signal neurons connected to it. Artificial neural networks are commonly employed to perform particular tasks, including clustering, classification, prediction, and pattern recognition. In neural networks, just as with the perceptron and sigmoid neuron, knowledge is acquired through learning.

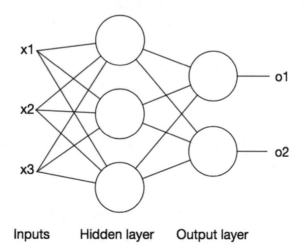

Figure 3-1. *Example of a neural network*

© Alexandre Bergel 2020
A. Bergel, *Agile Artificial Intelligence in Pharo*, https://doi.org/10.1007/978-1-4842-5384-7_3

Figure 3-1 shows a simple neural network made up of five neurons, three inputs, and two outputs. The left-most column is called the *input layer*. The input layer simply transmits some values to the hidden layer, without doing anything in particular. In Figure 3-1, the input layer is made up of three inputs—x1, x2, and x3. The middle of the network contains the hidden layers. This network contains only one hidden layer, made up of three neurons. However, a network may contain several hidden layers. The right-most column of the network is called *output layer,* and it contains two neurons.

All values transmitted between neurons are numerical values. Up to know, we have mostly been dealing with the numbers 0 and 1. However, sigmoid neurons accept and produce floating values. The output values, o1 and o2, are numbers ranging between 0 and 1. Since all the neurons we consider have a sigmoid activation function, only values ranging between 0 and 1 are transmitted between neuron layers.

The depicted neural network is called *fully-connected* since each neuron of the hidden layer is connected to *all* the neurons of the input layer and *all* the neurons of the output layer. Such a network corresponds to the simplest architecture. More sophisticated architecture include recurrent neural networks and convolutional neural networks, which are not covered in this book.

This chapter provides an implementation of abstraction we informally presented. The next chapter will uncover some theoretical aspects of the fully-connected network.

3.2 Neural Layer

We define a layer as a set of neurons. Layers are connected between them, and a set of layers form a neural network. We will represent a layer with the NeuronLayer class.

Each layer knows about the preceding layer using the previousLayer variable and the following layer using nextLayer. The learningRate variable refers to the learning rate of the layer. We define the NeuronLayer class as follows:

```
Object subclass: #NeuronLayer
        instanceVariableNames: 'previousLayer nextLayer neurons'
        classVariableNames: ''
        package: 'NeuralNetwork'
```

A layer contains some neurons, kept in the neurons variable. We can set the learning rate of a layer to 0.1 by default. A neuron layer may be initialized using the following method:

```
NeuronLayer>>initializeNbOfNeurons: nbOfNeurons nbOfWeights:
      nbOfWeights using: random
        "Main method to initialize a neuron layer
        nbOfNeurons : number of neurons the layer should be made of
        nbOfWeights : number of weights each neuron should have
        random : a random number generator

        "|
        weights |
        neurons := (1 to: nbOfNeurons) collect: [ :i |
          weights := (1 to: nbOfWeights) collect: [ :ii | random next * 4 - 2 ].
          Neuron new sigmoid; weights: weights; bias: (random next * 4 - 2) ].
        self learningRate: 0.1
```

The initializeNbOfNeurons:nbOfWeights:using: method accepts three arguments. The first one, nbOfNeurons, is an integer value and represents the number of neurons the layer should contain. The second argument, nbOfWeights, is an integer that indicates the number of weights each neuron should have. This number of weights reflects the number of input values the layer is accepting. The last argument, random, is a random number generator. As in the previous chapter, using a random number generator is useful to make the behavior deterministic. This random number generator is used to initialize each individual neuron.

The method first creates nbOfNeurons different neurons, each having nbOfWeights weight values. Each weight is a random number between −2 and +2. These boundaries are arbitrarily chosen. The expression random next produces a random number within 0 and 1. Multiplying it by four and subtracting two produces a value between -2 and +2. Each neuron has a sigmoid activation function, thanks to the sigmoid message.

Lastly, the method sets the learning rate of each neuron to 0.1. The learningRate: method is defined as follows:

```
NeuronLayer>>learningRate: aLearningRate
        "Set the learning rate for all the neurons
        Note that this method should be called after configuring the
              network, and _not_ before"
```

```
    self assert: [ neurons notEmpty ] description: 'learningRate:
        should be invoked after configuring the layer'.
    neurons do: [ : n | n learningRate: aLearningRate ]
```

Forward feeding the layer is an essential operation consisting of feeding each neuron and forwarding the values to the next layer. We define the feed: method as follows:

```
NeuronLayer>>feed: someInputValues
    "Feed the neuron layer with some inputs"

    | someOutputs |
    someOutputs := neurons collect: [ :n | n feed: someInputValues ] as
        : Array.
    ^ self isOutputLayer
        ifTrue: [ someOutputs ]
        ifFalse: [ nextLayer feed: someOutputs ]
```

The method invokes feed: on each of its neurons (the Neuron>>feed: method is detailed in the previous chapter). The results are then kept as an array. The method then checks if the layer is an output layer. If this is the case, the result of the method is simply the results of each neuron. If the layer is not an output (i.e., it is a hidden layer), we feed-forward the computed values to the next layer.

We need to determine if a neuron layer is the output layer or not. We can easily do this using the isOutputLayer predicate:

```
NeuronLayer>>isOutputLayer
    "Return true if the layer is the output layer (i.e., the last layer,
right-most, in the network)"
    ^ self nextLayer isNil
```

We will also need a way to hook layers together:

```
NeuronLayer>>nextLayer: aLayer
    "Set the next layer"
    nextLayer := aLayer
```

To access the next layer, we need the following method:

```
NeuronLayer>>nextLayer
        "Return the next layer connected to me"
        ^ nextLayer
```

Similarly, we need a way to set and access the previous layer:

```
NeuronLayer>>previousLayer: aLayer
        "Set the previous layer"
        previousLayer := aLayer
```

Similarly:

```
NeuronLayer>>previousLayer
        "Return the previous layer connected to me"
        ^ previousLayer
```

Neurons need to be accessed from a layer:

```
NeuronLayer>>neurons
        "Return the neurons I am composed of"
        ^ neurons
```

We also need the size of the layer to be accessible:

```
NeuronLayer>>numberOfNeurons
        "Return the number of neurons in the layer"
        ^ neurons size
```

We have now defined most of the NeuronLayer class. We can begin testing the class:

```
TestCase subclass: #NeuronLayerTest
        instanceVariableNames: ''
        classVariableNames: ''
        package: 'NeuralNetwork'
```

A simple test may be:

```
NeuronLayerTest>>testBasic
        | nl result r |
        r := Random seed: 42.
```

```
nl := NeuronLayer new.
nl initializeNbOfNeurons: 3 nbOfWeights: 4 using: r.

self assert: nl isOutputLayer.

result := nl feed: #(1 2 3 4).
self assert: result size equals: 3.
result
        with: #(0.03700050130978758 0.9051275824569505
            0.9815269659126287)
        do: [ :res :test | self assert: (res closeTo: test precision:
            0.0000000001) ]
```

The testBasic method creates a new neuron layer, composed of three neurons, each having four weights and one bias. The weights and biases are initialized using the random number generator, r.

We can also build a chain of layers and see how they perform:

```
NeuronLayerTest>>testOutputLayer
        | nl1 nl2 result random |
        random := Random seed: 42.
        nl1 := NeuronLayer new.
        nl1 initializeNbOfNeurons: 3 nbOfWeights: 4 using: random.
        nl2 := NeuronLayer new.
        nl2 initializeNbOfNeurons: 4 nbOfWeights: 3 using: random.
        nl1 nextLayer: nl2.
        self deny: nl1 isOutputLayer.
        self assert: nl2 isOutputLayer.
        result := nl1 feed: #(1 2 3 4).
        "Since nl2 has 4 neurons, we will obtain 4 outputs"
        self assert: result size equals: 4.
        result
                with: #(0.03089402289518759 0.9220488835263312
                    0.5200462953493654 0.20276557516858304)
                do: [ :r :test | self assert: (r closeTo: test precision:
                    0.0000000001) ]
```

We can now wrap a chain of layers into a neural network.

3.3 Modeling a Neural Network

We will represent a neural network as an instance of the NNetwork class:

```
Object subclass: #NNetwork
        instanceVariableNames: 'layers errors precisions'
        classVariableNames: ''
        package: 'NeuralNetwork'
```

We define a neural network simply as a container of layers. We also add an errors instance variable that will be useful for tracing the evolution of error during the learning phase.

The initialization of a network is done through the initialize method:

```
NNetwork>>initialize
        super initialize.
        layers := OrderedCollection new.
        errors := OrderedCollection new.
        precisions := OrderedCollection new.
```

The layers, errors, and precisions instance variables are initialized with an empty collection. The layers variable will refer to an instance of the NeuronLayer class. The errors and precisions variables will contain numerical values, representing the errors and precisions during the training process. We will exploit these variables when we classify data, in a future chapter.

Adding a layer is simply done through the addLayer: method, which takes a layer as an argument:

```
NNetwork>>addLayer: aNeuronLayer
        "Add a neural layer. The added layer is linked to the already added
                layers."
        layers ifNotEmpty: [
                aNeuronLayer previousLayer: layers last.
                layers last nextLayer: aNeuronLayer ].
        layers add: aNeuronLayer.
```

Layers are linked to each other. When a layer is added, it is linked to the previous layer and that layer is linked to the added layer.

Feeding a neural network involves simply feeding the first hidden layer:

```
NNetwork>>feed: someInputValues
        "Feed the first layer with the provided inputs"
        ^ layers first feed: someInputValues
```

We need a way to easily create a neural network. If we want to build a network with one hidden layer and one output layer, we can define the following method:

```
NNetwork>>configure: nbOfInputs hidden: nbOfNeurons nbOfOutputs:
        nbOfOutput
        "Configure the network with the given parameters
        The network has only one hidden layer"
        | random |
        random := Random seed: 42.
        self addLayer: (NeuronLayer new initializeNbOfNeurons: nbOfNeurons
                nbOfWeights: nbOfInputs using: random).
        self addLayer: (NeuronLayer new initializeNbOfNeurons: nbOfOutput
                nbOfWeights: nbOfNeurons using: random).
```

If we want to have two hidden layers and one output layer, we define the following:

```
NNetwork>>configure: nbOfInputs hidden: nbOfNeurons1 hidden:
        nbOfNeurons2 nbOfOutputs: nbOfOutput
        "Configure the network with the given parameters
        The network has only one hidden layer"
        | random |
        random := Random seed: 42.
        self addLayer: (NeuronLayer new initializeNbOfNeurons: nbOfNeurons1
                nbOfWeights: nbOfInputs using: random).
        self addLayer: (NeuronLayer new initializeNbOfNeurons: nbOfNeurons2
                nbOfWeights: nbOfNeurons1 using: random).
        self addLayer: (NeuronLayer new initializeNbOfNeurons: nbOfOutput
                nbOfWeights: nbOfNeurons2 using: random).
```

We also need a way to obtain the number of outputs a neural network can have (we will need this in the chapter about data classification):

```
NNetwork>>numberOfOutputs
        "Return the number of output of the network"
        ^ layers last numberOfNeurons
```

The NNetwork class defines the learningRate: method to set the learning rate for each layer:

```
NNetwork>>learningRate: aLearningRate
        "Set the learning rate for all the layers"
        layers do: [ :l | l learningRate: aLearningRate ]
```

The learningRate: method is useful for setting a unique learning rate for all the neurons in our network. The basic functionalities are now defined. We can test our network implementation, as follows:

```
TestCase subclass: #NNetworkTest
        instanceVariableNames: ''
        classVariableNames: ''
        package: 'NeuralNetwork'
```

Our first test could be as follows:

```
NNetworkTest>>testBasic
        | n |
        n := NNetwork new.
        n configure: 2 hidden: 2 nbOfOutputs: 1.
        self assert: ((n feed: #(1 3)) anyOne closeTo: 0.6745388083637036
            precision: 0.0000000001).
        self assert: n numberOfOutputs equals: 1
```

As you can see, testBasic is rather simplistic. It builds a simple network that expects two inputs. Furthermore, it is composed of one hidden layer made of two neurons, and an output layer with only one neuron. The test then runs the forward feeding.

So far, this network is pretty useless, as it can only feed-forward some values along a set of neurons that are randomly initialized. The output is therefore random values. The next section covers the learning mechanism for neural networks.

3.4 Backpropagation

Backpropagation is an algorithm commonly employed to train neural networks. The purpose of the backpropagation algorithm is to find a set of neuron weights and biases to reduce the network prediction error.

So far, we built a network as a set of neurons, each being initialized with random weights and random biases. Conceptually, backpropagation is an algorithm for supervised learning of gradient descent (the next few chapters will discuss this terminology). In practice, this algorithm will find adequate weights and biases to identify patterns from the input values. This section focuses on informally presenting the algorithm and providing an implementation of it. The next chapter will provide a theoretical foundation of the algorithm. This chapter covers mostly the implementation of this theory.

The backpropagation algorithm is composed of three steps:

1. *Forward feeding the inputs.* We first activate each neuron of our network to make the network produce an output. As we have previously seen, this forward feeding goes from the left-most layer to the output layer.

2. *Backward propagating the errors through the network.* The output produced in the previous step has to be compared to the actual training dataset. We can therefore compute the error made by the network. This error is key to determining how far our network is from correctly predicting the training set. This backward propagation goes from the right-most layer (i.e., the output layer) to the left-most layer (i.e., the first hidden layer).

3. *Updating the neurons weights and biases.* From the error computed in the previous step, we adequately adjust each neuron weight and bias to hopefully reduce the error made by the network. In our implementation, we will start from the left-most layer and go the output layer.

3.4.1 Step 1: Forward Feeding

The first step is mostly implemented by the NNetwork>>feed: method; however, we need to slightly improve the Neuron class to remember the produced output. During the forward feeding (i.e., when the feed: method is called), output is produced by each neuron. This output has to be compared to the expected output during the second step. Making the network learn is based on the difference between the actual output of a neuron and the expected output. Each neuron must keep a reference of its output.

We add two variables, delta and output, to the Neuron class. Therefore, our new definition of Neuron is as follows:

```
Object subclass: #Neuron
        instanceVariableNames: 'weights bias learningRate
            activationFunction delta output'

        classVariableNames: ''
        package: 'NeuralNetwork'
```

The delta value has to be accessible from the outside, as follows:

```
Neuron>>delta
        "Return the delta value computed when propagating the error"
        ^ delta
```

We also need to rewrite the feed: method in the Neuron class to remember the output value, as follows:

```
Neuron>>feed: inputs
        | z |
        z := (inputs with: weights collect: [ :x :w | x * w ]) sum + bias.
        output := activationFunction eval: z.
        ^ output
```

We also need to access the output value for a given neuron, as follows:

```
Neuron>>output
        "Return the output value, previous computed when doing a feed:"
        ^ output
```

At this stage, it is important to run the unit tests we previously defined. In particular, we need to make sure that the small changes we defined in the Neuron class do not break any invariant. We are now done with the first phase of the backpropagation.

EXERCISE: Run the unit tests written in the previous chapter. This is important to verify whether or not a functional invariant is affected by these recent modifications.

3.4.2 Step 2: Error Backward Propagation

The second step of the backpropagation consists of propagating the errors computed in the output layer back in the network. We define the following method:

```
NNetwork>>backwardPropagateError: expectedOutputs
        "expectedOutputs corresponds to the outputs we are training the
            network against"
        self outputLayer backwardPropagateError: expectedOutputs
```

The argument of backwardPropagateError: corresponds to the expected output values used during the learning phase.

We also define the following helper method:

```
NNetwork>>outputLayer
        "Return the output layer, which is also the last layer"
        ^ layers last
```

We add the backwardPropagateError: method to backpropagate the error from the output layer:

```
NeuronLayer>>backwardPropagateError: expected
        "This is a recursive method. The backpropagation begins with
            the output layer (i.e., the last layer)"
        "We are in the output layer"
        neurons with: expected do: [ :neuron :exp |
                | theError |
                theError := exp - neuron output.
                neuron adjustDeltaWith: theError ].

        "We iterate"
        self previousLayer notNil
            ifTrue: [
                    self previousLayer backwardPropagateError ].
```

The backwardPropagateError: method takes as arguments the expected output values. It computes the error for each neuron in the output layers and calls the adjustDeltaWith: method. We will soon see this method.

Once the neuron in the output layer has its delta value adjusted, previous layers have to be recursively updated. The backwardPropagateError method implements this behavior:

```
NeuronLayer>>backwardPropagateError
        "This is a recursive method. The backpropagation begins with the
            output layer (i.e., the last layer)"

        "We are in a hidden layer"
        neurons doWithIndex: [ :neuron :j |
                | theError |
                theError := 0.0.
                self nextLayer neurons do: [ :nextNeuron |
                    theError := theError + ((nextNeuron weights at: j) *
                    nextNeuron delta)
                ].
                neuron adjustDeltaWith: theError
        ].

        self previousLayer notNil
                ifTrue: [
                        self previousLayer backwardPropagateError ].
```

The recursion ends on the first hidden layer, which is the layer with no previous layer. Note that we do not explicitly model the input layer since it has no purpose. We also need the following helper method on the Neuron class:

```
Neuron>>adjustDeltaWith: anError
        delta := anError * (activationFunction derivative: output)
```

We are now done with the second phase. Only the third phase remains to be implemented in order to create a functional neural network.

3.4.3 Step 3: Updating Neuron Parameters

Luckily, the third phase is rather simple. We recursively update the weights and biases based on the delta computed in the previous step. The main method is updateWeight:, as follows:

```
NNetwork>>updateWeight: initialInputs
        "Update the weights of the neurons using the initial inputs"
        layers first updateWeight: initialInputs
```

This method simply invokes updateWeight: on each first hidden layer:

```
NeuronLayer>>updateWeight: initialInputs
        "Update the weights of the neuron based on the set of initial input.
                This method assumes that the receiver of the message invoking
                that method is the first hidden layer."
        | inputs |
        inputs := initialInputs.

        neurons do: [ :n |
                n adjustWeightWithInput: inputs.
                n adjustBias ].

        self nextLayer ifNotNil: [
                self nextLayer updateWeight ]
```

The recursion happens in the updateWeight method:

```
NeuronLayer>>updateWeight
        "Update the weights of the neuron based on the set of initial
                input. This method assumes that the receiver of the
                message invoking that method is the first hidden layer.
        We are now in the second hidden layers or in the output layer"
        | inputs |
        inputs := self previousLayer neurons collect: #output.

        self updateWeight: inputs
```

We need the following methods to update a neuron's weights:

```
Neuron>>adjustWeightWithInput: inputs
        inputs withIndexDo: [ :anInput :index |
                weights at: index put: ((weights at: index) + (learningRate *
                        delta * anInput)) ]
```

We also need to update the bias, as follows:

```
Neuron>>adjustBias
        bias := bias + (learningRate * delta)
```

This ends the third and final phase of the backpropagation algorithm. We are now ready to hook the backpropagation phases together:

```
NNetwork>>train: someInputs desiredOutputs: desiredOutputs
        "Train the neural network with a set of inputs and some
                expected output"
        self feed: someInputs.
        self backwardPropagateError: desiredOutputs.
        self updateWeight: someInputs
```

Voila! We have implemented the necessary steps to train a neural network.

We can now test the network with the XOR example:

```
NNetworkTest>>testXOR
        | n |
        n := NNetwork new.
        n configure: 2 hidden: 3 nbOfOutputs: 1.

        20000 timesRepeat: [
                n train: #(0 0) desiredOutputs: #(0).
                n train: #(0 1) desiredOutputs: #(1).
                n train: #(1 0) desiredOutputs: #(1).
                n train: #(1 1) desiredOutputs: #(0).
        ].

        self assert: (n feed: #(0 0)) first < 0.1.
        self assert: (n feed: #(0 1)) first > 0.9.
        self assert: (n feed: #(1 0)) first > 0.9.
        self assert: (n feed: #(1 1)) first < 0.1.
```

If you were to try to decrease 20000 to a low value, 1000 for example, the network would not receive enough training and the test would ultimately fail.

3.5 What Have We Seen in This Chapter?

This chapter covered the following topics:

- *The general architecture of a fully-connected network.* This architecture drove our implementation effort.

- *Implementation of a neural network library.* We built a small API to build neural networks.

- *Implementation of the backpropagation algorithm.* Making a neural network learn is a fundamental operation that gives meaning to a network. A properly trained network can identify patterns. This chapter ended with a trivial example, the XOR logical gate. The coming chapters will cover real and representative examples.

CHAPTER 4

Theory on Learning

Understanding the learning algorithm that's used with neural networks involves a fair dose of mathematical notations. This chapter details some relevant theoretical aspects of the way that neural networks operate. We will therefore review the notions of loss functions and gradient descent. Note that this chapter is by no means a complete description of how networks learn. As indicated at the end of this chapter, many other people have done an excellent job of accurately describing the theoretical foundation of learning and optimization mechanisms. Instead, this chapter is meant to back up some aspects of the implementation explained in the previous chapters, with the assumption that you are comfortable with basic differential calculus.

You can safely skip this chapter if the theory behind neural networks does not interest you.

This chapter intensively uses Roassal to visualize data. You therefore need to have it loaded, as indicated in the previous chapters, in order to run the scripts in this chapter.

4.1 Loss Function

A network needs to learn in order to reduce the amount of errors it makes when making a prediction. Such a prediction could be used either to classify data or to run regression analysis. It is therefore essential to have a way to measure the errors made by a network. This is exactly what a loss function does.

A *loss function* is a measure of the error made by a particular model. The loss function is also commonly called the *error function* or the *cost function*. To illustrate the use and need of a loss function, let's consider the following problem: for a given set of points, what is the straight line that is the closest to these points?

Consider a set of four points:

```
points :={(1 @ 3.0). (3 @ 5.2). (2 @ 4.1). (4 @ 7.5)}.
```

© Alexandre Bergel 2020
A. Bergel, *Agile Artificial Intelligence in Pharo*, https://doi.org/10.1007/978-1-4842-5384-7_4

```
g := RTGrapher new.
d := RTData new.
d dotShape color: Color red.
d points: points.
d x: #x; y: #y.
g add: d.
g
```

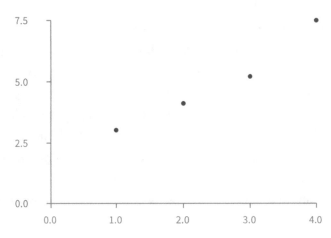

Figure 4-1. *Plotting four points*

Figure 4-1 shows the plot of these four points. Identifying a straight line that is close to these points means that we need to find the best value of a and b to have the function y = f(x) = a * x + b that is closest to these points. Since the points are not perfectly aligned, there is no line that exactly passes through all of them.

Let's pick an arbitrary a and b and draw a line:

```
points :={(1 @ 3.0). (3 @ 5.2). (2 @ 4.1). (4 @ 7.5)}.

a := 0.5.
b := 3.
f := [ :x | a * x + b ].

g := RTGrapher new.
d := RTData new.
d dotShape color: Color red.
d points: points.
```

```
d x: #x; y: #y.
g add: d.
d := RTData new.
d noDot; connectColor: Color blue.
d points: (0 to: 5).
d x: #yourself.
d y: f.
g add: d.
g
```

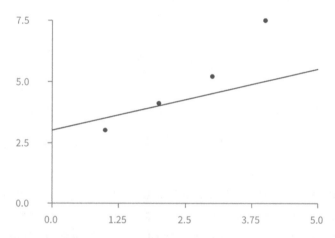

Figure 4-2. *Points and a line*

Figure 4-2 shows the points and the line that we arbitrarily defined. As you can see, the values we picked for a and b are not really good since the line is rather far away from the first and the fourth points. If we want to look for a better a and b, we need to translate in some way how far the line is from the points. We know our line is not great, but *how* bad is it? It is important that we have some way of measuring how good our approximation is.

A *loss function* is a mathematical function that maps an event, described as a set of values of one or more variables, into a numerical value. The numerical value given by the loss function intuitively represents the *cost* associated with the event, generally a numerical value. In this case, the loss function approximates the distance between the straight line with the four points. If the line is close to the four points, then the cost will be relatively low. Conversely, if it is far away from the points, the cost will be high. In our case, let's make the loss function tell us how off the straight line approximating the four points actually is.

A common loss function is the *mean squared error* (MSE). This function, in this case, is defined as the J function, as follows:

$$J(a,b) = \frac{1}{n} \sum_{i=1}^{n} \left(y_i - f_{a,b}(x_i) \right)^2$$

The J function is the mean squared difference between our line and each of the points. Note that J is always positive. The J function indicates how close the f function is to the points (x_i, y_i), for two given values of a and b. Note that the variables $x_1, \ldots, x_n$, $y_1, \ldots, y_n$ represent the data for which we would like to tune our model. In this case, these variables represent the points $(x_1, y_1), ..., (x_n, y_n)$. We can compute the value of J as follows:

```
points :={(1 @ 3.0) . (3 @ 5.2) . (2 @ 4.1) . (4 @ 7.5)}.
a := 0.5.
b := 3.
f := [ :x | a * x + b ].
j := (points collect: [ :p | (p y - (f value: p x)) squared ]) sum /
    points size.
```

The script returns 1.75. If we change a to 2 and b to -0.5, J equals 0.67. If you draw the line with a:=2 and b:=-0.5, you will see that it is closer to the red dots.

This example highlights an important use of the loss function. Changing parameters (a and b in this case) may increase or decrease the MSE. A smaller MSE indicates that our parameters are better since our model makes fewer mistakes.

How does this simple line relate to the learning mechanism of a neural network? The backpropagation algorithm is directly based on this mechanism, but on a larger scale. In this example we look for two values (a and b); in a neural network, we could look for thousands or millions of values, which correspond to the weights and biases.

Let's come back to the points and lines example. Our original problem was to find the straight line that is the closest to the points. This problem can therefore be translated into looking for an a and b that minimize the MSE value. Looking for these two values manually is rather tedious and laborious. The natural next step is automatically find the a and b values that minimize the loss function.

4.2 Gradient Descent

We know that modifying the a value changes the slope of our line, and modifying the b value moves the point in which the line intersects the Y axis. Therefore, each of the values modifies our line in a particular way. We are indeed searching for the best a and b, but we cannot try all the possibilities, essentially for two reasons: (i) it could be extremely expensive (trying all the combinations of possible values of a and b is a daunting task), and (ii) since a and b are continuous values, in theory, there is no finite set of values to try out.

In a general case, we have many parameters to search and it is not clear what each of them do. To express a small change in this model, we introduce the derivative. Since we focus on a small change of a single parameter in a multivariable function, we need to use a partial derivative.

The gradient descent is a general mechanism to look for an optimal model configuration. Gradient descent is intensively used in the field of mathematical optimization, including when making a neural network learn.

First, we need to calculate the partial derivative of MSE(a, b) with respect to each variable's value. Remember the J function:

$$J(a,b) = \frac{1}{n}\sum_{i=1}^{n}\left(y_i - f_{a,b}(x_i)\right)^2$$

If we expand the f function in J, we obtain the following:

$$J(a,b) = \frac{1}{n}\sum_{i=1}^{n}\left(y_i - (a.x_i + b)\right)^2$$

We can deduce the following partial derivatives with respect to a and b:

$$\frac{\partial J(a,b)}{\partial a} = \frac{-2}{n}\sum_{i}x_i.\left(y_i - (a.x_i + b)\right)$$

$$\frac{\partial J(a,b)}{\partial a} = \frac{-2}{n}\sum_{i}\left(y_i - (a.x_i + b)\right)$$

Applying the derivative functions $\frac{\partial J(a,b)}{\partial a}$ and $\frac{\partial J(a,b)}{\partial b}$ to a given a and b returns the direction to move the parameter in order to decrease the overall J(a, b).

We update a and b as follows:

$$a := a - \alpha \cdot \frac{\partial J(a,b)}{\partial a}(a,b)$$

$$b := b - \alpha \cdot \frac{\partial J(a,b)}{\partial b}(a,b)$$

The α value is the learning rate, indicating how fast the a and b should move toward the direction the derivative indicates.

Repeating the update of a and b will reduce the J loss function, which over time indicates that the model is improving. The following script demonstrates the whole process (we call α the learningRate):

```
points :={(1 @ 3.0) . (3 @ 5.2) . (2 @ 4.1) . (4 @ 7.5)}.


a := 0.5.
b := 3.
f := [ :x | x * a + b ].

learningRate := 0.01.
1000 timesRepeat: [
        deriMSEa := (2 / points size) * (points collect: [ :aPoint | aPoint
                x * (aPoint y - (f value: aPoint x)) negated ]) sum.
deriMSEb := (2 / points size) * (points collect: [ :aPoint | 1 * (
        aPoint y - (f value: aPoint x)) negated ]) sum.
        a := a - (learningRate * deriMSEa).
        b := b - (learningRate * deriMSEb).
].

g := RTGrapher new.
d := RTData new.
d dotShape color: Color red.
d points: points.
d x: #x; y: #y.
g add: d.
```

```
d := RTData new.
d noDot; connectColor: Color blue.
d dotShape color: Color blue.
d points: (0 to: 5).
d x: #yourself.
d y: f.
g add: d.
g
```

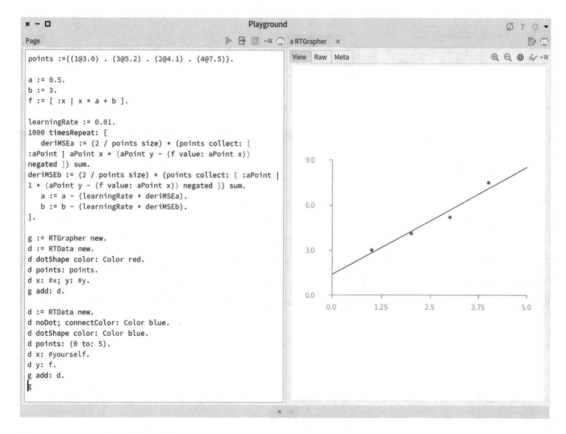

Figure 4-3. *Gradient descent*

Figure 4-3 gives the result of the script execution. The script computes the values of a and b that make the line closer to the four points. Said in other terms, the gradient descent technique is applied to minimize the J(a, b) cost function. Actually, after 1,000 iterations, we approximate the minimum of J at point (1.42, 1.39).

4.3 Parameter Update

The previous script may look a bit mysterious. We repeatedly decrease the a and b values with a little step, the result of multiplying a derivative value by learningRate. For some reason, the cost function decreases. Why is that? To answer this question, we need to dive deeper into some essential mathematical concepts.

Assuming a function f and a known value x, we write f(x). Knowing f(x), the Taylor series is used to approximate the value of f at x + e, where e is a very small value. Back at the beginning of the 18th Century, it was discovered that, in the case of an infinitely differentiable function (as neural networks operate with), we can approximate the value of f(x + e) as follows:

$$f(x+e) = f(x) + ef'(x)/1! + e^2 f''(x)/2! + \ldots$$

Why is computing f(x + e) such a thing? Well, a neural network is about making predictions/regressions, and learning is about determining which changes in the weights and biases make the network perform better, which is indirectly expressed as f(x + e). If f is the loss function, that means we would like to change weights and biases in such a way that f(x + e) is closer to 0 than f(x).

If we know f(x) and we search for f(x + e) to be less than f(x), we should change the parameters of the network to follow a descending slope of f. For a linear function, we can approximate up to the first derivative as f(x + e) = f(x) + ef'(x). Therefore, to minimize f(x + e), we need ef'(x) to decrease f(x). The only arbitrary value is e, so we need to find an e that minimizes f. The derivative ef'(x) with respect to e is:

$$\frac{d(e\ f'(x))}{de} = f'(x)$$

We can take e = f'(x). But in this case f maximizes, so we can choose e = −f'(x), which will minimize f. Replacing in our Taylor series:

$$f(x+e) = f(x) + ef'(x)$$
$$f(x - f'(x)) = f(x) + f'(x)^2$$

We can therefore deduce f(x − f'(x)) < f(x) since *we know* that f'(x)2 is a positive value (i.e., any value multiplied by itself is always positive). If we update x by subtracting the derivative of f, then f(x) is getting closer to 0. We can add the learning value with $e = -\alpha f'(x)$.

We can write the following expression:

$$x := x - \alpha f'(x)$$

This expression reduces the value of $f(x)$, if $f'(x) \neq 0$. Fortunately, we took care of choosing the cost function J to comply with these requirements. Otherwise, we would get stuck and stop learning.

Consider the following script:

```
points := {(1 @ 3.0) . (3 @ 5.2) . (2 @ 4.1) . (4 @ 7.5)}.

a := 0.5.
b := 3.

f := [ :x | x * a + b ].

learningRate := 0.01.

result := OrderedCollection new.
1000 timesRepeat: [
        deriMSEa := (2 / points size) * (points collect: [ :aPoint | aPoint
                x * (aPoint y - (f value: aPoint x)) negated ]) sum.
        deriMSEb := (2 / points size) * (points collect: [ :aPoint | 1 * (
                aPoint y - (f value: aPoint x)) negated ]) sum.
        a := a - (learningRate * deriMSEa).
        b := b - (learningRate * deriMSEb).

        mse := (points collect: [ :aPoint | (aPoint y - (f value: aPoint x)
                ) squared ]) sum / points size.
        result add: mse ].

g := RTGrapher new.
d := RTData new.
d noDot; connectColor: Color blue.
d points: result.
d y: #yourself.
g add: d.
g
```

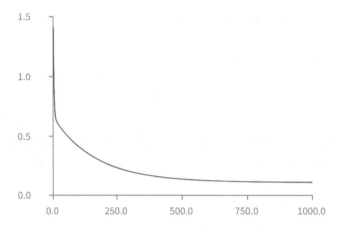

Figure 4-4. *Variation of the MSE cost function*

Figure 4-4 shows the variation of the cost function at each update of the a and b values. You can see that it gets closer to 0, but still remains far away. The reason is that since the points we used are not perfectly lined up, there is no a and b that make the cost value equal to 0. If you pick points that are perfectly lined up, (e.g., {(4@6.5). (2@3.5). (2@3.5). (2@3.5)}), then the cost function is asymptotic to 0.

4.4 Gradient Descent in Our Implementation

In Chapter 3, when we presented the activation function, we generalized the way an artificial neuron learns using the following rules:

$$\delta = (d - z) * \sigma'(z)$$
$$w_i(t+1) = w_i(t) + \delta * x_i * \alpha$$
$$b(t+1) = b(t) + \delta * \alpha$$

in which:

- δ is the difference between the desired output and the actual output of the neuron

- d is the example output, which is the desired value

- z is the actual output of the perceptron

- σ is the activation function (either the step or sigmoid function)

- σ' is the derivative function of σ

- i is the weight index, which ranges from 1 to N and is the number of weights contained in the neuron

- $w_i(t)$ is the weight i at a given time t

- $b(t)$ is the bias at a given time t

- x_i corresponds to the provided input at index i

- α is the learning rate, a small positive value close to 0

There is a strong similarity to the update rules we proposed for the a and b values. In this case, we have:

$$\frac{\partial J}{\partial w_i} = (d-z) * \sigma'(z) * x_i$$

$$\frac{\partial J}{\partial b} = (d-z) * \sigma'(z)$$

These formulas are exposed in the Neuron>>adjustDeltaWith:, NeuronLayer>> backwardPropagateError:, and NeuronLayer>>backwardPropagateError methods.

4.5 Stochastic Gradient Descent

The gradient descent computes the gradient of the loss function from the whole dataset. This is often difficult because minimum local points and saddle points may be found while searching for the global minimum. Furthermore, gradient descent adjusts the parameters based on the sum of the accumulated errors over all samples. This means that parameters are updated only after predicting each point of the whole dataset. This is becomes impracticable as soon as the dataset is large. You can see this in the previous section, where we used sum when computing deriMSEa and deriMSEb.

An alternative to *gradient descent* is *stochastic gradient descent* (SGD). With SCG, you first need to shuffle your training examples and divide them into small sets of datasets. Parameters are updated only after running a whole mini-batch. As a consequence, training over the whole dataset is faster using SGD. We will illustrate the idea with the current regression problem.

Consider the previous script, but slightly updated to take a larger dataset:

```
nbOfPoints := 100.
r := Random seed: 42.
points := (1 to: nbOfPoints) collect: [ :i | (i / nbOfPoints) asFloat @
        ((r next * 40 - 20 + i ) / nbOfPoints) asFloat ].

a := 0.5.
b := 3.
learningRate := 0.01.
f := [ :x | x * a + b ].

result := OrderedCollection new.
3000 timesRepeat: [
        deriMSEa := (2 / points size) * (points collect: [ :aPoint | aPoint
                x * (aPoint y - (f value: aPoint x)) negated ]) sum.
        deriMSEb := (2 / points size) * (points collect: [ :aPoint | 1 * (
                aPoint y - (f value: aPoint x)) negated ]) sum.
        a := a - (learningRate * deriMSEa).
        b := b - (learningRate * deriMSEb).

        mse := (points collect: [ :aPoint | (aPoint y - (f value: aPoint x)
                ) squared ]) sum / points size.
        result add: mse ].

g := RTGrapher new.
d := RTData new.
d noDot; connectColor: Color blue.
d points: result.
d y: #yourself.
g add: d.
g.
```

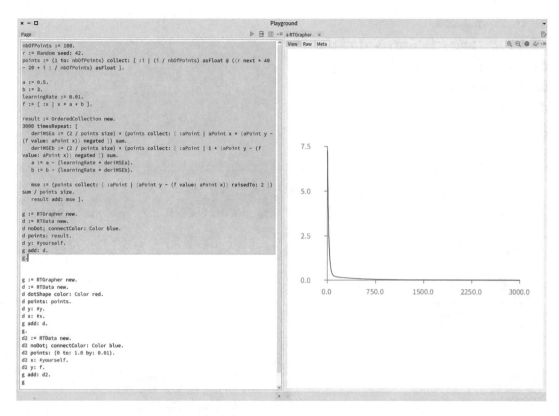

Figure 4-5. *Approximating a line passing by 100 points*

The script creates a dataset made up of 100 points. Points are located around the line y = x (the following script will illustrate this). Figure 4-5 indicates that our model is able to learn from the dataset using a gradient descent.

We can plot the 100 points and the line we found by appending the following script to the previous one:

```
...
g := RTGrapher new.
d := RTData new.
d dotShape color: Color red.
d points: points.
d y: #y.
d x: #x.
g add: d.
```

```
d2 := RTData new.
d2 noDot; connectColor: Color blue.
d2 points: (0 to: 1.0 by: 0.01).
d2 x: #yourself.
d2 y: f.
g add: d2.
g
```

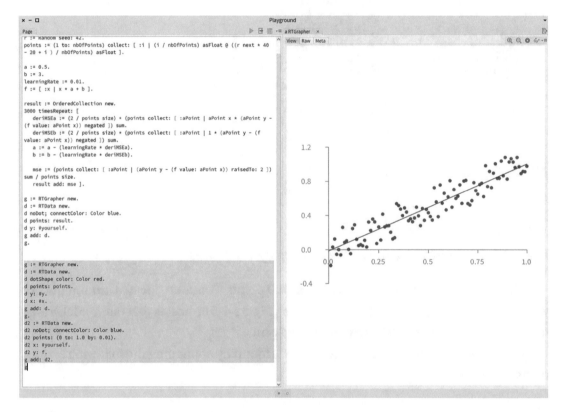

Figure 4-6. *Approximating a line passing by 100 points*

Figure 4-6 shows the layout of the dataset. Our model found a relatively good approximation.

Let's rewrite this script using a stochastic gradient descent algorithm:

```
nbOfPoints := 100.
r := Random seed: 42.
points := (1 to: nbOfPoints) collect: [ :i | (i / nbOfPoints) asFloat @
    ((r next * 40 - 20 + i ) / nbOfPoints) asFloat ].
```

```
currentBatch := OrderedCollection new.
miniBatches := OrderedCollection new.
batchSize := 5.
1 to: points size do: [ :index |
     currentBatch add: (points at: index).
    index \\ batchSize = 0
            ifTrue: [ miniBatches add: currentBatch copy. currentBatch :=
                OrderedCollection new. ]].
miniBatches.

a := 0.5.
b := 3.
learningRate := 0.01.
f := [ :x | x * a + b ].

result := OrderedCollection new.
1000 timesRepeat: [
     accumulatedMse := 0.
     miniBatches do: [ :pointsBatch |
            deriMSEa := (2 / pointsBatch size) * (pointsBatch collect: [ :
                aPoint | aPoint x * (aPoint y - (f value: aPoint x)) negated
                    ]) sum.
            deriMSEb := (2 / pointsBatch size) * (pointsBatch collect: [ :
                aPoint | 1 * (aPoint y - (f value: aPoint x)) negated ]) sum

                .
            a := a - (learningRate * deriMSEa).
            b := b - (learningRate * deriMSEb).

            mse := (pointsBatch collect: [ :aPoint | (aPoint y - (f value:
                aPoint x)) squared ]) sum / points size.
            accumulatedMse := accumulatedMse + mse
     ].
     result add: accumulatedMse ].
g := RTGrapher new.
d := RTData new.
d noDot; connectColor: Color blue.
```

```
d points: result.
d y: #yourself.
g add: d.
g.
```

This script is very similar to the version using gradient descent. The only differences are:

- The miniBatches variable contains batches of points. Each batch has a size of batchSize points.

- Instead of learning from points, the whole dataset, this script incrementally updates the a and b parameters after running over the pointsBatch mini-batch.

The result of the script is very similar to that of the gradient descent, as shown in Figure 4-7.

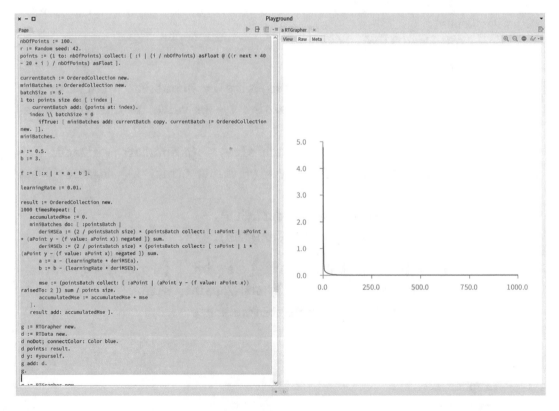

Figure 4-7. *Result of the stochastic gradient descent*

Figure 4-7 shows a very similar shape of the error function. This means this model is able to comfortably learn from our dataset, just as when we used the gradient descent.

The difference between the stochastic and non-stochastic algorithm is reflected when measuring performance.

Consider this script, which use the gradient descent algorithm:

```
[ nbOfPoints := 30000.
r := Random seed: 42.
points := (1 to: nbOfPoints) collect: [ :i | (i / nbOfPoints) asFloat @
        ((r next * 40 - 20 + i ) / nbOfPoints) asFloat ].

a := 0.5.
b := 3.
f := [ :x | x * a + b ].
learningRate := 0.01.

result := OrderedCollection new.
3000 timesRepeat: [
        deriMSEa := (2 / points size) * (points collect: [ :aPoint | aPoint
                x * (aPoint y - (f value: aPoint x)) negated ]) sum.
        deriMSEb := (2 / points size) * (points collect: [ :aPoint | 1 * (
            aPoint y - (f value: aPoint x)) negated ]) sum.
        a := a - (learningRate * deriMSEa).
        b := b - (learningRate * deriMSEb).

        mse := (points collect: [ :aPoint | (aPoint y - (f value: aPoint x)
                ) squared ]) sum / points size.
        result add: mse ]. ] timeToRun
```

The previous script returns 0:00:00:27.479 on our computer. Running the script takes over 27 seconds using 3.2GHz Intel Core i5, with 16GB of RAM.

Consider the stochastic version:

```
[ nbOfPoints := 30000.
r := Random seed: 42.
points := (1 to: nbOfPoints) collect: [ :i | (i / nbOfPoints) asFloat @
        ((r next * 40 - 20 + i ) / nbOfPoints) asFloat ].

currentBatch := OrderedCollection new.
```

```
miniBatches := OrderedCollection new.
batchSize := 5.
1 to: points size do: [ :index |
      currentBatch add: (points at: index).
     index \\ batchSize = 0
           ifTrue: [ miniBatches add: currentBatch copy. currentBatch :=
                OrderedCollection new. ]].

a := 0.5.
b := 3.
f := [ :x | x * a + b ].
learningRate := 0.01.

result := OrderedCollection new.
1000 timesRepeat: [
    accumulatedMse := 0.
    miniBatches do: [ :pointsBatch |
         deriMSEa := (2 / pointsBatch size) * (pointsBatch collect: [ :
              aPoint | aPoint x * (aPoint y - (f value: aPoint x))
              negated
              ]) sum.
         deriMSEb := (2 / pointsBatch size) * (pointsBatch collect: [ :
              aPoint | 1 * (aPoint y - (f value: aPoint x)) negated ]) sum
              .
         a := a - (learningRate * deriMSEa).
         b := b - (learningRate * deriMSEb).

         mse := (pointsBatch collect: [ :aPoint | (aPoint y - (f value:
              aPoint x)) squared ]) sum / points size.
         accumulatedMse := accumulatedMse + mse
    ].
    result add: accumulatedMse ].
] timeToRun
```

The script returns $0:00:00:18.847$. This takes almost 10 seconds less than the previous script, without significantly reducing the quality of the training.

4.6 The Derivative of the Sigmoid Function

The SigmoidAF>>derivative: method is defined as follows:

```
SigmoidAF>>derivative: output
        ^ output * (1 - output)
```

This section describes why this method is defined that way. As we previously saw, we have $\partial(x) = \dfrac{1}{1+e^{-x}}$.

Therefore, we also have the following:

$$\frac{d}{dx}\partial(x) = \frac{d}{dx}\frac{1}{1+e^{-x}}$$

$$= \frac{d}{dx}\left(1+e^{-x}\right)^{-1}$$

Since the derivative of x_n is nx^{n-1}, we have

$$= -(1+e^{-x})^{-2}(-e^{-x})$$

By rearranging the terms, we get

$$= \frac{e^{-x}}{\left(1+e^{-x}\right)^2}$$

$$= \frac{1}{1+e^{-x}} \cdot \frac{e^{-x}}{1+e^{-x}}$$

$$= \frac{1}{1+e^{-x}} \cdot \frac{\left(1+e^{-x}\right)-1}{1+e^{-x}}$$

$$= \frac{1}{1+e^{-x}} \cdot \left(\frac{1+e^{-x}}{1+e^{-x}} - \frac{1}{1+e^{-x}}\right)$$

$$= \frac{1}{1+e^{-x}} \cdot \left(1 - \frac{1}{1+e^{-x}}\right)$$

$$= \sigma(x) \cdot (1 - \sigma(x))$$

This result is expressed in the SigmoidAF>>derivative: method, which was shown in the previous chapters.

4.7 What Have We Seen in This Chapter?

This chapter presented some of theoretical foundations of the implementation found in the previous chapters. In particular, we learned about:

- The loss function as a measure of the amount of error made by a particular model, such as a neural network.

- The notion of gradient descent and the benefits of stochastic gradient descent.

- Connecting some aspects of our implementation with some theoretical properties of making a network learn.

4.8 Further Reading

A number of excellent bibliographical references exist. *Deep Learning* by Goodfellow, et al., published by MIT Press, is a reference of the field. Note that this book does not mention programming and implementation detail. It lays out the theoretical foundation of deep learning. A free version of the *Deep Learning* book is available from `www.deeplearningbook.org`.

CHAPTER 5

Data Classification

Neural networks have an incredibly large range of applications. Classifying data is a prominent one, and this chapter is devoted to it.

5.1 Training a Network

In the previous chapter, we saw that we can obtain a trained neural network to express the XOR logical gate. In particular, we saw the following script:

```
n := NNetwork new.
n configure: 2 hidden: 3 nbOfOutputs: 1.

20000 timesRepeat: [
        n train: #(0 0) desiredOutputs: #(0).
        n train: #(0 1) desiredOutputs: #(1).
        n train: #(1 0) desiredOutputs: #(1).
        n train: #(1 1) desiredOutputs: #(0).
].
```

After evaluating this script, the expression `n feed: #(1 0)` evaluates to `#(0.9530556769505442)`, which is an array having an expected float value close to 1. If we step back a bit, we see that the script is actually very verbose. For example, why should we manually handle the repetition? Why is the message `train:desiredOutputs:` sent so many times? We can greatly simplify the way networks are trained by providing a bit of infrastructure.

Consider the following method:

```
NNetwork>>train: train nbEpochs: nbEpochs
        "Train the network using the train dataset."
        | sumError outputs expectedOutput epochPrecision t |
```

89

© Alexandre Bergel 2020
A. Bergel, *Agile Artificial Intelligence in Pharo*, https://doi.org/10.1007/978-1-4842-5384-7_5

```
    1 to: nbEpochs do: [ :epoch |
        sumError := 0.
            epochPrecision := 0.
        train do: [ :row |
        outputs := self feed: row allButLast.
        expectedOutput := (1 to: self numberOfOutputs) collect: [ :
            notUsed | 0 ].
        expectedOutput at: (row last) + 1 put: 1.
         (row last = (self predict: row allButLast)) ifTrue: [
            epochPrecision := epochPrecision + 1 ].
        t := (1 to: expectedOutput size)
                collect: [ :i | ((expectedOutput at: i) - (outputs
                    at: i)) squared ].
        sumError := sumError + t sum.
        self backwardPropagateError: expectedOutput.
        self updateWeight: row allButLast.
    ].
    errors add: sumError.
        precisions add: (epochPrecision / train size) asFloat.
]
```

Predicting the output for a given set of input values may be implemented using a predict: method:

```
NNetwork>>predict: inputs
    "Make a prediction. This method assumes that the number of
        outputs is the same as the number of different values
        the network can output"
    "The index of a collection begins at 1 in Pharo"
    | outputs |
    outputs := self feed: inputs.
    ^ (outputs indexOf: (outputs max)) - 1
```

These two methods make the network training significantly less verbose. The script that trains a network with XOR logical gate may now be written as follows:

```
n := NNetwork new.
n configure: 2 hidden: 3 nbOfOutputs: 2.
```

```
data := {#(0 0 0) .
      #(0 1 1) .
      #(1 0 1) .
      #(1 1 0) }.
n train: data nbEpochs: 20000
```

The data variable is an array of arrays of numbers. Each row represents an example and it contains the input values and the output value. For example, the row #(0 1 1) represents the line ntrain: #(0 1)desiredOutputs: #(1). Note that the neural network has two output neurons.

This is the result of using a one-hot encoding for the output. The examples have two different output values, either 0 or 1. So if we use the one-hot encoding, we have two output neurons, each neuron for a particular value. Later in this chapter we will detail this encoding.

Another example of using the syntax we have just introduced follows:

```
n := NNetwork new.
n configure: 3 hidden: 8 nbOfOutputs: 8.

data := {#(0 0 0 0).
      #(0 0 1 1).
      #(0 1 0 2).
      #(0 1 1 3).
      #(1 0 0 4).
      #(1 0 1 5).
      #(1 1 0 6).
      #(1 1 1 7) }.
n train: data nbEpochs: 1000.
```

This code builds a neural network trained to convert binary numbers into a decimal number. The binary number is encoded using three bits, so we need a neural network with three inputs. Since the decimal value ranges from 0 to 7, we need eight output neurons of the network. As an example, to convert the binary number, you can evaluate the following expression after the previous script:

```
...
n predict: #(0 1 1)
```

This last expression returns 3, thus indicating a good conversion. The way `train:nbEpochs:` and `predict:` are implemented enforces the training data to follow some rules. Each element contained in `data` must be a collection of numbers. All but the last numbers represent the inputs values. The last value of an example, presented as an array, is the expected output value. For example, considering the example `#(0 1 1 3)`, the value 3 is the expected value when `#(0 1 1)` is provided as input. The expected output is a positive value ranging from 0 to the number of outputs of the neural network minus one.

5.2 Neural Network as a Hashmap

Let's step back a bit. We spent six chapters to motivate, describe, and incrementally build neural networks. But we are using a neural network pretty much the way we would use a regular hashmap. Consider the following example:

```
data := {#(0 0 0 0).
    #(0 0 1 1).
    #(0 1 0 2).
    #(0 1 1 3).
    #(1 0 0 4).
    #(1 0 1 5).
    #(1 1 0 6).
    #(1 1 1 7) }.

d := Dictionary new.
data do: [ :anExample |
    d at: anExample allButLast put: anExample last ].
d at: #(0 1 1)
```

The script produces 3. The `d` variable is a dictionary filled with the example data. The values we used as input in the neural network are used as keys in the dictionary. Indeed, using a dictionary has many benefits here: filling a dictionary is significantly faster than training a neural network (by several orders of magnitude!), and getting a value for a particular key is also significantly faster than feed-forwarding a network.

However, a hashmap requires the exact same key (or at least adequately answers to the message =). A neural network does not require the exact same input values. Consider the following script:

```
n := NNetwork new.
n configure: 3 hidden: 8 nbOfOutputs: 8.

data := {#(0 0 0 0).
    #(0 0 1 1).
    #(0 1 0 2).
    #(0 1 1 3).
    #(1 0 0 4).
    #(1 0 1 5).
    #(1 1 0 6).
    #(1 1 1 7) }.
n train: data nbEpochs: 1000.
n predict: #(0.4 0.7 0.6)
```

By returning the value 3, the network can match the input values #(0.4 0.7 0.6) to #(0 1 1). A hashmap cannot make such a connection without the programmer explicitly telling it to do so, and that is the whole point of neural networks: establishing connections between input data and identifying the most relevant data, without intervention from the programmer.

5.3 Visualizing the Error and the Topology

We saw that the first step of the backpropagation is to evaluate the network with the provided inputs. The output values are then compared with the expected output values. The difference between the actual output and the expected output is then used to adjust the weights and biases by backpropagating these differences to the network.

The NNetwork>>train:nbEpochs: method contains the statements errors add: sumError and precisions add: (epochPrecision / train size)asFloat. These two lines of code have the effect of recording the value of sumError, indicating how well the network has performed for the provided example, and the value of precision per epoch. These two collections of numbers can be visualized as a helper to characterize the overall learning process for a given network and example set.

We define the viewLearningCurve method on the NNetwork class:

```
NNetwork>>viewLearningCurve
        "Draw the error and precision curve"
        | b ds |
        "No need to draw anything if the network has not been run"
        errors ifEmpty: [ ^ RTView new
                            add: (RTLabel elementOn: 'Should first run
                                the network');
                            yourself ].
        b := RTDoubleGrapher new.

        "We define the size of the charting area"
        b extent: 500 @ 300.
        ds := RTData new.
        "A simple optimization that Roassal offers"
        ds samplingIfMoreThan: 2000.
        "No need of dots, simply a curve"
        ds noDot; connectColor: Color blue.
        ds points: (errors collectWithIndex: [ :y :i | i -> y ]).
        ds x: #key.
        ds y: #value.
        ds dotShape rectangle color: Color blue.
        b add: ds.
        ds := RTData new.
        ds samplingIfMoreThan: 2000.
        ds noDot.
        ds connectColor: Color red.
        ds points: (precisions collectWithIndex: [ :y :i | i -> y ]).
        ds x: #key.
        ds y: #value.
        ds dotShape rectangle color: Color blue.
        b addRight: ds.
        b axisX noDecimal; title: 'Epoch'.
        b axisY title: 'Error'.
        b axisYRight title: 'Precision'; color: Color red.
        ^ b
```

The following method defines a visualization of the errors and precisions variables:

```
NNetwork>>viewLearningCurveIn: composite
        <gtInspectorPresentationOrder: -10>
        composite roassal2
                title: 'Learning';
                initializeView: [ self viewLearningCurve ]
```

The NNetwork>>viewLearningCurveIn: method uses the GTInspector framework to add a particular tab in the inspector.

Inspecting the following code snippet displays the error curve (see Figure 5-1):

```
n := NNetwork new.
n configure: 2 hidden: 3 nbOfOutputs: 2.

data := {#(0 0 0) .
     #(0 1 1) .
     #(1 0 1) .
     #(1 1 0) }.
n train: data nbEpochs: 10000.
```

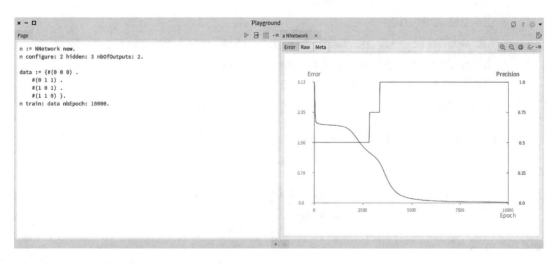

Figure 5-1. *Visualizing the learning*

The learning curve indicates the effect of the number of epochs in making the neural network learn. The fact that the blue line is close to 0 is a strong indicator that the neural network is properly learning. The red line reaches 1.0, which means that the network is accurate.

Similarly, we can visualize the topology of the network using the following method:

```
NNetwork>>viewNetwork
        | b lb |
        b := RTMondrian new.

        b nodes: layers forEach: [ :aLayer |
                b shape circle size: 20.
                b nodes: aLayer neurons.
                b layout verticalLine.
        ].

        b shape arrowedLine; withShorterDistanceAttachPoint.
        b edges connectTo: #nextLayer.
        b layout horizontalLine gapSize: 30; center.

        b build.

        lb := RTLegendBuilder new.
        lb view: b view.
        lb addText: self numberOfNeurons asString, ' neurons'.
        lb addText: self numberOfInputs asString, ' inputs'.
        lb build.
        ^ b view
```

We need to define the helper method, as follows:

```
NNetwork>>numberOfInputs
        "Return the number of inputs the network has"
        ^ layers first neurons size
```

and the method:

```
NNetwork>>numberOfNeurons
        "Return the total number of neurons the network has"
        ^ (layers collect: #numberOfNeurons) sum
```

Similarly, we need to extend GTInspector to consider the visualization within GTInspector (see Figure 5-2):

```
NNetwork>>viewNetworkIn: composite
        <gtInspectorPresentationOrder: -5>
        composite roassal2
                title: 'Network';
                initializeView: [ self viewNetwork ]
```

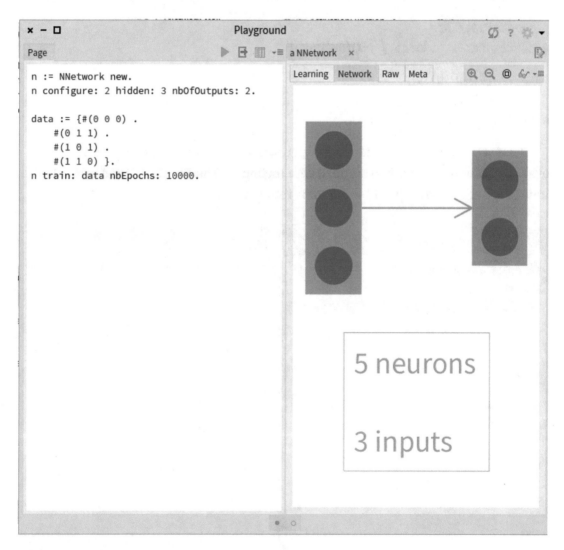

Figure 5-2. *Visualizing the network topology*

You can click a neuron to reveal its weights and bias.

5.4 Contradictory Data

The blue error curve quantifies the error made by the network during the learning phase. It may happen that the error has some plateaus. In such a case, increasing the number of epochs may have the effect of lowering the error curve.

In some cases, if the error curve cannot get close to 0, it may indicate a contradiction in the data.

Consider the following example:

```
n := NNetwork new.
n configure: 2 hidden: 3 nbOfOutputs: 2.

data := {#(0 0 0) .
       #(0 0 1) }.
n train: data nbEpochs: 1000.
```

The script trains a neural network with two contradictory examples. The first example trains the network to output 0 with the inputs 0 and 0. The second example trains the network to output 1 for the same input values.

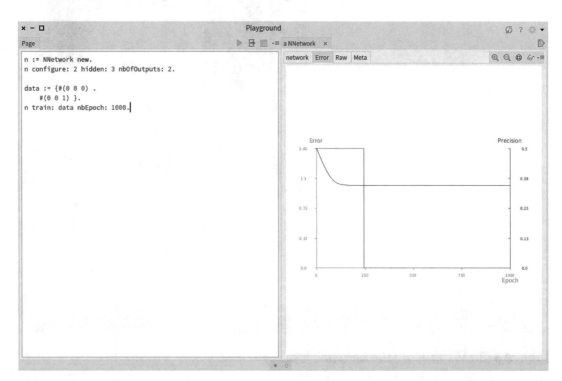

Figure 5-3. *Data contradiction*

Figure 5-3 illustrates the error and precision curves in presence of contradicting data. The script makes the neural network learn two different outputs for exactly the same input values. As a consequence, the network will have to make mistakes during the learning phase.

In a real and non-trivial dataset it is likely that this situation will happen. If the contradictory occurrences are not common, the network will then consider this contradiction as pure noise and will have a tendency to diminish it.

5.5 Classifying Data and One-Hot Encoding

Classification can be defined as grouping elements based on their features. Elements sharing similar features are grouped together. The previous XOR dataset may be considered a (simple) classification model in which each group is made of two elements. Group 0 is made of the elements [0, 0] and [1, 1], while group 1 is made of [0, 1] and [1, 0].

Have you noticed that to learn the XOR dataset we used a neural network with two outputs? The reason is that we encode the output value using the *one-hot encoding*.

One-hot encoding is a simple mechanism that converts a categorical variable into a numerical form, eligible to be fed into a neural network. Consider the variable v, which represents a word within the set { "hello", "bonjour", "Buenos dias" }. Applying one-hot encoding would assign a unique number to each word. For example, "hello" is associated with the index 0, "bonjour" associated with index 1, and "Buenos dias" with 2. The value of v can then be encoded with three different bits, since the dataset has three different words. We can then encode the words:

- "hello" = [1, 0, 0]

- "bonjour" = [0, 1, 0]

- "Buenos dias" = [0, 0, 1]

If the variable v has to be provided to a neural network, then three neurons can be used for that purpose.

We have defined the XOR dataset as follows:

```
n := NNetwork new.
n configure: 2 hidden: 3 nbOfOutputs: 2.
```

```
data := {#(0 0 0) .
     #(0 1 1) .
     #(1 0 1) .
     #(1 1 0) }.
n train: data nbEpochs: 10000
```

Since there are two different values of the datasets, 0 and 1, we have two output neurons: the value 0 is encoded [1, 0], and 1 is encoded [0, 1].

Now that we explained the one-hot encoding, we can proceed with a larger dataset.

5.6 The Iris Dataset

The Iris flower dataset is a popular dataset used by the machine learning community (see http://archive.ics.uci.edu/ml/datas). This dataset was collected in 1936 by Ronald Fisher and presented in the seminal paper entitled, "The Use of Multiple Measurements in Taxonomic Problems." The dataset contains 50 samples of three families of Iris, called *Iris setosa*, *Iris virginica,* and *Iris versicolor*. We refer to these families as *classes*.

We provide a copy of this dataset on https://agileartificialintelligence. github.io/Datasets/iris.csv. Within Pharo, you can fetch the dataset using the following expression:

```
(ZnEasy get: 'https://agileartificialintelligence.github.io/Datasets/
        iris.csv') contents.
```

The code fetches the iris.csv file and returns its content. The file structure, as given in the CSV header, is as follows:

```
sepal_length,sepal_width,petal_length,petal_width,species
```

However, fetching the file is just the first small step toward making the file able to be processed by a neural network. For example, we need to convert each row of the file into a set of numerical values (remember that neural networks can only accept numbers as input).

In order to feed a network with the IRIS dataset, we need to perform the following steps:

1. Fetch the file from the Internet.

2. Cut the file content, represented as very long text, into textual lines.

3. Ignore the first line of the file since it contains the CSV header, which is not relevant to the network.

4. Parse the CSV file.

5. In the table, replace each flower name with a numerical value, which could be 0, 1, or 2.

The following script performs these five steps:

```
"The execution of this script initializes the variable irisData.
This variable is used in the subsequent scripts of this chapter"
irisCSV := (ZnEasy get: 'https://agileartificialintelligence.github.io/
        Datasets/iris.csv') contents.
lines := irisCSV lines.
lines := lines allButFirst.
tLines := lines collect: [ :l |
            | ss |
            ss := l substrings: ','.
            (ss allButLast collect: [ :w | w asNumber ]), (Array with: ss
                last) ].

irisData := tLines collect: [ :row |
            | l |
            row last = 'setosa' ifTrue: [ l := #( 0 ) ].
            row last = 'versicolor' ifTrue: [ l := #( 1 ) ].
            row last = 'virginica' ifTrue: [ l := #( 2 ) ].
            row allButLast, l ].

irisData.
```

To summarize, the script converts a very long string, similar to the following:

```
'sepal_length,sepal_width,petal_length,petal_width,species
5.1,3.5,1.4,0.2,setosa
4.9,3.0,1.4,0.2,setosa
4.7,3.2,1.3,0.2,setosa
...
'
```

Into a collection of numbers, as follows:

#(#(5.1 3.5 1.4 0.2 0) #(4.9 3.0 1.4 0.2 0) #(4.7 3.2 1.3 0.2 0) ...

The result of the script is the value of the irisData variable. In the remainder of the chapter, when we will refer to the Iris dataset, we actually mean the irisData value.

5.7 Training a Network with the Iris Dataset

Training a network is actually easy since we carefully prepared the battlefield. The remainder of the chapter assumes that the variable irisData is defined as shown in the previous section. Consider the following code:

```
n := NNetwork new.
n configure: 4 hidden: 6 nbOfOutputs: 3.
n train: irisData nbEpochs: 1000.
```

This code builds a network with four input values, one hidden layer with six neurons, and an output layer with three neurons. The number of inputs represents the size of a row in the Iris dataset minus one, which is the expected output value, which is not part of the input. We pick an arbitrary six as the size of the hidden layer. A general rule of thumb for the hidden layer size is to include 50% more neurons than the number of inputs. We have three neurons in the output layers since there are three different families of Iris.

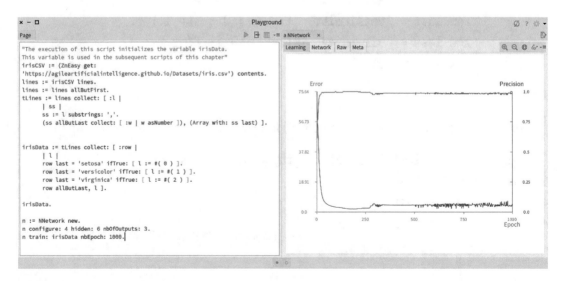

Figure 5-4. *Learning the Iris dataset*

Figure 5-4 represents the error curve of the network. The blue curve is very close to 0, which indicates that the network is learning and the dataset does not have a contradiction. The red curve is very close to 1.0, which means that the network has excellent precision. The network is able to learn and achieve good precision during that learning process.

The configuration of our network has two parameters: the number of neurons in the hidden layers, and the number of epochs to consider. There are no general rules on how to pick these parameters. For now, experiments and ad hoc tries remain the easiest approach to configure a network. The third part of the book, about neuroevolution, will cover the search for hyperparameters using genetic algorithms.

5.8 The Effect of the Learning Curve

When we defined the Neuron class, in Chapter 2, we defined the learningRate: method to set the learning rate of the neuron. In general, for a single neuron, the higher the learning rate, the quicker it will learn. We can easily illustrate this effect in the following example (see Figure 5-5):

```
g := RTGrapher new.
#(0.001 0.01 0.1 0.2 0.3)
        doWithIndex: [ :lr :index |
                learningCurveNeuron := OrderedCollection new.
                0 to: 1000 do: [ :nbOfTrained |
                        r := Random new seed: 42.
                        p := Neuron new.
                        p weights: #(-1 -1).
                        p bias: 2.
                        p learningRate: lr.
                        nbOfTrained
                                timesRepeat: [ p train: #(0 0) desiredOutput: 0.
                                        p train: #(0 1) desiredOutput: 0.
                                        p train: #(1 0) desiredOutput: 0.
                                        p train: #(1 1) desiredOutput: 1 ].
                        res := ((p feed: #(0 0)) - 0) abs + ((p feed: #(0 1)) - 0)
                                abs
```

```
                    + ((p feed: #(1 0)) - 0) abs + ((p feed: #(1 1)) - 1)
                    abs.
                learningCurveNeuron add: res / 4 ].
            d := RTData new.
            d label: 'Sigmoid neuron lr = ' , lr asString.
            d noDot.
            d connectColor: (RTPalette c1 at: index).
            d points: learningCurveNeuron.
            d y: #yourself.
            g add: d ].
g legend addText: 'Learning rate effect'.
g
```

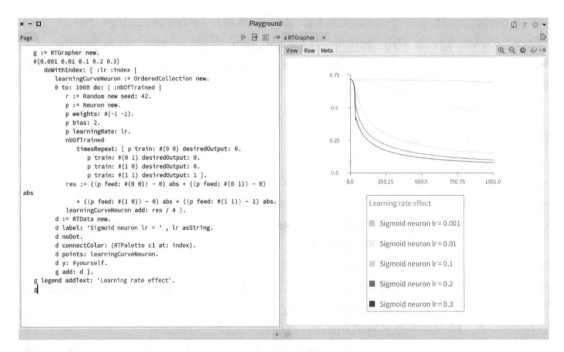

Figure 5-5. *The effect of the learning rate on a single neuron*

Figure 5-5 represents the error curves during the training of five different values of the learning rate (0.001, 0.01, 0.1, 0.2, and 0.3). The graph indicates that the higher the learning rate, the quicker it learns.

The effect observed on a single sigmoid neuron *cannot* be observed on a whole network. We can train a network for the Iris dataset for different values of the learning rate. Consider the following script:

```
n := NNetwork new.
n configure: 4 hidden: 6 nbOfOutputs: 3.
n learningRate: 0.3. " Repeat the script with a different value"
n train: irisData nbEpochs: 1000.
```

We run the script for the 0.001, 0.01, 0.1, and 0.3 values. The results are presented in Figure 5-6.

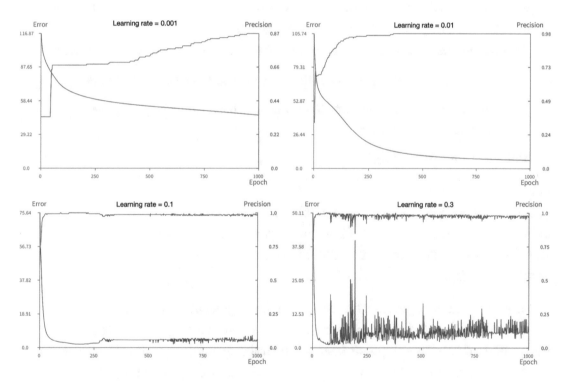

Figure 5-6. *The effect of the learning rate for a neural network on the Iris dataset*

We clearly see that with a low learning rate, the precision and error curves are rather stable. With a relatively high learning rate, we experience very frequent peaks.

Unfortunately, there is no general methodology to identify the adequate learning rate or the architecture of the network. Manual tuning is the norm so far. Some optimization algorithms, such as the Adam optimization algorithm, vary the learning rate during training.

5.9 Testing and Validation

So far, we have built a network trained on the whole Iris dataset: we use all the entries in the .csv file to train the network. The network seems to properly learn, as the network makes fewer errors while increasing precision along the epochs (i.e., the error curve is getting very close to 0).

The error curve indicates how well the network is learning the provided dataset. If we wish to know how well the network classifies data, it would not make much sense to test it on data it was trained with. Asking a network how well it performs in the presence of the very same data used to train it is not much of a challenge. However, an important question is how well does the network behave in the presence of data that it has never seen? In other words, how well does the network classify unknown data?

One way to answer this question is to divide the Iris dataset in two distinct parts:

- *Training dataset*: A portion of the .csv file used to train the network.

- *Test dataset*: A second portion of the file is used to see how effective the trained network is.

Consider the following script:

```
cut := 0.8.
cutTraining := (irisData size * cut) rounded.
cutTest := (irisData size * (1 - cut)) rounded.
trainingData := irisData first: cutTraining.
testData := irisData last: cutTest.
```

The cut variable represents the portion of the original Iris dataset used for the training: 80% of irisData is used for training. The cutTraining variable represents the number of irisData elements used for the training. Similarly, cutTest represents the number of elements for the test. The rounded message, when sent to a float value, returns the integer nearest to the float value (e.g., 4.6 rounded returns 5, 4.3 rounded returns 4, and 4.5 rounded returns 5).

We can train a network based on the trainingData:

```
...
n := NNetwork new.
n configure: 4 hidden: 6 nbOfOutputs: 3.
n train: trainingData nbEpochs: 1000.
```

We see that the network can properly learn trainingData, as the error curve is close to 0, similar to Figure 5-4.

Consider this script (it assumes the existence of the previously seen variable irisData):

```
cut := 0.8.
cutTraining := (irisData size * cut) rounded.
cutTest := (irisData size * (1 - cut)) rounded.
trainingData := irisData first: cutTraining.
testData := irisData last: cutTest.
n := NNetwork new.
n configure: 4 hidden: 6 nbOfOutputs: 3.
n train: trainingData nbEpochs: 1000.

(((testData collect: [ :d |
    (n predict: d allButLast) = d last
]) select: [ :d | d = true]) size / testData size) asFloat round: 2
```

Evaluating the script returns 0.9, which represents the accuracy of our network: 90% of the elements contained in testData are correctly predicted.

We will now detail the last part of the script:

```
(((testData collect: [ :d |
    (n predict: d allButLast) = d last
]) select: [ :d | d = true]) size / testData size) asFloat round: 2
```

For all the elements of testData, we predict the classification of the input (dallButLast) and compare the network result with the expected result (dlast). The result of the collect: instruction is a list of binary values (true or false). We only select the true values and count how many there are (size). We then compute the ratio with the size of the test data (/testDatasize). Finally, we only consider a float value with two decimals.

EXERCISE: Determine the accuracy of the network with a cut of 0.6, 0.5, and 0.4. Consider a cut of 0.7, as illustrated in the script:

```
cut := 0.7.
cutTraining := (irisData size * cut) rounded.
cutTest := (irisData size * (1 - cut)) rounded.
trainingData := irisData first: cutTraining.
testData := irisData last: cutTest.
```

```
n := NNetwork new.
n configure: 4 hidden: 6 nbOfOutputs: 3.
n train: trainingData nbEpochs: 1000.

(((testData collect: [ :d |
    (n predict: d allButLast) = d last
]) select: [ :d | d = true]) size / testData size) asFloat round: 2
```

The result is 0.0, indicating that the network cannot make a prediction. Why not? When we reduce the size of the training data (for example, if the cut equals 0.5), the accuracy of the network increases. This is an effect of the data organization.

If we inspect the 150 values of irisData, we see that they are actually ordered: the first 50 entries are Iris setosa (the expected value is 0), the subsequent 50 entries are Iris versicolor (the expected value is 1), and the last 50 entries are Iris virginica (the expected value is 2). The fact that the original dataset is ordered has an impact on the accuracy of the network. Luckily, this problem is easy to solve: a simple shuffling of the original data will prevent the network from suffering the entry order.

Consider this new script:

```
shuffledIrisData := irisData shuffleBy: (Random seed: 42).
cut := 0.8.
cutTraining := (shuffledIrisData size * cut) rounded.
cutTest := (shuffledIrisData size * (1 - cut)) rounded.
trainingData := shuffledIrisData first: cutTraining.
testData := shuffledIrisData last: cutTest.
n := NNetwork new.
n configure: 4 hidden: 6 nbOfOutputs: 3.
n train: trainingData nbEpochs: 1000.

(((testData collect: [ :d |
    (n predict: d allButLast) = d last
]) select: [ :d | d = true]) size / testData size) asFloat round: 2
```

The script introduces a new variable, called shuffledIrisData. It is initialized with irisData shuffleBy: (Random seed: 42), which creates a copy of irisData shuffled using a random number. If we wish not to use a random number generator and therefore have a slightly different result at each run, we could simply use shuffled instead of shuffleBy: (Random seed: 42).

5.10 Normalization

When we presented the perceptron and the sigmoid neuron, we saw that the activation function was applied to the value $z = w.x + b$. Applied to a neuron with two inputs, we have $z = x_1.w_1 + x_2.w_2 + b$. In the examples, all the xi and output values range in the same interval, from 0 to 1. In the logical gate example, each xi is either 0 or 1. In the Iris dataset, we can compute the minimum and maximum for each input value:

```
max := OrderedCollection new.
min := OrderedCollection new.
(1 to: 4) collect: [ :i |
    max add: (irisData collect: [ :d | d at: i ]) max.
    min add: (irisData collect: [ :d | d at: i ]) min.
].
{ max . min }
```

The result of this script indicates that overall, the value ranges from 0.1 to 7.9. In other words, all the input values have a range within the same magnitude.

Why is this important? Consider the example we previously saw when converting binary numbers to decimals:

```
n := NNetwork new.
n configure: 3 hidden: 8 nbOfOutputs: 8.

data := {#(0 0 0 0).
      #(0 0 1 1).
      #(0 1 0 2).
      #(0 1 1 3).
      #(1 0 0 4).
      #(1 0 1 5).
      #(1 1 0 6).
      #(1 1 1 7) }.
n train: data nbEpochs: 1000.
```

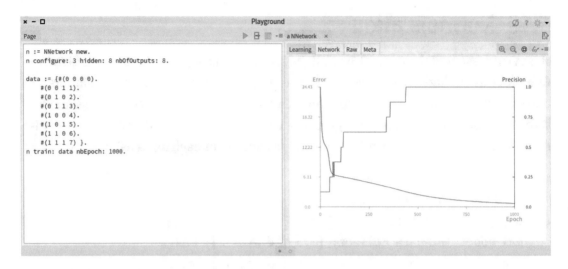

Figure 5-7. *Learning the Iris dataset*

Figure 5-7 shows the error curve of the network. Each input value is either 0 or 1. We will produce a different, but equivalent, dataset by changing the scale of each column. In this revised example, we will make the first input either 0 or 0.1, and the second input either 0 or 1000. Consider the following:

```
n := NNetwork new.
n configure: 3 hidden: 8 nbOfOutputs: 8.

data := {#(0 0 0 0).
      #(0 0 1 1).
      #(0 1000 0 2).
      #(0 1000 1 3).
      #(0.1 0 0 4).
      #(0.1 0 1 5).
      #(0.1 1000 0 6).
      #(0.1 1000 1 7) }.
n train: data nbEpochs: 10000.
```

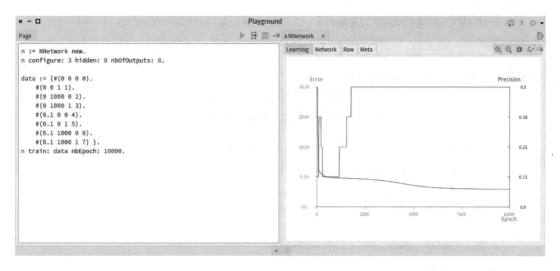

Figure 5-8. *The Iris dataset, oddly scaled*

Figure 5-8 shows the error curve and the precision along the epochs. The evolution of the error has reached a plateau and the precision does not go above 0.5. This is because changing the scale of a particular input value affects the relevance of these values.

The sigmoid function returns a value between 0 and 1. Having the same range for the input improves the learning performance. One way to avoid data distortion is to have each input range between 0 and 1. The process of transforming data from an arbitrary range to a restricted range is called *normalization*. Luckily, normalizing data is rather simple. Consider the function f:

$$f(x) = \frac{(x - d_L)(n_H - n_L)}{d_H - d_L} + n_L$$

The function f(x) normalizes a value, x. The variable d represents the high and low values of the data. The variable n represents the desired high and low normalization range. In most cases, we will have n_L = 0 and r_H = 1.

We can therefore implement the following utility class:

```
Object subclass: #Normalization
        instanceVariableNames: ''
        classVariableNames: ''
        package: 'NeuralNetwork'
```

We then define the normalizeData: method, which takes as an argument some training data:

```
Normalization>>normalizeData:
    aCollectionOfTrainingDataWithExpectedOutput
    "Normalize the data provided as argument"

    | nbOfColumns min max |
    "We exclude the expected output"
    nbOfColumns := aCollectionOfTrainingDataWithExpectedOutput first
        size - 1.

    min := OrderedCollection new.
    max := OrderedCollection new.
    1 to: nbOfColumns do: [ :index |
        | column |
        column := aCollectionOfTrainingDataWithExpectedOutput collect:
            [ :row | row at: index ].
        min add: column min.
        max add: column max ].

    ^ self normalizeData: aCollectionOfTrainingDataWithExpectedOutput
        min: min max: max
```

The real work happens in this second method:

```
Normalization>>normalizeData:
    aCollectionOfTrainingDataWithExpectedOutput min: minimumValues max:
    maximumValues
    | nbOfColumns result mn mx |
    nbOfColumns := aCollectionOfTrainingDataWithExpectedOutput first
        size - 1.

    result := OrderedCollection new.
    aCollectionOfTrainingDataWithExpectedOutput do: [ :row |
        | t v |
        t := OrderedCollection new.
        1 to: nbOfColumns do: [ :index |
```

```
            v := row at: index.
            mn := minimumValues at: index.
            mx := maximumValues at: index.
            t add: ((v - mn) / (mx - mn)) asFloat
        ].
        t add: row last.
        result add: t asArray ].
    ^ result asArray
```

We can test these methods. First we can create a unit test called NormalizationTest:

```
TestCase subclass: #NormalizationTest
        instanceVariableNames: ''
        classVariableNames: ''
        package: 'NeuralNetwork'

NormalizationTest>>testSimpleNormalization
        | input expectedNormalizedInput |
        input := #( #(10 5 1) #(2 6 0) ).
        expectedNormalizedInput := Normalization new normalizeData: input.
        self assert: expectedNormalizedInput equals: #(#(1.0 0.0 1) #(0.0
            1.0 0))
```

This small test method illustrates the result of a simple normalization. For example, the first column of the two entries of input has 10 as the highest value and 2 as the lowest. The normalization replaces the highest value by 1.0 and the lowest by 0.0.

Note that the normalization makes sense only if two or more entries are provided as input. We can test erroneous cases:

```
NormalizationTest>>testError
        self should: [ Normalization new normalizeData: #( #(10 5 1) ) ]
            raise: Error.
NormalizationTest>>testEmptyError
        self should: [ Normalization new normalizeData: #() ] raise: Error.
```

When a neural network is used for regression, returned values are normalized. We therefore need to *denormalize* them. Consider the function g:

$$g(x) = \frac{(d_L - d_H)x - (n_H d_L) + d_H n_L}{n_L - n_H}$$

We give the denormalization function for sake of completeness. We will not use it since we excluded data regression from this chapter.

5.11 Integrating Normalization into the NNetwork Class

The previous section described the normalization functionality. Currently, it is disconnected from the NNetwork class. Integrating normalization into our neural network is the natural next step to seamlessly benefit from it. The `train:nbEpochs:` method can be redefined as follows:

```
NNetwork>>train: train nbEpochs: nbEpochs
        "Train the network using the train dataset."
        | sumError outputs expectedOutput epochPrecision t normalizedTrain
            |
        normalizedTrain := Normalization new normalizeData: train.
        1 to: nbEpochs do: [ :epoch |
            sumError := 0.
                epochPrecision := 0.
            normalizedTrain do: [ :row |
                    outputs := self feed: row allButLast.
                    expectedOutput := (1 to: self numberOfOutputs) collect: [ :
                        notUsed | 0 ].
                    expectedOutput at: (row last) + 1 put: 1.
                    (row last = (self predict: row allButLast)) ifTrue: [
                        epochPrecision := epochPrecision + 1 ].
                    t := (1 to: expectedOutput size)
                            collect: [ :i | ((expectedOutput at: i) -
                            (outputs at: i)) squared ].
```

```
                    sumError := sumError + t sum.
                    self backwardPropagateError: expectedOutput.
                    self updateWeight: row allButLast.
            ].
            errors add: sumError.
        precisions add: (epochPrecision / train size) asFloat.
]
```

The revision of the method normalizes the input data with the Normalization **new** normalizeData: train expression. The result of this expression is used to train the network. Running the following script indicates that high precision is quickly reached (see Figure 5-9):

```
n := NNetwork new.
n configure: 3 hidden: 8 nbOfOutputs: 8.

data := {#(0 0 0 0).
    #(0 0 1 1).
    #(0 1000 0 2).
    #(0 1000 1 3).
    #(0.1 0 0 4).
    #(0.1 0 1 5).
    #(0.1 1000 0 6).
    #(0.1 1000 1 7) }.
n train: data nbEpochs: 10000.
```

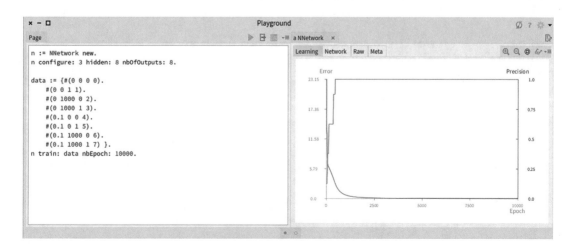

Figure 5-9. *The network is able to quickly learn the data once normalized*

Figure 5-9 shows the precision reaching 1.0. Thanks to the normalization, all the input values have the same relevance for the network. As a consequence, the network is able to learn properly. Note that in this example we use a linear normalization. It may be that a nonlinear transformation would improve the learning, especially in presence of outlier values in the training data. However, we consider nonlinear data transformation out of the scope of this book. Keep in mind that you may need it if you have a dataset with relevant outliers.

5.12 What Have We Seen in This Chapter?

This chapter was like a long road exploring different aspects of data manipulation. In particular, it explored:

- A simple visualization to monitor network learning

- The one-hot encoding technique that makes a network operate on non-numeric data

- The Iris dataset as a complete example of applying a neural network to classify data

- The relevance of normalizing data before processing it

We invite the reader to explore different datasets. The https://datasetsearch. research.google.com website includes many relevant datasets to be employed with a neural network or any other machine learning algorithm.

CHAPTER 6

A Matrix Library

In the previous chapters, we presented an implementation of a neural network made of layers and neurons (i.e., instances of NeuronLayer and Neuron). Although instructive, that implementation does not reflect classical ways of implementing a neural network. A layer can be expressed as a matrix of weights and a vector of biases. This is how most libraries that build neural networks (e.g., TensorFlow and PyTorch) actually operate.

This chapter lays out a small library to build and manipulate matrices. This chapter is an important foundation for the subsequent chapter, which is about how networks can be implemented using matrices. Matrices are a particular data structure for which operations cannot efficiently be implemented in Pharo. We will write these costly operations in C but make them accessible within Pharo.

In addition to defining a matrix library, this chapter highlights one particular aspect of Pharo, which is the use of Foreign Function Interface (FFI). This is a relevant mechanism whenever one wishes to make Pharo use external libraries written using the C or C++ programming languages. For example, TensorFlow is written in C++, which may be accessed from Pharo using the very same technique presented in this chapter.

This chapter is long and contains many inter-dependent methods. The chapter needs to be fully implemented before being functional.

6.1 Matrix Operations in C

Pharo does not provide built-in features to manipulate matrices. Although we could implement them in Pharo, it would suffer from very poor performance. Instead, we will code a small library in C to support the elementary C operations. Create a file named matrix.c with the following C code:

```
void dot(double *m1, int m1_nb_rows, int m1_nb_columns, double *m2,
                    int m2_nb_rows, int m2_nb_columns,
                    double *res) {
```

© Alexandre Bergel 2020
A. Bergel, *Agile Artificial Intelligence in Pharo*, https://doi.org/10.1007/978-1-4842-5384-7_6

```
    int col, row, k;
    for (col = 0; col < m2_nb_columns; col++) {
        for (row = 0; row < m1_nb_rows; row++) {
            double tmp = 0;
        for (k = 0; k < m2_nb_rows; k++)
            tmp += m1[row * m1_nb_columns + k] * m2[k *
                m2_nb_columns + col];
            res[row * m2_nb_columns + col] = tmp;
} } }
void sub(double *m1, int nb_rows, int nb_columns,
                    double *m2, double *res) {
    int col, row;
    for (col = 0; col < nb_columns; col++) {
            for (row = 0; row < nb_rows; row++) {
                res[row * nb_columns + col] =
                m1[row * nb_columns + col] - m2[row * nb_columns + col];
} } }
void add(double *m1, int nb_rows, int nb_columns,
                    double *m2, double *res) {
    int col, row;
     for (col = 0; col < nb_columns; col++) {
            for (row = 0; row < nb_rows; row++) {
                    res[row * nb_columns + col] =
                m1[row * nb_columns + col] + m2[row * nb_columns + col];
} } }
```

This small library is composed of three C functions:

- dot performs the multiplication of matrices

- sub subtracts one matrix from another

- add sums the two matrices

We will not go into details about this C file. It simply applies some basic matrix operations. Each function takes as an argument a pointer to some matrices along with their shape. The library has to be compiled, which means that inevitably we have to get closer to the operating system. This chapter will cover MacOS and Linux only. Both platforms offer the gcc standard compiler. Assuming the gcc tool suite is installed and you're using MacOS, you should type the following in a terminal:

```
gcc -dynamiclib -o matrix.dylib matrix.c
```

On Linux, you need to execute this instead:

```
gcc -c -Wall -Werror -fpic matrix.c
gcc -shared -o libmatrix.so matrix.o
```

Our matrix file is compiled as a dynamic library, loadable within Pharo. The compilation produces a dynamic library. On OSX, the generated file is named `matrix.dylib`, and it's called `libmatrix.so` on Linux. Either way, this file *has to be* located next to the `.image` file, within the same folder.

6.2 The Matrix Class

We can now write the Pharo class called `MMatrix`, which will use our C library. Note that Pharo 7 contains a deprecated class called `Matrix`, which is not really useful for our purposes. That's why our class is prefixed with an additional `M` character. In a new package called `Matrix`, we define the class:

```
Object subclass: #MMatrix
        instanceVariableNames: 'nbRows nbColumns array'
        classVariableNames: ''
        package: 'Matrix'
```

The two first variables describe the shape of the matrix, while the `array` variable refers to an array containing the actual values of the matrix, in a linear fashion. This array will have to be accessible both from Pharo and from our C library.

On the class side of the class `MMatrix`, we define a number of useful methods to create matrices. You need to switch the class browser to the class mode to define class methods. The `newFromArrays:` method creates a matrix from a collection of arrays:

```
MMatrix class>>newFromArrays: arrays
        "Create a matrix from an array containing the structured
        values of the matrix. Example of matrix creations:
        MMatrix newFromArrays: #(#(1 2 3) #(4 5 6))
```

```
    MMatrix newFromArrays: #(#(1 2 3))
    MMatrix newFromArrays: #(#(1) #(2) #(3))
    "

    ^ self basicNew
        initializeRows: arrays size columns: arrays first size;
        fromContents: (arrays flatCollect: #yourself);
        yourself
```

We also need a lower level to create a matrix, simply by providing the shape of the matrix. This assumes that the matrix content is set later. Consider this new class method:

```
MMatrix class>>newRows: numRows columns: numColumns
    "Create a matrix with a given shape"
    ^ self basicNew
    initializeRows: numRows columns: numColumns;
    yourself
```

We then define a method to initialize a matrix:

```
MMatrix>>initializeRows: numRows columns: numColumns
        self initialize.
        nbRows := numRows.
        nbColumns := numColumns.
        array := self newArray
```

The array is useful to keep the matrix content and is defined using newArray:

```
MMatrix>>newArray
        "Create an array used to contains the store the matrix content"
        ^ FFIExternalArray
            newType: 'double'
            size: nbColumns * nbRows
```

The FFIExternalArray class represents an array for which its elements are values of some external type. In our case, we will encode matrix values as a double, which is a float value encoded on 64 bits. The array has to be accessed from other objects:

```
MMatrix>>array
        "The array containing matrix' values"
        ^ array
```

Foreign objects, living within the Pharo memory space, need to be accessible from our external library. A useful class represents the memory address that is used by the C library. The FFIExternalArray class offers the getHandle method to access the memory location:

```
MMatrix>>getHandle
        "Return the handle of the foreign object.
        This allows the array to be accessed from C"
        ^ array getHandle
```

The handy asArray method is useful in the test. We will use it when verifying that a matrix is properly created:

```
MMatrix>>asArray
        "Return a linear array of the matrix values"
        ^ array asArray
```

In some situations, a handle has to be provided when a matrix is created. The following method addresses this:

```
MMatrix class>>newHandle: aHandle rows: numRows columns: numColumns
        "Create a matrix with a provided content. Useful when creating
            a matrix after an FFI operation"
        ^ self basicNew
            initializeHandle: aHandle rows: numRows columns: numColumns;
            yourself
```

The initializeHandle:rows:columns: method initializes a matrix with a handle and a particular shape:

```
MMatrix>>initializeHandle: aHandle rows: numRows columns: numColumns
        "Initialize the matrix"
        self initialize.
        nbRows := numRows.
        nbColumns := numColumns.
        array := self newArrayFromHandle: aHandle
```

The following factory method creates an external array using a given handle:

```
MMatrix>>newArrayFromHandle: aHandle
        "Create an external array using a handle"
```

```
^ FFIExternalArray
        fromHandle: aHandle
        type: 'double'
        size: nbColumns * nbRows
```

We need a few utility methods to access the shape of the matrix:

```
MMatrix>>nbRows
        "Number of rows defined in the matrix"
        ^ nbRows
```

and

```
MMatrix>>nbColumns
        "Number of columns defined in the matrix"
        ^ nbColumns
```

The number of values of the matrix is accessed using size, as follows:

```
MMatrix>>size
        "The number of values contained in the matrix"
        ^ nbColumns * nbRows
```

A matrix may be *filled* with a linear set of values:

```
MMatrix>>fromContents: content
        "Initialize the matrix with a linear content"
        self assert: [ content size = (nbColumns * nbRows) ] description:
            'size mismatch'.
        content doWithIndex: [ :v :i | array at: i put: v ]
```

These methods will be properly tested in the following subsections.

6.3 Creating the Unit Test

We can now write a unit test. The MMatrixTest class will contain all our tests about MMatrix. Consider the following class:

```
TestCase subclass: #MMatrixTest
        instanceVariableNames: ''
        classVariableNames: ''
        package: 'Matrix'
```

As a first test, we can vary the proper behavior of the `creation` method, defined on `MMatrix`:

```
MMatrixTest>>testCreation
        | m |
        m := MMatrix newFromArrays: #(#(1 2) #(3 4)).
        self assert: m asArray equals: #(1.0 2.0 3.0 4.0)
```

In the remainder of the chapter we will expand the `MMatrixTest` class.

6.4 Accessing and Modifying the Content of a Matrix

Being able to easily update the matrix content is the first step we should consider. The contents of a matrix can be accessed using the `at:` message. This method takes as an argument a point, as follows:

```
MMatrix>>at: aPoint
        "Access an element of the matrix"
        ^ array at: ((aPoint x - 1) * nbColumns + (aPoint y - 1)) + 1
```

We can test the `at:` method as follows:

```
MMatrixTest>>testAt
        | m |
        m := MMatrix newFromArrays: #(#(1 2) #(3 4)).
        self assert: (m at: 1 @ 1) equals: 1.
        self assert: (m at: 1 @ 2) equals: 2.
        self assert: (m at: 2 @ 1) equals: 3.
        self assert: (m at: 2 @ 2) equals: 4.
```

Similarly, we need to provide a way to modify the contents of a matrix. The `at:put:` method inserts a value at a given position:

```
MMatrix>>at: aPoint put: aNumber
        "Modify an element of the matrix"
        array at: ((aPoint x - 1) * nbColumns + (aPoint y - 1)) + 1 put:
            aNumber asFloat
```

To ease the testing, we add a convenient conversion method:

```
MMatrix>>asStructuredArray
        "Return a structured array that describe the matrix"
        ^ (1 to: nbRows) collect: [ :i | self atRow: i ] as: Array
```

The atRow: method returns the horizontal values for a given index.

```
MMatrix>>atRow: rowNumber
        "Return a particular row"
        (rowNumber between: 1 and: rowNumber)
                ifFalse: [ self error: 'index out of range' ].
        ^ (1 to: nbColumns) collect: [ :x | self at: rowNumber @ x ]
```

A simple test illustrates the use of at:put::

```
MMatrixTest>>testAtPut
        | m |
        m := MMatrix newFromArrays: #(#(1 2) #(3 4)).
        m at: 2 @ 1 put: 10.0.
        self assert: (m at: 2 @ 1) equals: 10.0.
        self assert: m asStructuredArray equals: #(#(1 2) #(10 4))
```

Note that we refer to an element using a coordinate row @ column. This way of accessing a matrix element is close to the mathematical notation traditionally used in linear algebra.

When we do the prediction in a network, we will need to obtain the maximum value of a matrix. We can simply define this as follows:

```
MMatrix>>max
        "Return the maximum value of the matrix"
        ^ self asArray max
```

The corresponding test is as follows:

```
MMatrixTest>>testMax
        | m |
        m := MMatrix newFromArrays: #(#(1 2) #(3 4)).
        self assert: m max equals: 4.
```

We have laid out the necessary infrastructure to define some operations. The following sections cover the operations we will employ in our neural network.

6.5 Summing Matrices

Two matrices may be summed. The operation assumes that the two matrices have exactly the same dimensions. We can define the sum with the + method. This method accepts another matrix of the same size as the receiver, or a vertical, vector (i.e., a matrix with only one column):

```
MMatrix>>+ matrixOrVector
        "Add either a matrix or a vector to the receiver.
        The argument could either be a matrix of the same size or
        a vector. A new matrix is returned as result"
        | m |
         ((nbRows = matrixOrVector nbRows) and: [ nbColumns = matrixOrVector
                nbColumns ])
                ifTrue: [ ^ self add: matrixOrVector ].
        matrixOrVector nbColumns ~= 1 ifTrue: [ self error: 'not a n * 1
                vector' ].
        m := matrixOrVector stretchToColumns: nbColumns.
        ^ self + m
```

The addition involves several steps due to the complexity of the operation. We define the add: method:

```
MMatrix>>add: aMatrix
        "Add two matrices, the receiver and the argument, and produces
                a new matrix"
        | result resultArray |
        nbColumns = aMatrix nbColumns ifFalse: [self error: 'dimensions
                do not conform'].
        nbRows = aMatrix nbRows ifFalse: [self error: 'dimensions do not
                conform'].

        resultArray := ByteArray new: (nbRows * aMatrix nbColumns * 8).
        self assert: [ nbRows * nbColumns = array size ].
        self assert: [ aMatrix nbRows * aMatrix nbColumns = aMatrix size ].
        self assert: [ nbRows * aMatrix nbColumns * 8 = resultArray size ].
        self
```

```
        add: self getHandle with: nbRows with: nbColumns with: aMatrix
            getHandle
        in: resultArray.
    result := MMatrix newHandle: resultArray rows: nbRows columns:
        nbColumns.
    ^ result
```

The add: method creates a new matrix and invokes the add function from our C library. On MacOS, you need to define the method as follows:

```
MMatrix>>add: m1 with: nb_rows with: nb_columns with: m2 in: res
    ^ self
        ffiCall: #(void add(double *m1, int nb_rows, int nb_columns,
                    double *m2,
                    double *res))
        module: 'matrix.dylib'
```

Note that on Linux, you need to replace 'matrix.dylib' with 'libmatrix.so'. We can test this by summing two matrices:

```
MMatrixTest>>testAddition1
    | m1 m2 |
    m1 := MMatrix newFromArrays: #(#(1 2 3) #(4 5 6)).
    m2 := MMatrix newFromArrays: #(#(4 5 6) #(1 2 3)).
    self assert: (m1 + m2) asStructuredArray equals: #(#(5.0 7.0 9.0)
        #(5.0 7.0 9.0))
```

We can also try adding a matrix to itself:

```
MMatrixTest>>testAddition2
    | m |
    m := MMatrix newFromArrays: #(#(1 2 3) #(4 5 6)).
    self assert: (m + m) asStructuredArray equals: #(#(2.0 4.0 6.0)
        #(8.0 10.0 12.0))
```

Elements of a matrix may be horizontally summed up. As we will see in the next chapter, this operation is important when we implement the backpropagation algorithm. Consider the following sumHorizontal method:

```
MMatrix>>sumHorizontal
        "Horizontal summing"
        | result sum |
        result := MMatrix newRows: nbRows columns: 1.
        1 to: nbRows do: [ :y |
            sum := 0.
            1 to: nbColumns do: [ :x |
                sum := sum + (self at: y @ x) ].
            result at: y @ 1 put: sum ].
        ^ result
```

An example of sumHorizontal is provided in the following test method:

```
MMatrixTest>>testSumHorizontal
        | m expectedResult |
        m := MMatrix newFromArrays: #(#(1.0 2.0) #(3.0 4.0) #(5.0 6.0)).
        expectedResult := MMatrix newFromArrays: #(#(3.0) #(7.0) #(11.0)).
        self assert: m sumHorizontal asStructuredArray equals:
            expectedResult asStructuredArray
```

6.6 Printing a Matrix

Being able to print a matrix is essential to seeing how the matrix is made. The printOn:
method returns a textual representation of the object that received the corresponding
message. We will therefore redefine it in the MMatrix class:

```
MMatrix>>printOn: aStream
        "Print the matrix in the stream, with 4 decimal for each value"
        self printOn: aStream round: 4
```

We will handle matrices with 64-bit float values. To make the printing effective, we
need to limit the number of decimals:

```
MMatrix>>printOn: aStream round: nbDecimals
        "Print the receiver matrix into a stream. All numerical value are
            truncated to a fixed number of decimals"
        aStream nextPutAll: '('.
        (1 to: nbRows)
```

```
            do: [ :r |
                        (self atRow: r)
                                do: [ :each | aStream nextPutAll: (each round:
                                        nbDecimals) printString ]
                                separatedBy: [ aStream space ]]
                separatedBy: [ aStream cr ].
        aStream nextPutAll: ' )'.
```

We can now test our code in a playground. Consider the following code snippet:

```
m := MMatrix newFromArrays: #(#(1 2 3) #(4 5 6)).
m + m
```

Printing this code should produce the following:

```
(2.0 4.0 6.0
8.0 10.0 12.0)
```

6.7 Expressing Vectors

A *vector* is a matrix with only one column. For example, the expression
MMatrixnewFromArrays: #(#(1)#(2)#(3)) creates a vector of three elements. We
provide a utility method to define a vector:

```
MMatrix class>>newFromVector: array
        "Create a Nx1 matrix from an array of numbers (N = array size)"
        ^ self basicNew
            initializeRows: array size columns: 1;
            fromContents: array;
            yourself
```

The newFromVector: method expects a flat Pharo array. Here is an example:

```
MMatrixTest>>testVectorCreation
        | v |
        v := MMatrix newFromVector: #(1 2 3).
        self assert: v nbColumns equals: 1.
        self assert: v nbRows equals: 3.
        self assert: v asStructuredArray equals: #(#(1) #(2) #(3))
```

The backpropagation algorithm must stretch a vector into a matrix. It converts a vector into a matrix by juxtaposing the vector several times. We define the following method:

```
MMatrix>>stretchToColumns: nbOfColumns
        "Stretch a vertical vector in a column."
        | content result |
        content := OrderedCollection new.
        1 to: nbRows do: [ :row |
            1 to: nbOfColumns do: [ :columns |
                content add: (self at: row @ 1) ] ].
        result := MMatrix newRows: nbRows columns: nbOfColumns.
        result fromContents: content.
        ^ result
```

Printing the expression (MMatrixnewFromVector: => #(1 2 3 4)) stretchToColumns: 5 results in the following:

```
(1.0 1.0 1.0 1.0 1.0
2.0 2.0 2.0 2.0 2.0
3.0 3.0 3.0 3.0 3.0
4.0 4.0 4.0 4.0 4.0 )
```

A test can be defined as follows:

```
MMatrixTest>>testStretching
        | m |
        m := (MMatrix newFromVector: #(1 2 3 4)) stretchToColumns: 5.
        self assert: m nbRows equals: 4.
        self assert: m nbColumns equals: 5.
        self assert: (m atRow: 1) equals: #(1 1 1 1 1).
        self assert: (m atRow: 3) equals: #(3 3 3 3 3).
```

6.8 Factors

Being able to transform a matrix and multiply matrices is essential during several parts of the backpropagation algorithm. We will first define a generic way to transform a matrix:

```
MMatrix>>collect: aOneArgBlock
        "Return a new matrix, for which each matrix element is
            transformed using the provided block"
        | result |
        result := MMatrix newRows: nbRows columns: nbColumns.
        1 to: nbRows do: [ :y |
            1 to: nbColumns do: [ :x |
                result at: y @ x put: (aOneArgBlock value: (self at: y @ x))
            ] ].
        ^ result
```

Here's a simple test that adds a value to each matrix element:

```
MMatrixTest>>testCollect
        | m expectedMatrix |
        m := MMatrix newFromArrays: #(#(1 2 3) #(4 5 6)).
        expectedMatrix := MMatrix newFromArrays: #(#(2 3 4) #(5 6 7)).
        self assert: (m collect: [ :v | v + 1]) asStructuredArray equals:
            expectedMatrix asStructuredArray
```

Elements of a matrix may be multiplied by a numerical factor. For that purpose, we define the ∗ method:

```
MMatrix>>* aFactor
        "Multiply each element of the matrix by a factor"
        ^ self collect: [ :v | v * aFactor ]
```

We can test this method when it's applied to a vector:

```
MMatrixTest>>testMultiplicationOnVector
        | x |
        x := MMatrix newFromVector: #(1 2 3 4).
        self assert: (x * 5) asStructuredArray equals: #(#(5.0) #(10.0)
            #(15.0) #(20.0))
```

Similarly, we can test the multiplication on a matrix:

```
MMatrixTest>>testMultiplicationOnMatrix
        | x |
        x := MMatrix newFromArrays: #(#(1 2 3 4) #(10 20 30 40)).
        self assert: (x * 5) asStructuredArray
            equals: #(#(5.0 10.0 15.0 20.0) #(50.0 100.0 150.0 200.0))
```

Another relevant operation is to multiply two matrices element-wise:

```
MMatrix>>multiplyPerElement: mat
        "Multiply two matrices element-wise"
        | r |
        self assert: [ nbRows = mat nbRows ].
        self assert: [ nbColumns = mat nbColumns ].
        r := MMatrix newRows: nbRows columns: nbColumns.
        r fromContents: (self asArray with: mat array asArray collect: [ :a
            :b | a * b ]).
        ^ r
```

The method could be tested as follows:

```
MMatrixTest>>testMultiplicationPerElement
        | v1 v2 expectedVector |
        v1 := MMatrix newFromVector: #(1 2 3).
        v2 := MMatrix newFromVector: #(10 20 30).
        expectedVector := MMatrix newFromVector: #(10 40 90).
        self assert: (v1 multiplyPerElement: v2) asArray
                equals: expectedVector asArray
```

6.9 Dividing a Matrix by a Factor

In the same fashion as in the previous section, we can divide a matrix by a factor:

```
MMatrix>>/ value
        "Divide each element of the matrix by a value"
        ^ self collect: [ :v | v / value ]
```

This method can be tested using the following:

```
MMatrixTest>>testDivision
    | m |
    m := MMatrix newFromArrays: #(#(1 2 3) #(4 5 6)).
    self assert: (m / 2) asStructuredArray equals: #(#(0.5 1.0 1.5)
        #(2.0 2.5 3.0))
```

6.10 Matrix Product

We defined the matrix product using two methods +* and dot:. The first is a shortcut to the latter:

```
MMatrix>>+* anotherMatrix
    "Shortcut for the dot operator between matrices"
    ^ self dot: anotherMatrix
```

The dot: method is defined as follows:

```
MMatrix>>dot: anotherMatrix
    "Compute the dot product between the receiving matrix and the
        argument"
    | result resultArray |
    nbColumns = anotherMatrix nbRows ifFalse: [self error:
        'dimensions do not conform'].
    self assert: [ nbRows * nbColumns = array size ].
    self assert: [ anotherMatrix nbRows * anotherMatrix nbColumns =
        anotherMatrix size ].
    resultArray := ByteArray new: (nbRows * anotherMatrix nbColumns * 8).
    self
        dot: self getHandle with: nbRows with: nbColumns
        with: anotherMatrix getHandle
        with: anotherMatrix nbRows with: anotherMatrix nbColumns in:
            resultArray.
    result := MMatrix
        newHandle: resultArray
        rows: nbRows
```

```
        columns: anotherMatrix nbColumns.
    ^ result
```

The connection between the Pharo code and the C library is defined in the following method:

```
MMatrix>>dot: array1 with: m1_nb_rows with: m1_nb_columns with: array2
        with: m2_nb_rows with: m2_nb_columns in: res
        "Invoke the C library to perform the dot operator"
        ^ self
            ffiCall: #(void dot(
                void *array1, int m1_nb_rows, int m1_nb_columns,
                void *array2, int m2_nb_rows, int m2_nb_columns, void *res))
            module: 'matrix.dylib'
```

On Linux, you need to replace `'matrix.dylib'` with `'libmatrix.so'`. You can test this code using the following test method:

```
MMatrixTest>>testMatrixProduct
    | m1 m2 |
    m1 := MMatrix newFromArrays: #(#(1 2 3 4) #(5 6 7 8)).
    m2 := MMatrix newFromArrays: #(#(1 2) #(3 4) #(5 6) #(7 8)).
    self assert: (m1 +* m2) asStructuredArray equals: #(#(50.0 60.0)
        #(114.0 140.0))
```

6.11 Matrix Subtraction

Subtracting matrices is another relevant operation in machine learning in general. We define the following shortcut:

```
MMatrix>>- anotherMatrix
        "Subtract a matrix from the receiver matrix"
        ^ self sub: anotherMatrix
```

This shortcut calls the `sub:` method:

```
MMatrix>>sub: anotherMatrix
        | result resultArray |
        nbColumns = anotherMatrix nbColumns ifFalse: [self error: '
```

```
            dimensions do not conform'].
    nbRows = anotherMatrix nbRows ifFalse: [self error: 'dimensions
        do not conform'].

    resultArray := ByteArray new: (nbRows * anotherMatrix nbColumns *8).

    self assert: [ nbRows * nbColumns = array size ].
    self assert: [ anotherMatrix nbRows * anotherMatrix nbColumns =
        anotherMatrix size ].
    self assert: [ nbRows * anotherMatrix nbColumns * 8 = resultArray
        size ].

    self
        sub: self getHandle with: nbRows with: nbColumns with:
            anotherMatrix getHandle
        in: resultArray.
    result := MMatrix newHandle: resultArray rows: nbRows columns:
        nbColumns.
    ^ result
```

Our C library is used via the following method:

```
MMatrix>>sub: m1 with: nb_rows with: nb_columns with: m2 in: res
    ^ self
        ffiCall: #(void sub(double *m1, int nb_rows, int nb_columns,
                    double *m2, double *res))
        module: 'matrix.dylib'
```

Note that on Linux, you need to replace 'matrix.dylib' with 'libmatrix.so'. A simple test illustrates the behavior of matrix subtraction:

```
MMatrixTest>>testSub
    | m1 m2 |
    m1 := MMatrix newFromArrays: #(#(1 2 3 4) #(5 6 7 8)).
    m2 := MMatrix newFromArrays: #(#(4 2 1 3) #(7 6 8 5)).
    self assert: (m1 - m2) asStructuredArray equals: #(#(-3 0 2 1)
                #(-2 0 -1 3))
```

6.12 Filling the Matrix with Random Numbers

The initial state of a neural network is mostly random. We therefore need a way to randomly initialize a matrix. Consider this method:

MMatrix>>random

```
    "Fill the matrix with random numbers"
    ^ self random: Random new
```

It could be convenient to provide a random generator for the initialization:

MMatrix>>random: randomNumberGenerator

```
    "Fill the matrix with random numbers. Takes a random number
        generator as argument"
    self fromContents: ((1 to: nbRows * nbColumns) collect: [ :vv |
        randomNumberGenerator next ])
```

Executing the expression (MMatrixnewRows: 4columns: 5)random illustrates its use:

```
(0.2073 0.7154 0.3008 0.06 0.0865
0.3493 0.6396 0.7285 0.4873 0.1947
0.7951 0.3034 0.6066 0.8358 0.1445
0.5454 0.2504 0.2012 0.9086 0.5719 )
```

6.13 Summing the Matrix Values

Values contained in a matrix may be summed. This is useful for evaluating the cost function when training a neural network:

MMatrix>>sum

```
    "Return the sum of the matrix values"
    | sum |
    sum := 0.
    1 to: nbRows do: [ :y |
        1 to: nbColumns do: [ :x |
            sum := sum + (self at: y @ x)
        ]
    ].
    ^ sum
```

The use of sum is illustrated in the test:

```
MMatrixTest>>testSum
    | m |
    m := MMatrix newFromArrays: #(#(1 2 3 4) #(5 6 7 8)).
    self assert: m sum equals: (1 to: 8) sum
```

6.14 Transposing a Matrix

Transposing a matrix is an operation that consists of flipping a matrix along its diagonal axis. We can define the operation as follows:

```
MMatrix>>transposed
    "Transpose the matrix"
    | result |
    result := MMatrix newRows: nbColumns columns: nbRows.
    1 to: nbRows do: [ :row |
        1 to: nbColumns do: [ :column |
            result at: column @ row put: (self at: row @ column)
        ]
    ].
    ^ result
```

The following test illustrates the behavior of the transposed method:

```
MMatrixTest>>testTransposedOnMatrix
        | m expectedResult |
    m := MMatrix newFromArrays: #(#(1 2 3 4) #(5 6 7 8)).
    expectedResult := MMatrix newFromArrays: #(#(1 5) #(2 6) #(3 7) #(4 8)).
    self assert: m transposed asStructuredArray equals: expectedResult
            asStructuredArray
```

Transposing a vector produces a matrix of one row, as the following test method illustrates:

```
MMatrixTest>>testTransposedOnVector
        | m |
    m := MMatrix newFromVector: #(1 2 3).
        self assert: m transposed asStructuredArray equals: #(#(1 2 3))
```

6.15 Example

We can illustrate the use of matrices in a simple backpropagation implementation. The following script creates two random sets of values and trains a neural network to map the input values to the output values. It illustrates the "essence" of forward and backward propagation:

```
n := 8.                 "Number of examples"
din := 10.              "Number of input values"
h := 20.                "Size of the hidden layer"
dout := 5.              "Number of output values"

r := Random seed: 42.
x := (MMatrix newRows: n columns: din) random: r.
y := (MMatrix newRows: n columns: dout) random: r.
w1 := (MMatrix newRows: din columns: h) random: r.
w2 := (MMatrix newRows: h columns: dout) random: r.

learningRate := 1e-6.
losses := OrderedCollection new.
1500 timesRepeat: [
        hh := x +* w1.
        hrelu := hh collect: [ :v | v max: 0 ].
        ypred := hrelu +* w2.
        "Compute and print loss"
        loss := ((ypred - y) collect: [:vv | vv * vv ]) sum.
        losses add: loss.

        "Backprop to compute gradients of w2 and w2 with respect to loss"
        gradYPred := (ypred - y) * 2.0.
        gradW2 := hrelu transposed +* gradYPred.
        gradHRelu := gradYPred +* w2 transposed.
        gradH := gradHRelu collect: [ :v | v max: 0 ].
        gradW1 := x transposed +* gradH.

        w1 := w1 - (gradW1 * learningRate).
        w2 := w2 - (gradW2 * learningRate)
].
```

```
g := RTGrapher new.
d := RTData new.
d noDot; connectColor: Color blue.
d points: losses.
d y: #yourself.
g add: d.
g axisX title: 'Epoch'.
g axisY title: 'Error'.
g
```

The last part of the script uses RTGrapher to show the evolution of the loss value along epochs (see Figure 6-1).

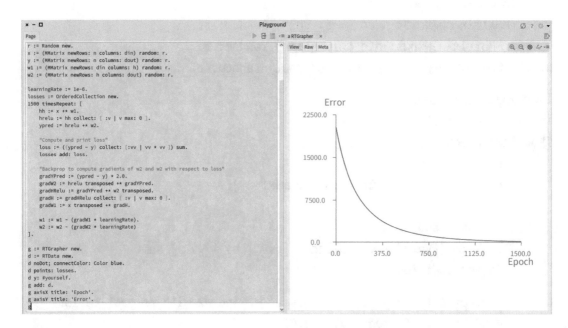

Figure 6-1. *A simple implementation of backpropagation*

6.16 What Have We Seen in This Chapter?

The chapter covered the following topics:

- *Definition of a minimal C library.* Neural networks, and deep learning in general, employ matrices to perform their computations.

- *Definition of the MMatrix class.* This class models the mathematical notion of a matrix. Note that we designed our class to offer relevant operations for neural networks. It is by no means a definitive generic matrix implementation.

This was a dense chapter. However, the matrix library we created will greatly simplify the revised version of our neural network in the next chapter.

Modern libraries that build neural networks employ matrices to carry out their numerical computations. However, the GPU is traditionally used instead of the CPU, as we are doing here. We could have used CUDA or OpenCL to perform the matrix operations on the GPU. However, that would have considerably lengthened the amount of code. This is why we restrict ourselves to computations carried out by the CPU.

In the next chapter, we will rewrite the neural network implementation to use the matrix.

CHAPTER 7

Matrix-Based Neural Networks

This chapter revises the implementation of our neural network. In this revision, our network will use matrices to compute the forward and backward propagation algorithms. Overall, our matrix-based implementation is composed of two classes, NMLayer and NMNetwork. Since most of the computation is delegated to the matrix library we defined in the previous chapter, our new version of the neural network is rather light in terms of code.

7.1 Defining a Matrix-Based Layer

A neural network is composed of layers. We describe a layer as an instance of the NMLayer class, defined as follows:

```
Object subclass: #NMLayer
    instanceVariableNames: 'w b delta output previous next lr
        numberOfExamples'
    classVariableNames: ''
    package: 'NeuralNetwork-Matrix'
```

The NMLayer class does not contain neurons, as we saw in our first implementation. Instead, a matrix describing weights is used and kept in the w variable, and another matrix is used to keep the bias vector, kept in the b variable.

The initialization of a layer simply consists of setting the default learning rate:

```
NMLayer>>initialize
    super initialize.
    lr := 0.1
```

© Alexandre Bergel 2020
A. Bergel, *Agile Artificial Intelligence in Pharo*, https://doi.org/10.1007/978-1-4842-5384-7_7

The NMLayer class contains many accessors and mutator methods. First, a layer contains a matrix for the weight. It is set using w::

```
NMLayer>>w: matrixForWeights
    "Take a MMatrix as argument"
    w := matrixForWeights
```

The weight matrix is accessible using w, as follows:

```
NMLayer>>w
    "Return the MMatrix representing the weights"
    ^ w
```

Similarly, the bias vector is set using b:, as follows:

```
NMLayer>>b: biasVector
    "Set a vector, instance of MMatrix, as the bias vector"
    b := biasVector
```

The bias vector is accessible using the following:

```
NMLayer>>b
    "Return the bias vector"
    ^ b
```

The delta matrix is stored in the delta variable, as follows:

```
NMLayer>>delta: deltaMatrix
    delta := deltaMatrix
```

It is read using an accessor:

```
NMLayer>>delta
    ^ delta
```

The learning rate, a very small positive number, is globally set to a layer:

```
NMLayer>>lr: aLearningRate
    lr := aLearningRate
```

Layers are chained to each other. We use the classical representation of layers: the network is fed from the left-most layer, the input layer. Output is produced from the right-most layer, the output layer. For a given layer l, the next layer of l is the layer to the right of l, and the previous is the layer to the left of l. The next layer is set using the following:

```
NMLayer>>next: aLayer
    "Set the next layer"
    next := aLayer
```

The next layer is retrieved using the following:

```
NMLayer>>next
    "Return the next layer"
    ^ next
```

Similarly, the previous layer is set using the following:

```
NMLayer>>previous: aLayer
    "Set the previous layer"
    previous := aLayer
```

The previous layer is obtained using the following:

```
NMLayer>>previous
    "Return the previous layer"
    ^ previous
```

The output of the layer is obtained using its accessor, as follows:

```
NMLayer>>output
    "Return the output matrix, computed during the feed forward phase"
    ^ output
```

The number of examples needs to be accessible to compute the cost derivative. It is set using the numberOfExamples: method, which is defined as follows:

```
NMLayer>>numberOfExamples: aNumber
    numberOfExamples := aNumber
```

The number of examples is read using the corresponding accessor:

```
NMLayer>>numberOfExamples
    ^ numberOfExamples
```

The layer is initialized by providing the number of neurons it should contain and the number of outputs. The random number generator is also provided to initialize the weight and bias matrices. We define the initialization method as follows:

```
NMLayer>>nbInputs: nbOfInputs nbOutputs: nbOfOutputs random: random
    "Initialize the layer"
    w := MMatrix newRows: nbOfOutputs columns: nbOfInputs.
    w random: random.
    b := MMatrix newRows: nbOfOutputs columns: 1.
    b random: random.
```

Feed forwarding a layer is carried out using the feed: method:

```
NMLayer>>feed: inputMatrix
    "Feed the layer with the input matrix"
    output := (w +* inputMatrix + b) collect: [ :v | 1 / (1 + v negated exp) ].
^ output
```

Once the error is backpropagated, weights and biases can be updated:

```
NMLayer>>update
    "Update the weights and biases using the delta value"
    w := w - ((delta +* previous output transposed) * lr /
    numberOfExamples).
    b := b - (delta sumHorizontal * lr / numberOfExamples).
    next ifNotNil: [ next update ]
```

The very first layer uses the input vector to update its parameters:

```
NMLayer>>update: input
    "Update the weights and biases using the input value"
    w := w - ((delta +* input transposed) * lr / numberOfExamples).
    b := b - (delta sumHorizontal * lr / numberOfExamples).
    next update
```

Our definition of layer is now complete. We can next propose a definition of the NMNetwork class.

7.2 Defining a Matrix-Based Neural Network

We will call NMNetwork the class describing a matrix-based neural network. Here is its definition:

```
Object subclass: #NMNetwork
    instanceVariableNames: 'random errors layers'
    classVariableNames: ''
    package: 'NeuralNetwork-Matrix'
```

The variables are similar to our first version of the neural network. The random variable contains a random number generator, which is useful to initialize the layers. The errors variable contains the error values produced during the training. The layers variable contains instances of NMLayer.

The network is initialized with no layer and a random number generator:

```
NMNetwork>>initialize
    "Initialize the network with no layer and a proper random generator"
    super initialize.
    layers := OrderedCollection new.
    random := Random seed: 42.
```

When a layer is added to the network, a chain of layers has to be maintained:

```
NMNetwork>>addLayer: aLayer
    "Add a layer to the network. Note that layers form a bidirectional
    chain."
    layers ifNotEmpty: [
        layers last next: aLayer.
        aLayer previous: layers last ].
    layers add: aLayer
```

A central method of the learning process is backwardX:y:, which computes the error and backpropagates it along the layers:

```
NMNetwork>>backwardX: x y: y
    "Compute and backpropagate the error"
    | lastLayer dz currentLayer |
```

```
    lastLayer := layers last.
    dz := lastLayer output - y.
    lastLayer delta: dz.
    currentLayer := lastLayer previous.
    [ currentLayer notNil ] whileTrue: [
        dz := (currentLayer next w transposed +* dz)
                multiplyPerElement: (currentLayer output collect: [:v |
                v * (1 - v) ]).
        currentLayer delta: dz.
        currentLayer := currentLayer previous.
    ].
```

The cost function is computed for two given vectors:

```
NMNetwork>>computeCost: v1 and: v2
    "Compute the cost function for two provided vectors"
    ^ ((v1 - v2) collect: [ :v | v * v ]) sum
```

The configuration of the network is performed through a number of utility methods. The following method configures a network with one hidden layer:

```
NMNetwork>>configure: nbOfInputs hidden: nbOfNeurons nbOfOutputs:
    nbOfOutputs
    "Configure the network with the given parameters
    The network has only one hidden layer"
    self addLayer: (NMLayer new nbInputs: nbOfInputs nbOutputs:
        nbOfNeurons random: random).
    self addLayer: (NMLayer new nbInputs: nbOfNeurons nbOutputs:
        nbOfOutputs random: random).
```

Similarly, two hidden layers may be configured using the following method:

```
NMNetwork>>configure: nbOfInputs hidden: nbOfNeurons1 hidden:
    nbOfNeurons2 nbOfOutputs: nbOfOutputs
    "Configure the network with the given parameters. The network has two
    hidden layers"
    self addLayer: (NMLayer new nbInputs: nbOfInputs nbOutputs:
        nbOfNeurons1 random: random).
```

```
self addLayer: (NMLayer new nbInputs: nbOfNeurons1 nbOutputs:
    nbOfNeurons2 random: random).
self addLayer: (NMLayer new nbInputs: nbOfNeurons2 nbOutputs:
    nbOfOutputs random: random).
```

The forward feeding is simply done using the feed: method:

```
NMNetwork>>feed: inputs
    "Feed the network with the provided inputs vector
    Return the output value as a matrix"
    | mat |
    mat := inputs.
    layers do: [ :l | mat := l feed: mat ].
    ^ mat
```

The learning rate of the network is defined using a dedicated method, as follows:

```
NMNetwork>>lr: aLearningRateAsFloat
    "Globally set the learning rate"
    layers do: [ :l | l lr: aLearningRateAsFloat ]
```

The training is performed using the following method:

```
NMNetwork>>trainX: x y: y nbOfEpochs: nbEpochs
    "Train the network with a set of inputs against the expected values"
    | cost output |
    "We need to tell to each layer the number of examples they have"
    layers do: [ :l | l numberOfExamples: y nbColumns ].
    errors := OrderedCollection new.
    nbEpochs timesRepeat: [
        output := self feed: x.
        cost := self computeCost: output and: y.
        self backwardX: x y: y.
        self update: x.
        errors add: cost.
    ].
    ^ cost
```

The update of the weights and biases is done using the following method:

```
NMNetwork>>update: input
    "Update the weights and bias using the provided input vector"
    layers first update: input
```

Note that the layer performs the job of updating its parameters. Prediction can be achieved by simply copying the predict: method from our original implementation:

```
NMNetwork>>predict: inputs
    "Make a prediction. This method assumes that the number of outputs
        is the same as the number of different values the network can
        output"
    "The index of a collection begins at 1 in Pharo,
    which is why we need to substrate 1"
    | outputs |
    outputs := self feed: inputs.
    ^ (outputs asArray indexOf: (outputs max)) - 1
```

We define the train:nbEpochs: method, which is useful for training a model using a labeled dataset:

```
NMNetwork>>train: data nbEpochs: nbEpochs
    "Data is provided as a collection of arrays.
    The example data needs to be labeled using a numerical value"
    | x y labels numberOfOutputs |
    x := (MMatrix newFromArrays: (data collect: #allButLast))
        transposed.
    layers do: [ :l | l numberOfExamples: data size ].
    labels := data collect: #last.
    numberOfOutputs := labels asSet size.
    labels := labels collect: [ :row |
        | expectedOutput |
        expectedOutput := Array new: numberOfOutputs withAll: 0.
        expectedOutput at: row + 1 put: 1.
        expectedOutput
    ].
    y := (MMatrix newFromArrays: labels) transposed.
    ^ self trainX: x y: y nbOfEpochs: nbEpochs
```

At that stage, we have a matrix-based network, which can learn from a labeled dataset. Consider the following example:

```
xor := #(#(0 0 0)
         #(0 1 1)
         #(1 0 1)
         #(1 1 0)).
n := NMNetwork new.
n configure: 2 hidden: 3 nbOfOutputs: 2.
n train: xor nbEpochs: 5000.
n predict: (MMatrix newFromVector: #(1 0)).
```

The result of the prediction is 1. Similarly, evaluating the expression n predict: (MMatrix newFromVector: #(1 1)). returns 0. The following section presents a simple way to draw the error function.

7.3 Visualizing the Results

We will extend the NMNetwork class to visualize the evolution of the error along the epochs. Simply the define this method:

```
NMNetwork>>viewLearningCurve
    | b ds |
    errors
        ifEmpty: [ ^ RTView new
                add: (RTLabel elementOn: 'Should first run the network');
                yourself ].
b := RTGrapher new.
"We define the size of the charting area"
b extent: 500 @ 300.
ds := RTData new.
ds samplingIfMoreThan: 2000.
ds noDot.
ds connectColor: Color blue.
ds points: (errors collectWithIndex: [ :y :i | i -> y ]).
ds x: #key.
ds y: #value.
```

```
ds dotShape rectangle color: Color blue.
b add: ds.
b axisX noDecimal; title: 'Epoch'.
b axisY title: 'Error'.
^ b
```

The hook into the GTInspector framework is done using the following method:

```
NMNetwork>>viewLearningCurveIn: composite
    <gtInspectorPresentationOrder: -10>
    composite roassal2
        title: 'Cost';
        initializeView: [ self viewLearningCurve ]
```

Evaluating the training instruction in the previous section should output the error curve shown in Figure 7-1.

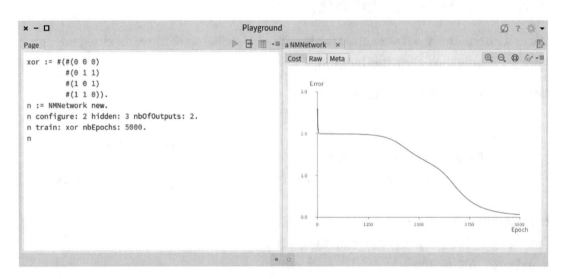

Figure 7-1. *Visualizing the cost function*

7.4 Iris Flower Dataset

We can now adapt the script to train a neural network on the Iris flower dataset. Consider this script:

```
"The execution of this script initializes the variable irisData.
    This variable is used in the subsequent scripts of this chapter"
irisCSV := (ZnEasy get: 'https://agileartificialintelligence.github.io/
    Datasets/iris.csv') contents.
lines := irisCSV lines.
lines := lines allButFirst.
tLines := lines collect: [ :l |
            | ss |
            ss := l substrings: ','.
            (ss allButLast collect: [ :w | w asNumber ]), (Array with: ss
            last) ].
irisData := tLines collect: [ :row | |l|
            row last = 'setosa' ifTrue: [ l := #( 0 ) ].
            row last = 'versicolor' ifTrue: [ l := #( 1 ) ].
            row last = 'virginica' ifTrue: [ l := #( 2 ) ].
            row allButLast, l ].
irisData.

n := NMNetwork new.
n configure: 4 hidden: 6 nbOfOutputs: 3.
n train: irisData nbEpochs: 3000.
n
```

The result is the same one we previously saw.

7.5 What Have We Seen in This Chapter?

This chapter revised our previous implementation of a neural network. Our revised implementation employs matrices to model the state of the network, which greatly simplifies its implementation. However, it raises the level of abstractness since matrices are not at the core. The chapter explored:

- *The use of matrices to implement forward and backward propagation.*
  It uses the matrix library presented in the previous chapter.

- *Using the Iris classification example to illustrate the new neural network classes.*

PART II

Genetic Algorithms

CHAPTER 8

Genetic Algorithms

The first part of the book is about neural networks, a computational metaphor about how the brain operates. This chapter, the first of the second part of the book, focuses on evolution. In particular, it will cover genetic algorithms, a computational metaphor for how genetic information is recombined and passed through generations. This algorithm focuses on the pillars of how evolution naturally happens.

This chapter is self-contained: having knowledge of the previous chapters is therefore not a prerequisite to enjoy this chapter and the following ones in this part.

8.1 Algorithms Inspired from Natural Evolution

We, as human beings, are the result of thousands of years of evolution. Biological evolution refers to some alteration of heritable characteristics and attributes of biological populations over successive generations. Most of the characteristics are the expressions of genes that are passed on from parent to offspring during reproduction.

Darwinian natural selection stipulates that in order to have natural evolution, it is necessary to have the following ingredients:

- *Heredity:* A child receives a number of properties from its parents. In particular, if the parents are robust and can live long enough to procreate, the child should too.

- *Variation:* Some variations may be introduced in offspring. As such, a child will not be an identical copy of its parents.

- *Selection:* Some members of a population must have the opportunity to be parents and have offspring in order to pass on their genetic information. The selection is typically referred to as "survival of the fittest."

© Alexandre Bergel 2020
A. Bergel, *Agile Artificial Intelligence in Pharo*, https://doi.org/10.1007/978-1-4842-5384-7_8

Computer scientists have a great interest in the way that natural evolution happens. Why? In very broad terms, consider the following: if humans are on Earth to solve a problem, then it is surely a very complex problem. And that is exactly the reason why natural evolution is so appealing to computer scientists, to solve incredibly complex problems. Following that line, a number of algorithms have been proposed by computer scientists to simulate evolution. For example:

- *An ant colony optimization* is based on the idea that ants forage by pheromone communication to form a path. Such an algorithm is suitable for graph-related problems.

- A *bee algorithm* is based on the honey bee's foraging behavior. This algorithm is suitable for scheduling and ordering problems.

- A *genetic algorithm* is a simulation of evolution based on manipulating genetic information. This chapter is about this algorithm.

A Genetic Algorithm (GA) is an evolutionary algorithm that simulates the evolution of DNA information across a population. Genetic algorithms have three important properties that we will exploit in the book:

- GAs are efficient at solving optimization problems.

- GAs are easily implemented and do not require a strong theoretical background.

- GAs can be easily combined with neural networks. We will go into detail about this in the third part of the book when we focus on neuroevolution.

8.2 Example of a Genetic Algorithm

The overall idea of genetic algorithms is pretty simple. Imagine that a friend asks you to solve the following challenge: "You must find the three-letter word I have in mind. For each try, I will tell you the number of letters correctly positioned." Assume that the secret word is cat, for example. At first, we guess any randomly generated words made of three letters, such as cow, poc, and gaz.

The word *cow* has exactly one letter in common with *cat*, the secret word. We therefore say that *cow* has a score of 1. The word *poc* has a score of 0 since it has no matching letters with the secret word. The word *gaz* has also a score of 1 since the letter *a* matches the second letter of the secret word.

Since we have not found the solution (i.e., *cow*, *poc*, nor *gaz* is the secret word), we can produce a new generation of words by combing some of the words we already have. In particular, *gaz* and *cow* can be combined into *gow* (formed with the first letter of *gaz* and the last two letters of *cow*) and *caz* (first letter of *cow* and the two last letters of *gaz*). From these two new words, the word *caz* has a score of two and is very close to the secret word. We say that this second generation of words is better than the previous one since it is closer to the solution.

A third generation can be formed in which the word *caz* can produce the word *cat*, in which the *z* is randomly mutated into *t*. This small example illustrates the overall idea of a genetic algorithm: each individual in a set of randomly formed individuals is evaluated to compute a score value. Individuals with a high score, which are the ones close to solving the problem, are recombined to form new individuals. Before detailing the algorithm, we will clarify the vocabulary we will use in this chapter.

8.3 Relevant Vocabulary

We have to introduce a few terms to describe the concepts we will use in this chapter. We will rephrase the example given using these appropriate concepts.

We refer to an *individual* as an element that contains genetic information. Such genetic information is described as a sequential collection of *genes*. A *gene* represents a unit of information and it may represent anything, literally. In the previous example, a gene is simply a letter. An individual is a three-letter word.

A *population* is a fixed number of individuals. The population has a constant size, but its composing individuals are replaced at each generation.

The *fitness function* indicates how "strong" an individual is. The fitness function is a simple function that takes as an argument an individual and produces a numerical value. The whole idea of a genetic algorithm is to build and search for individuals that maximize the fitness function.

8.4 Modeling Individuals

This chapter contains the complete implementation of a genetic algorithm in Pharo. All the presented code is assumed to be part of the package called GeneticAlgorithm.

We will first model individuals. We will therefore model a class called GAIndividual. We will create the GAIndividual subclass of the custom class GAObject. We define GAObject as a subclass of Object, which has a random variable.

Almost all elements involved in a genetic algorithm require generating random numbers. It is therefore convenient to have the variable defined in the root hierarchy used in our implementation:

```
Object subclass: #GAObject
    instanceVariableNames: 'random'
    classVariableNames: ''
    package: 'GeneticAlgorithm-Core'
```

As usual, we define the getter as follows:

```
GAObject>>random
    "Return the random number generator associated to the object"
    ^ random
```

And the setter as follows:

```
GAObject>>random: aRandomNumberGenerator
    "Set the random number generator associated to the object. The
        argument must be an instance of Random."
    random := aRandomNumberGenerator
```

The random: method expects an instance of the Random class as an argument. We also define a utility method to generate a number between 0.0 and 1.0:

```
GAObject>>randomNumber
    "Return a number between 0.0 and 1.0"
    ^ random next
```

We can define a small utility method used by the subclasses to ensure a random number generator is set:

```
GAObject>>checkForRandomNumber
```

```
self
    assert: [ random notNil ]
    description: 'Need to provide a random number generator'
```

We are ready to model individuals using the GAIndividual class:

```
GAObject subclass: #GAIndividual
    instanceVariableNames: 'genes fitness'
    classVariableNames: ''
    package: 'GeneticAlgorithm-Core'
```

An individual is simply composed of its genes and its fitness value. The fitness variable acts as a cache value. Computing the fitness of an individual is an essential piece of the genetic algorithm:

```
GAIndividual>>computeFitnessUsing: fitnessBlock
    "Compute the fitness of myself if not already computed"
    self assert: [ genes notNil ] description: 'Need to have some genes
    first'.

    "Simply exit if already computed"
    fitness ifNotNil: [ ^ self ].

    "Compute the fitness score"
    fitness := fitnessBlock value: genes
```

We will use a one-argument block to compute its fitness, and this block takes as an argument the genes of the individual. When evaluated, the block returns a numerical value, which is the fitness, of the provided genes.

The computeFitnessUsing: method sets the fitness variable with that value. We will see some examples shortly.

Once the fitness value is computed, other parts of the genetic algorithm, including the selection algorithm, will have to access it. The fitness is accessible via an accessor method, as follows:

```
GAIndividual>>fitness
    "Return the fitness value of the individual"
    ^ fitness
```

Genes from an individual have to be accessible. In particular, a fitness function requires an individual's genes to compute the individual fitness. We define an accessor method to access the genes from an individual:

```
GAIndividual>>genes
    "Return the individual's genes"
    ^ genes
```

When a crossover genetic operation is carried out, the new computed genes have to be set in an individual. We therefore need a dedicated method to allow this:

```
GAIndividual>>genes: someGenes
    "Set the genes of the individual. Used by the genetic operations."
    genes := someGenes
```

The number of genes may be obtained using a dedicated method. This will be useful for the genetic operations:

```
GAIndividual>>numberOfGenes
    "Return the number of genes the individual has"
    ^ self genes size
```

An essential ability of the GAIndividual class is to generate genetic information. For that purpose, we define a gene factory as a Pharo block closure that accepts three arguments—the random number generator, the index of the gene, and the individual. We define the set:genesUsing: method for that purpose:

```
GAIndividual>>set: numberOfGenes genesUsing: geneBlockFactory
    "Public method - Generate the genes of the individual"

    self checkForRandomNumber.
    genes := (1 to: numberOfGenes)
    collect: [ :index | geneBlockFactory cull: random cull: index cull:
    self ]
```

The first argument of set:genesUsing: is an integer. The second argument is a block that expects three arguments:

- *The random number generator:* This is useful for letting the gene factory randomly choose values.

- *The index of the genes to be created:* This is often useful when not all the genes have to be the same. In that case, the gene factory block may choose some values based on the gene index.

- *The individual itself:* It may happen that the individual has to be accessed when computing a gene.

The set:genesUsing: method is evaluated using cull:. As such, if the block has missing arguments, then they are simply ignored. For example, we have the following execution:

```
[ :x :y | x + y ] cull: 10 cull: 20 cull: 30. "=> 20"
[ :x :y :z | x + y + z] cull: 10 cull: 20 cull: 30. "=> 60"
[ 42 ] cull: 10 cull: 20 cull: 30. "=> 42"
```

We can now create a useful factory method for a group of individuals, as a class method:

```
GAIndividual class>>create: numberOfIndividuals
    individualsAndInitialize: numberOfGenes genesWith: geneBlockFactory
    using: randomNumberGeneration
    "Factory method to easily create a population of Individuals.
        numberOfIndividuals : number of individuals to return
        numberOfGenes : number of genes each individual should have
        geneBlockFactory : a one-argument block to generate a gene.
            It takes a random generator as an argument
        randomNumberGeneration : a random generator"
    | someIndividuals ind |
    someIndividuals := OrderedCollection new.
    numberOfIndividuals timesRepeat: [
        ind := self new.
        ind random: randomNumberGeneration.
        ind set: numberOfGenes genesUsing: geneBlockFactory.
        someIndividuals add: ind ].
    ^ someIndividuals
```

This method is designed to create individuals. It therefore acts as a factory of individuals. The random number generator may be omitted using the factory method:

```
GAIndividual class>>create: numberOfIndividuals
    individualsAndInitialize: numberOfGenes genesWith: geneBlockFactory
    "Factory method to easily create a number of Individuals.
        numberOfIndividuals : the number of individuals to return
        numberOfGenes : number of genes each individual should have
        geneBlockFactory : is a one-argument block to generate a gene.
            It takes a random generator as an argument"
    ^ self create: numberOfIndividuals individualsAndInitialize:
        numberOfGenes genesWith: geneBlockFactory using: (Random new seed: 42)
```

This factory method returns a group of initialized individuals. We can now test the GAIndividual class. We create the GAIndividualTest test, which is a subclass of TestCase, for that purpose:

```
TestCase subclass: #GAIndividualTest
    instanceVariableNames: ''
    classVariableNames: ''
    package: 'GeneticAlgorithm-Tests'
```

As a simple test, we can create 100 individuals, each having 10 genes:

```
GAIndividualTest>>testCreationWithCharacters
    | r individuals f ind |
    r := Random seed: 42.
    f := [ :random | ($a to: $z) atRandom: random ].
    individuals := GAIndividual
        create: 100
        individualsAndInitialize: 10
        genesWith: f
        using: r.

    self assert: individuals size equals: 100.
    self assert: (individuals collect: #numberOfGenes) asSet asArray
        equals: #(10).

    ind := individuals anyOne.
    self assert: (ind genes allSatisfy: [ :c | ($a to: $z) includes: c ]).
```

In the example of genetic algorithm we first gave, the algorithm had to guess the word *cat*. We can now use some individuals to guess that word.

Consider the following script:

```
inds := GAIndividual
            create: 1000
            individualsAndInitialize: 3
            genesWith: [ :r | ($a to: $z) atRandom: r ].
fitnessBlock := [ :genes |
    (genes with: 'cat' asArray collect: [ :a :b | (a == b)
        ifTrue: [ 1 ]
        ifFalse: [ 0 ] ]) sum ].
inds do: [ :i | i computeFitnessUsing: fitnessBlock ].
```

The script first creates some individuals, each having three letters as genes. Notice that the block to create a gene takes as an argument a random number generator. Evaluating the expression will create *the exact same* individuals even if random numbers are employed. The fitness of each individual is then computed. The fitness value returns a score that describes how close to the solution the individual is.

After executing this short script, each individual has a fitness value. Overall, the fitness value ranges from 0 to 3. An individual with a fitness of 3 matches the solution, which means its genes are equal to #($c $a $t).

As a simple and intuitive way to estimate the performance of each individual, we can render a histogram of the fitness of the individuals (see Figure 8-1):

```
...
data := ((inds collect: #fitness) groupedBy: #yourself) associations
            collect: [ : as | as key -> as value size ].

g := RTGrapher new.
d := RTData new.
d points: data.
d barChartWithBarTitle: #key.
d y: [ :as | as value ].
d yLog.
g add: d.
g axisY noDecimal.
g axisX noTick.
g
```

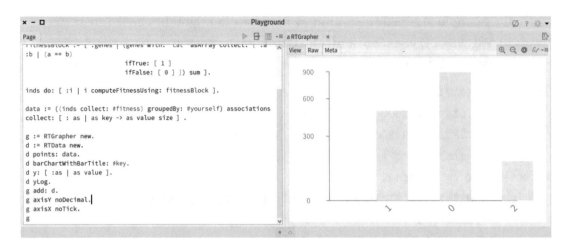

Figure 8-1. *Visualizing the fitness distribution of 1,000 individuals*

Using a vertical logarithmic scale, the graphic shows that from the 1000 initial individuals, 880 individuals have a fitness of 0, 113 individuals have a fitness of 1, and only seven individuals have a fitness of 2. None have a fitness of 3.

If we step back a bit, we are loosking for the word *cat*, composed of three letters. This means that we can formulate the space of search as a three-dimensional space in which each dimension ranges from 1 to 26. The word *cat* is one single point in that space.

In the previous script, we had only 1,000 words, and therefore it is not a surprise that we did not find the secret word. Let's try again with 100,000 individuals this time. The complete script is as follows (see Figure 8-2):

```
inds := GAIndividual
           create: 100000
           individualsAndInitialize: 3
           genesWith: [ :r | ($a to: $z) atRandom: r ].

fitnessBlock := [ :genes | (genes with: 'cat' asArray collect: [ :a :b | (a == b)
           ifTrue: [ 1 ]
           ifFalse: [ 0 ] ]) sum ].

inds do: [ :i | i computeFitnessUsing: fitnessBlock ].

data := ((inds collect: #fitness) groupedBy: #yourself) associations
    collect: [ : as | as key -> as value size ].
```

```
g := RTGrapher new.
d := RTData new.
d points: data.
d barChartWithBarTitle: #key.
d y: [ :as | as value ].
d yLog.
g add: d.
g axisY noDecimal.
g axisX noTick.
g
```

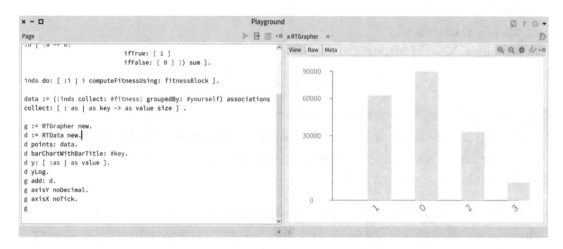

Figure 8-2. *Visualizing the fitness distribution of 100,000 individuals individuals*

Moving the mouse cursor to above bar 3 reveals that four individuals with the secret words have been created. We will see that by using a genetic algorithm, significantly fewer individuals have to be created to find the secret word.

8.5 Crossover Genetic Operations

A genetic algorithm uses genetic operations to produce new individuals. Biology recognizes two operations: *crossover,* which combines two individual to form a new one, and *mutation,* which produces a new individual with sporadic gene variations.

We will provide an implementation of these two operators, but it is important to have our implementation open to new genetic operations. Some particular operations may be crucial to significantly accelerate the convergence toward a solution. In this chapter, we focus on mutation and crossover. When we cover neuroevolution in Chapters 14 and 15 , we will need different mutations and crossover operations.

We can define the GAOperation class as the root class of all operations.

```
GAObject subclass: #GAOperation
    instanceVariableNames: ''
    classVariableNames: ''
    package: 'GeneticAlgorithm-Core'
```

We can define a hierarchy of the crossover as follows:

```
GAOperation subclass: #GAAbstractCrossoverOperation
    instanceVariableNames: ''
    classVariableNames: ''
    package: 'GeneticAlgorithm-Core'
```

We can now implement the crossover operation with the following method:

```
GAAbstractCrossoverOperation>>crossover: partnerA with: partnerB
    "Return a new child, which is the result of mixing myself with the argument"
    ^ self crossover: partnerA with: partnerB midpoint: (self
pickCutPointFor: partnerA)
```

The crossover:with: method takes two individuals as an argument. A new individual is produced and the genetic information of the parents are mixed. Consider this method:

```
GAAbstractCrossoverOperation>>crossover: partnerA with: partnerB
    midpoint: midpoint
    "Return a new child, which is the result of mixing myself with the argument"

    | child crossOverGenes |
    child := GAIndividual new.
    child random: random.
    crossOverGenes := (partnerA genes first: midpoint),
        (partnerB genes allButFirst: midpoint).
    child genes: crossOverGenes.
    ^ child
```

The `crossover:with:midpoint:` method accepts a cutting point as the third argument. The `first:midpoint` call returns the first `midpoint` elements, and the `allButFirst:midpoint` call returns the elements after the first `midpoint` elements. For example, `'abcdefghi'` `first: 3` returns `'abc'` and `'abcdefghi'allButFirst: 3` returns `'defghi'`.

We define an abstract method, which will be implemented in subclasses:

```
GAAbstractCrossoverOperation>>pickCutPointFor: anIndividual
    "Need to be overridden in subclasses"
    self subclassResponsibility
```

The `pickCutPointFor:` method has to be overridden in each subclass. We define the `GACrossoverOperation` class as follows:

```
GAAbstractCrossoverOperation subclass: #GACrossoverOperation
    instanceVariableNames: ''
    classVariableNames: ''
    package: 'GeneticAlgorithm-Core'
```

The `GACrossoverOperation` class overrides the `pickCutPointFor:` method:

```
GACrossoverOperation>>pickCutPointFor: partnerA
    "Simply returns a random number between 1 and the number of genes of
    the individual provided as an argument"
    ^ random nextInt: partnerA numberOfGenes
```

We can now test our crossover operation:

```
TestCase subclass: #GACrossoverOperationTest
    instanceVariableNames: 'i1 i2 op'
    classVariableNames: ''
    package: 'GeneticAlgorithm-Tests'
```

The test defines three variables—i1, i2, and op. These variables define the test fixture and they are initialized in the `setUp` method:

```
GACrossoverOperationTest>>setUp
    super setUp.
    i1 := GAIndividual new genes: 'abcd'.
    i2 := GAIndividual new genes: 'defg'.
    op := GACrossoverOperation new.
```

We can now test different combinations. In the first scenario, the midpoint is 2, which means that the resulting genes will have the first two letters of i1 and the last two letters of i2:

GACrossoverOperationTest>>testCrossover1

```
    | i3 |
    i3 := op crossover: i1 with: i2 midpoint: 2.
    self assert: i3 genes equals: 'abfg'
```

In this second scenario, the midpoint is 1:

GACrossoverOperationTest>>testCrossover2

```
    | i3 |
    i3 := op crossover: i1 with: i2 midpoint: 1.
    self assert: i3 genes equals: 'aefg'
```

In this third scenario, the midpoint is 0, which means that the resulting individual has all the letters of i2:

GACrossoverOperationTest>>testCrossover3

```
    | i3 |
    i3 := op crossover: i1 with: i2 midpoint: 0.
    self assert: i3 genes equals: 'defg'
```

We can also test the crossover:with: method using the following test:

GACrossoverOperationTest>>testCrossover4

```
    | i3 |
    op random: (Random seed: 42).
    i3 := op crossover: i1 with: i2.
    self assert: i3 genes equals: 'aefg'
```

We now have provided a complete implementation of the crossover operation. The effect of the crossover operation is to make the population converge toward a specific point in the search space. In a genetic algorithm, *exploitation* is often referred to as the ability to lead a population toward good solutions, and hopefully, to the global optimum.

8.6 Mutation Genetic Operations

A proper configuration of a genetic algorithm is to have a balance between *exploitation* and *exploration*, two important concepts. Exploitation is the result of applying crossover. The algorithm is exploiting the genetic information contained in the individuals by recombining them.

On the other hand, exploration is tied to mutation. Mutation is about exploring new areas in the search space, which has the effect of avoiding convergence.

Numerous mutations operations may be defined. We will therefore make our codebase open to new mutation operations. The natural way to do so using an object-oriented programming language such as Pharo is to express these operations as a hierarchy of classes. Consider the following abstract class:

```
GAOperation subclass: #GAAbstractMutationOperation
    instanceVariableNames: 'mutationRate'
    classVariableNames: ''
    package: 'GeneticAlgorithm-Core'
```

All the mutation operations we will define have at least one common variable, the mutation rate. We therefore define this rate as an instance variable. Typically, the value of that variable is a small positive number, close to `0.0` and significantly less than `1.0`. We set it per default:

```
GAAbstractMutationOperation>>initialize
    super initialize.
    self mutationRate: 0.01
```

The `0.01` value indicates that 1% of the genes of each individual will be modified. The mutation rate is a low value that enables exploring some particular area. Rate values are low, but any particular guideline is closely tied to the problem to be solved. As such, one has to try different values to find the most adequate rate.

The `mutationRate` variable may be accessed by using:

```
GAAbstractMutationOperation>>mutationRate
    "Return the used mutation rate. Typically, a small positive number,
     close to 0.0 and significantly less than 1.0"
    ^ mutationRate
```

The `mutationRate` variable may be set by using:

```
GAAbstractMutationOperation>>mutationRate: aFloat
    "Set the mutation rate. Typically, a small positive number, close to
     0.0 and significantly less than 1.0"
    mutationRate := aFloat
```

The key method of the `mutation` operation class is `mutate:`, which takes as an argument an individual and *produces a new individual*, which is the result of mutating the argument:

```
GAAbstractMutationOperation>>mutate: individual
    "Return a new individual (different object than the argument),
        result of a mutation from the individual provided as an argument."
    | newIndividual |
    newIndividual := GAIndividual new.
    newIndividual random: random.
    newIndividual genes: individual genes copy.
    self doMutate: newIndividual.
    ^ newIndividual
```

The `mutate:` method takes an individual as an argument and produces a new individual, which is the result of mutating the argument. The method simply copies the argument and calls the `doMutate:` method. The `doMutate:` method is abstract:

```
GAAbstractMutationOperation>>doMutate: individual
    "To be overridden"
    self subclassResponsibility
```

Most of the mutation operations require a way to create an individual gene. We add the empty method, as follows:

```
GAAbstractMutationOperation>>geneFactoryBlock: oneArgBlock
    "Do nothing. May be overridden if necessary"
```

The method has to be overridden in subclasses. Note that this method is called by `GAEngine`, which we will see later in this chapter. We can now define the standard mutation operation. Consider this class:

```
GAAbstractMutationOperation subclass: #GAMutationOperation
    instanceVariableNames: 'geneFactoryBlock'
    classVariableNames: ''
    package: 'GeneticAlgorithm-Core'
```

The mutation operator requires a way to define a new gene. We will use the same requirement expressed using the GAIndividual class. The geneFactoryBlock variable refers to a one-argument block to create a gene. The block receives a random number as an argument. The geneFactoryBlock: method sets the block to the operation:

```
GAMutationOperation>>geneFactoryBlock: oneArgBlock
    "The block receives a random number as an argument"
    geneFactoryBlock := oneArgBlock
```

The block may be accessed by using the following:

```
GAMutationOperation>>geneFactoryBlock
    "Return the three-arg block used to create a gene, following the
        pattern
    [ :rand :index :ind | ... ]
    rand is the random number generator,
    index is index of the gene,
    ind is the individual being filled"

    ^ geneFactoryBlock
```

As we have previously seen, the geneFactoryBlock variable refers to a three-argument block for which the first argument is the random number, the second is the index of the gene, and the third is the individual.

For help when using the mutation operation, we define a utility method to raise an error in case the geneFactoryBlock is not set. Such a method is useful for trapping common errors:

```
GAMutationOperation>>checkForGeneFactory
    self
        assert: [ geneFactoryBlock notNil ]
        description: 'Need to provide a block to create gene'
```

The core method of GAMutationOperation is doMutate:. We define it as follows:

```
GAMutationOperation>>doMutate: individual
    "Mutate genes of the argument"
    self checkForRandomNumber.
    self checkForGeneFactory.
    1 to: individual genes size do: [ :index |
        self randomNumber <= mutationRate
            ifTrue: [ individual genes at: index put: (geneFactoryBlock
                cull: random cull: index cull: individual) ] ]
```

The GAMutationOperation class can be properly tested. Consider this class:

```
TestCase subclass: #GAMutationOperationTest
    instanceVariableNames: 'i op'
    classVariableNames: ''
    package: 'GeneticAlgorithm-Tests'
```

The setUp method is defined as follows:

```
GAMutationOperationTest>>setUp
    super setUp.
    i := GAIndividual new genes: 'abcd' asArray.
    op := GAMutationOperation new.
```

We can test the mutation with the following:

```
GAMutationOperationTest>>testMutation
    | i2 |
    op random: (Random seed: 7).
    op geneFactoryBlock: [ :r | ($a to: $z) atRandom: r ].
    op mutationRate: 0.5.

    i2 := op mutate: i.
    self assert: i2 genes equals: 'xfcd' asArray.

    i2 := op mutate: i2.
    self assert: i2 genes equals: 'tfcd' asArray.

    i2 := op mutate: i2.
    self assert: i2 genes equals: 'tfjd' asArray.
```

The erroneous cases can be tested by using the following:

```
GAMutationOperationTest>>testRandomAndGeneFactoryMustBeSet
    self should: [ op mutate: i ] raise: AssertionFailure.

    op random: Random new.
    self should: [ op mutate: i ] raise: AssertionFailure.

    op geneFactoryBlock: [ :r | 42 ].
    self shouldnt: [ op mutate: i ] raise: AssertionFailure.
```

The mutation operator is now implemented. Our next move involves the selection mechanism.

8.7 Parent Selection

Being able to select an individual and promote it as a parent is essential. Some individuals deserve to enter the reproduction phase, and the selection algorithm is central to it.

Because several selection mechanisms exist, we will define a hierarchy of selection mechanisms. The GASelection class is a relatively large and complex class. It is closely tied to the GAEngine class, which we will present later in this chapter.

The GASelection class may be defined as follows:

```
Object subclass: #GASelection
    instanceVariableNames: 'population fittest initialPopulation
        fitnessBlock populationSize compareFitness engine'
    classVariableNames: ''
    package: 'GeneticAlgorithm-Core'
```

GASelection references a population of GAIndividual instances. The purpose of GASelection is to pick the fittest individual based on a strategy, implemented by a subclass of GASelection. The selection is also aware of the initialPopulation, which is necessary to deduce a new population of a size populationSize. The fitnessBlock tells the selection the way the fitness of each individual is computed. The compareFitness variable references a two-argument block that indicates which of two fitness values is the best. In some situations, a high fitness value indicates a good individual; in other situations, a high fitness value may indicate a bad individual. The engine variable references the genetic algorithm engine.

First, we provide a simple constructor for GASelection, as follows:

```
GASelection>>initialize
    super initialize.
    population := OrderedCollection new.
```

We provide some accessors and some mutator methods. Consider the engine method:

```
GASelection>>engine
    "Return the GAEngine to which the selection is associated"
    ^ engine
```

The mutator of engine may be as follows:

```
GASelection>>engine: theEngine
    "Set the GAEngine to which I have to be associated with"
    engine := theEngine.
    self checkIfEngineSet
```

We provide a simple guard, defined as follows:

```
GASelection>>checkIfEngineSet
    self assert: [ engine notNil ] description: 'Should set the engine'
```

The population may be accessed using the following:

```
GASelection>>population
    "Return the new population"
    ^ population
```

The fitness block may be accessed using fitnessBlock::

```
GASelection>>fitnessBlock: aOneArgBlock
    "The argument is evaluated on the genes of each individual.
    The block argument has to compute the fitness."
    fitnessBlock := aOneArgBlock
```

The fitness block may be accessed using fitnessBlock, as follows:

```
GASelection>>fitnessBlock
    "Return the one-arg block used to compute fitness of each
        individual"
    ^ fitnessBlock
```

The fittest element is accessible using the `fittest` method:

```
GASelection>>fittest
    "Return the fittest individual from the new population"
    ^ fittest
```

The initial population may be set using a dedicated method:

```
GASelection>>initialPopulation: aPopulationAsIndividuals
    "Set the initial population. This is used to create the new
        population"
    initialPopulation := aPopulationAsIndividuals.
    self checkIfInitialPopulationSet
```

We provide a new utility method to catch errors early:

```
GASelection>>checkIfInitialPopulationSet
    self assert: [ initialPopulation notNil ]
        description: 'Should set the initial population'.
    self assert: [ initialPopulation isCollection ]
        description: 'Has to be a collection'.
    self assert: [ initialPopulation notEmpty ]
        description: 'Cannot be empty'
```

The `checkIfInitialPopulationSet` method raises an error if the initial population is incorrectly set. The way fitness values are compared may be set as follows:

```
GASelection>>compareFitness: aTwoArgBlock
    "Take as an argument a two-argument block that compares the
        fitness of two individuals"
    compareFitness := aTwoArgBlock
```

The population size may be read by using the following:

```
GASelection>>populationSize
    "Return the population size"
    ^ initialPopulation size
```

The population size is set using the following:

```
GASelection>>populationSize: anInteger
    "Set the population size"
    populationSize := anInteger
```

Subsequently, we define a number of essential methods that describe the logic of the selection. The abstract method createNewPopulation has to be overridden in subclasses. Its purpose is to create a new population:

```
GASelection>>createNewPopulation
    "Create a new population"
    self subclassResponsibility
```

An essential method of the GASelection class is to be able to perform the selection. This is what the doSelection method does:

```
GASelection>>doSelection
    "Produce a new population using the selection algorithm"
    self checkIfEngineSet.
    self checkIfInitialPopulationSet.
    populationSize := initialPopulation size.
    fittest := initialPopulation first.
    initialPopulation
        do: [ :ind |
            ind computeFitnessUsing: fitnessBlock.
            (self isIndividual: ind betterThan: fittest)
                ifTrue: [ fittest := ind ] ].
    self createNewPopulation.
    initialPopulation := population.
```

The method first begins by performing some sanity checks. These checks are intended to help users correctly use the provided code.

We will define a number of utility methods to simplify the way the algorithm logic is expressed. For example, the crossover operation may be delegated by using:

```
GASelection>>crossover: partnerA with: partnerB
    "Return one child, result of the crossover over the two arguments"
    ^ engine crossover: partnerA with: partnerB
```

Comparison between individuals may be defined as follows:

```
GASelection>>isIndividual: ind betterThan: fittestIndividual
    "Is the first individual better than the second?"
    ^ engine isIndividual: ind betterThan: fittestIndividual
```

The mutation operation may be invoked by using the following:

```
GASelection>>mutate: child
    "Perform a mutation on the argument"
    ^ engine mutate: child
```

To produce a random number within a particular interval, we need to produce random numbers:

```
GASelection>>randomNumber: value
    "Return a number between 1 and value"
    ^ engine randomNumber: value
```

Several selections strategies are available to select an individual from a population to be a parent. One popular and efficient selection strategy is called *tournament,* which operates as follows: it randomly picks a number of individuals from a population and identifies the individual with the best fitness. This identification acts as a competition between pairs of individuals. The competition is carried out over a small number of individuals. Arbitrarily, we will consider each tournament to be five individuals. The winning individual is returned from the algorithm.

We define the GATournamentSelection class as follows:

```
GASelection subclass: #GATournamentSelection
    instanceVariableNames: 'tournamentSize'
    classVariableNames: ''
    package: 'GeneticAlgorithm-Core'
```

In our case, the tournamentSize variable indicates how large the tournament should be. Per default, the value is set to 5:

```
GATournamentSelection>>initialize
    super initialize.
    tournamentSize := 5
```

We implement the algorithm as follows:

```
GATournamentSelection>>getGoodIndividual
    "Return the best individual from tournamentSize individual randomly
        chosen from the population"
    | best ind |
    best := nil.
    tournamentSize timesRepeat: [
        ind := initialPopulation at: (self randomNumber:
            initialPopulation size).
        (best isNil or: [ compareFitness value: ind fitness value: best
            fitness ])
            ifTrue: [ best := ind ] ].
    ^ best
```

Finally, a new population may be created using the following:

```
GATournamentSelection>>createNewPopulation
    "Return a new population made of newly breed individual"
    | partnerA partnerB child |
    population := (1 to: self populationSize) collect: [ :seed |
      engine random: (Random seed: seed).
      partnerA := self getGoodIndividual.
      partnerB := self getGoodIndividual.
      child := self mutate: (self crossover: partnerA with: partnerB).
      child computeFitnessUsing: engine fitnessBlock.
      child.
    ]
```

The `createNewPopulation` method implements the logic of the genetic algorithm: it picks two elements from the population, does a crossover between them, mutates the result, and computes the fitness of each new element added to the new population.

8.8 Evolution Monitoring

Being able to monitor the execution of the algorithm is essential. For example, it's important to have a termination condition to indicate when the algorithm has to stop. We will produce a dedicated class to monitor progress made by the algorithm. Consider the GALog class:

```
Object subclass: #GALog
    instanceVariableNames: 'generationNumber timeToProduceGeneration
        fittestIndividual worseFitness averageFitness'
    classVariableNames: ''
    package: 'GeneticAlgorithm-Core'
```

An instance of GALog is associated with a generation and contains relevant information to indicate progresses of the genetic algorithm.

It is highly relevant to identify the best individual from a population:

```
GALog>>fittestIndividual
    "Return the best individual of the generation I represent"
    ^ fittestIndividual
```

The best individual will be set by the genetic algorithm engine, which we will soon see:

```
GALog>>fittestIndividual: anIndividual
    "Set the best individual of the generation I represent"
    fittestIndividual := anIndividual
```

The fitness method returns the fitness value of the best individual of the population:

```
GALog>>bestFitness
    "Return the best fitness value of a generation I am representing"
    ^ fittestIndividual fitness
```

The average fitness of the population is obtained using the averageFitness method:

```
GALog>>averageFitness
    "Return the average fitness value of a generation I am representing"
    ^ averageFitness
```

The average fitness may be set by using the following:

```
GALog>>averageFitness: aNumber
    "Set the average fitness value of a generation I am representing"
    averageFitness := aNumber
```

Similarly, the lowest fitness score is obtained by using the following:

```
GALog>>worseFitness
    "Return the worse fitness value of a generation I am representing"
    ^ worseFitness
```

The worst fitness score is set by the engine by using the following:

```
GALog>>worseFitness: aNumber
    "Set the worst fitness value of a generation I am representing"
    worseFitness := aNumber
```

The number of generations also has to be tracked. The generationNumber indicates the number of the generation the log object is referring to:

```
GALog>>generationNumber
    "Return the generation number I represent"
    ^ generationNumber
```

Similar to the fittest individual, the generation number is set by the engine, as we will soon see:

```
GALog>>generationNumber: generationNumberAsInteger
    "Set the generation number I am representing"
    generationNumber := generationNumberAsInteger
```

It's also wise to monitor the consumed resources in some cases. The time taken to produce a new generation is important to track:

```
GALog>>timeToProduceGeneration
    "Time to produce the generation I represent"
    ^ timeToProduceGeneration
```

Again, the engine will set this value:

```
GALog>>timeToProduceGeneration: anInteger
    "Set the time to produce the generation I am representing"
    timeToProduceGeneration := anInteger
```

A simple way of printing the result is useful. The `Object` class defines the `printOn:` method, which is responsible for providing a textual representation of the object. By overriding this method, we will make the textual representation of a log object more meaningful:

```
GALog>>printOn: str
    "Printing the log object"
    super printOn: str.
    str nextPut: $<.
    str nextPutAll: fittestIndividual genes asString.
    str nextPut: $>.
```

We have now established a solid foundation on which we can implement the algorithm.

8.9 The Genetic Algorithm Engine

The engine is a central class that uses the genetic algorithm. It offers methods that configure and run the genetic algorithm. We can define the class as follows:

```
GAObject subclass: #GAEngine
    instanceVariableNames: 'fitnessBlock createGeneBlock numberOfGenes
        populationSize logs population terminationBlock compareFitness
        mutationOperator crossoverOperator selection
        beforeCreatingInitialIndividual'
    classVariableNames: ''
    package: 'GeneticAlgorithm-Core'
```

`GAEngine` is a complex and relatively long class. It has a number of variables:

- `fitnessBlock` is a one-argument block. It takes the genes of each individual as an argument and returns the fitness of the individual.

- `createGeneBlock` refers to a gene block factory.

- `numberOfGenes` indicates the number of genes each individual has.

- `populationSize` is the size of the population.

- `logs` refers to a collection of instances of GALog. This variable keeps the evolutionary history of the algorithm.

- `population` refers to the individual population.

- `terminationBlock` is a block that indicates when the algorithm has to stop. The block represents the termination condition and does not take an argument.

- `compareFitness` is a two-argument block, taking two fitness values. The block indicates which fitness is better than the other.

- `mutationOperator` is the mutation operator.

- `crossoverOperator` is the crossover operator.

- `selection` refers to a selection algorithm.

- `beforeCreatingInitialIndividual` contains a one-argument block that is evaluated before an individual of the initial population is created. The block takes a random number generator as an argument.

Some accessors are necessary to let the user configure the algorithm. Note that an example of using the algorithm is provided at the end of the chapter. The createGeneBlock: method is used to indicate how a gene has to be created:

```
GAEngine>>createGeneBlock: threeArgBlock
    "Three arguments must be provided rand, index, and the individual
        being filled"
    createGeneBlock := threeArgBlock.
    mutationOperator geneFactoryBlock: threeArgBlock
```

The fitnessBlock: method is used to indicate how fitness is computed:

```
GAEngine>>fitnessBlock: aOneArgBlock
    "The argument is evaluated on the genes of each individual.
    The block argument has to compute the fitness."
    fitnessBlock := aOneArgBlock
```

The fitnessBlock may be obtained using a method (the selection algorithm uses it):

```
GAEngine>>fitnessBlock
    "Return the fitness block used by the engine"
    ^ fitnessBlock
```

We also provide an accessor of the beforeCreatingInitialIndividual: variable using this method:

```
GAEngine>>beforeCreatingInitialIndividual: aOneArgBlock
    "Set the behavior to be executed before creating an individual.
    The block takes a random number generator as an argument."
    beforeCreatingInitialIndividual := aOneArgBlock
```

The mutation rate may be set by using the following:

```
GAEngine>>mutationRate: aFloat
    "Set the mutation rate used by the engine. The default value is 0.01"
    mutationOperator mutationRate: aFloat.
```

The number of genes per individual is set as follows:

```
GAEngine>>numberOfGenes: anInteger
    "Set the number of genes each individual will have"
    numberOfGenes := anInteger
```

The crossover operation may be set using the crossoverOperator: method:

```
GAEngine>>crossoverOperator: aCrossoverOperator
    "Set the crossover operator used in the algorithm"
    crossoverOperator := aCrossoverOperator.
    crossoverOperator random: random
```

The mutation operation may be set as follows:

```
GAEngine>>mutationOperator: aMutationOperator
    mutationOperator := aMutationOperator.
    aMutationOperator random: random
```

The size of the population is configured using the following:

```
GAEngine>>populationSize: anInteger
    "Set the population size"
    populationSize := anInteger
```

The selection operator may be set using a dedicated method, as follows:

```
GAEngine>>selection: aSelection
    "Set the selection method to be used to create a new population"
    selection := aSelection.
    aSelection engine: self.
```

A tournament object is used as an argument of selection:. The selection variable may be accessed by using:

```
GAEngine>>selection
    "Return the selection operator"
    ^ selection
```

In many situations, a better individual is the one with the highest fitness value:

```
GAEngine>>maximizeComparator
    "A better individual is the one with the highest fitness value"
    compareFitness := [ :f1 :f2 | f1 > f2 ]
```

However, it may happen that a better individual is the one with the lowest value:

```
GAEngine>>minimizeComparator
    "A better individual is the one with the lowest fitness value"
    compareFitness := [ :f1 :f2 | f1 < f2 ]
```

The constructor of the engine is as follows:

```
GAEngine>>initialize
    super initialize.
    logs := OrderedCollection new.
    random := Random seed: 42.
    self endForMaxNumberOfGeneration: 10.
    populationSize := 10.
    self maximizeComparator.
```

184

```
mutationOperator := GAMutationOperation new.
mutationOperator mutationRate: 0.01.
mutationOperator random: random.

crossoverOperator := GACrossoverOperation new.
crossoverOperator random: random.

self selection: GATournamentSelection new.

beforeCreatingInitialIndividual :=
        [ :rand | "do nothing per default" ]
```

As you can see, several parameters have a default value. The fitnessBlock is passed from the engine to the selection:

GAEngine>>beforeRun

```
"Method executed before creating the initial population"
self checkIfReadyToRun.
selection fitnessBlock: fitnessBlock.
selection populationSize: populationSize
```

The checkIfReadyToRun method raises an exception if the algorithm is not properly set up:

GAEngine>>checkIfReadyToRun

```
"Raise an exception if the configuration is not ready to be run"
self assert: [ fitnessBlock notNil ]
    description: 'Need to set a fitnessBlock'.
self assert: [ createGeneBlock notNil ]
    description: 'Need to set a createGeneBlock'.
self assert: [ numberOfGenes notNil ]
    description: 'Need to set how many genes you wish to have,
        using numberOfGenes:'.
self assert: [ logs isEmpty ]
    description: 'Already been run'.
```

In particular, the algorithm can be run if it has a fitnessBlock, a createGeneBlock, and a numberOfGenes. Moreover, it should not have been previously run (i.e., the logs variable has to be empty).

When the engine is asked to perform a crossover operation, it simply delegates it to the operation object:

```
GAEngine>>crossover: partnerA with: partnerB
    "Perform a crossover operation between the two arguments"
    ^ crossoverOperator crossover: partnerA with: partnerB
```

Similarly, when the engine is asked to mutate an individual, it simply delegates it to the corresponding operator:

```
GAEngine>>mutate: individual
    "Mutate the child provided as an argument"
    ^ mutationOperator mutate: individual
```

The initial population is defined using the following:

```
GAEngine>>initializePopulation
    self checkForRandomNumber.
    population := OrderedCollection new.
    populationSize timesRepeat: [
        | ind |
        beforeCreatingInitialIndividual value: random.
        ind := GAIndividual new.
        population add:
            (ind
                random: random;
                set: numberOfGenes genesUsing: createGeneBlock) ]
```

It is essential to determine which of two individuals is better. We use the following method:

```
GAEngine>>isIndividual: anIndividual betterThan: aFittestIndividual
    "Compare an individual against the fittest individual of the population"
    ^ compareFitness value: anIndividual fitness value:
        aFittestIndividual fitness
```

The logs may be obtained using simple variable accessors:

```
GAEngine>>logs
    "Return the logs of the run"
    ^ logs
```

Here is the central method of the algorithm. The GAEngine>>run method is the entry point of the algorithm:

```
GAEngine>>run
    "Public method -- Run the genetic algorithm"

    | t log |
    self beforeRun.
        self initializePopulation.
    selection initialPopulation: population.
    selection compareFitness: compareFitness.
    UIManager default
        informUserDuring: [ :bar |
            | gen |
            gen := 0.
            [ self shouldTerminate ] whileFalse: [ gen := gen + 1.
                bar label: gen asString.
                self microPause.
                t := Time now asSeconds.
                self produceNewPopulation.

                log := GALog new.
                log generationNumber: gen.
                log fittestIndividual: selection fittest.
                log worseFitness: ((population collect: #fitness)
                    inject: log bestFitness into: [ :wFit :current | (
                    compareFitness value: wFit value: current) ifTrue: [
                    current ] ifFalse: [ wFit ] ]).
                log averageFitness: (population collect: #fitness)
                    average asFloat.
                log timeToProduceGeneration: Time now asSeconds - t.
                logs add: log ] ]
```

When the algorithm runs, it is essential to let the system broadcast its own progress. We therefore add the microPause method, which makes it possible for the current running thread to let the other threads do some work:

```
GAEngine>>microPause
    "Useful when you wish to log in the Transcript and see progresses"
    (Delay forMilliseconds: 1) wait.
    World doOneCycleNow.
```

The produceNewPopulation method is central to the engine:

```
GAEngine>>produceNewPopulation
    "This method
        - produces a new population, set in the variable 'population'
        - select the fittest element of the population"
    selection doSelection.
    population := selection population.
```

We also employ a small utility method to produce random numbers:

```
GAEngine>>randomNumber: maxNumber
    "Return a number between 1 and maxNumber"
    ^ random nextInt: maxNumber
```

The result of the algorithm is accessed using the result method:

```
GAEngine>>result
    "Return the genes of the fittest individual. This method is
        expected to be executed after #run has completed"
    ^ self logs last fittestIndividual genes
```

8.10 Terminating the Algorithm

We are now entering the last batch of methods to complete the implementation of our algorithm. One important aspect when configuring a genetic algorithm is determining when the algorithm execution has to stop.

Terminating the algorithm execution is a sensitive aspect that should be carefully considered. For example, if we can unambiguously say it has found the solution, then the termination condition is trivial: just stop when we find the solution. However, for many problems, we have no idea what the optimal solution looks like. In such cases, we can ask the algorithm to stop after a particular number of generations, or stop if the fitness does not get better after a few generations. The condition that should be met in order to stop the algorithm may depend on a number of different factors (e.g., if the exact solution exists and may be found).

The shouldTerminate method indicates whether the algorithm has to terminate. If no log has been registered, it means that the algorithm was not run, and in that case, we evaluate the terminationBlock variable:

```
GAEngine>>shouldTerminate
    logs ifEmpty: [ ^ false ].
    ^ terminationBlock value
```

The following method defines the terminationBlock variable according to a particular strategy. The endForMaxNumberOfGeneration: method defines a termination condition based on the number of generations. The algorithm stops after a particular number of created generations:

```
GAEngine>>endForMaxNumberOfGeneration: nbOfGenerations
    "End the algorithm after a fixed number of generations"
    terminationBlock :=
        [ logs last generationNumber >= nbOfGenerations ]
```

It may happen that if the fitness is above a particular value, the fittest individual may be considered an acceptable solution. In such a case, there is no reason to pursue the execution of the algorithm:

```
GAEngine>>endIfFitnessIsAbove: aFitnessValueThreshold
    "End the algorithm if the best fitness value is above a particular
        threshold"
    terminationBlock :=
        [ logs last fittestIndividual fitness >= aFitnessValueThreshold
            ]
```

Another strategy is to stop the algorithm if no better solution is found for a given number of generations:

```
GAEngine>>endIfNoImprovementFor: nbOfGenerations
    "End if no improvement occurred within a given number of
        generations"
    ^ self endIfNoImprovementFor: nbOfGenerations withinRangeOf: 0
```

Complex strategy may be formulated. For example, endIfNoImprovementFor:withi nRangeOf: defines a condition based on the number of generations and a range of delta values:

```
GAEngine>>endIfNoImprovementFor: nbOfGenerations withinRangeOf: delta
    "End if no improvement occurred (within a delta value) within a
        given number of generations"
    terminationBlock := [
        (logs last generationNumber >= nbOfGenerations) and: [
            | fs |
            fs := (logs last: nbOfGenerations) collect: [ :aLog | aLog
                fittestIndividual fitness ].
            (fs max - fs min) <= delta
            ] ]
```

We have implemented the essential features of this algorithm and can now test it.

8.11 Testing the Algorithm

We will define a unit test that focuses on this algorithm. Consider the GAEngineTest class:

```
TestCase subclass: #GAEngineTest
    instanceVariableNames: ''
    classVariableNames: ''
    package: 'GeneticAlgorithm-Tests'
```

We can now implement the introductory example we use for searching a secret word:

```
GAEngineTest>>testExamples01
    | g |
    g := GAEngine new.
    g populationSize: 1000.
    g numberOfGenes: 4.
    g createGeneBlock: [ :rand :index :ind | ($a to: $z) atRandom: rand ].
    g fitnessBlock: [ :genes |
```

```
    (#($g $a $t $o) with: genes collect: [ :a :b |
        a = b ifTrue: [ 1 ] ifFalse: [ 0 ] ]) sum ].
g run.
self assert: g logs first fittestIndividual fitness equals: 2.
self assert: g logs first fittestIndividual genes equals: #($g $l $t $s).
self assert: g logs fourth fittestIndividual fitness equals: 4.
self assert: g logs fourth fittestIndividual genes equals: #($g $a $t $o).
```

The testExamples01 test creates an engine, configured with a population size of 1,000. Each individual has four genes. The gene block factory picks a random letter, and the fitness block is the number of matching letters. In the first generation, the best individual has a fitness of 2, and in the fourth generation the answer is found.

8.12 Visualizing Population Evolution

Visualizing the execution of the algorithm is an essential feature. We extend the GAEngine class to visualize the historical data kept in the log objects.

The visualize method uses Roassal to draw three curves. At each generation, the best, average, and lowest score is kept. Consider the following method definition:

```
GAEngine>>visualize
    "Visualize the evolution of the population"
    | g d |
    g := RTGrapher new.
    d := RTData new.
    d label: 'Best fitness'.
    d interaction popupText: [ :assoc | assoc value bestFitness ].
    d connectColor: Color blue.
    d noDot.
    d points: self logs.
    d y: #bestFitness.
    d x: #generationNumber.
    g add: d.
```

```
d := RTData new.
d label: 'Worst fitness'.
d interaction popupText: [ :assoc | assoc value worseFitness ].
d connectColor: Color red.
d noDot.
d points: self logs.
d y: #worseFitness.
d x: #generationNumber.
g add: d.

d := RTData new.
d label: 'Average fitness'.
d interaction popupText: [ :assoc | assoc value averageFitness ].
d connectColor: Color green.
d noDot.
d points: self logs.
d y: #averageFitness.
d x: #generationNumber.
g add: d.
g legend addText: 'Fitness evolution'.
g axisY title: 'Fitness'.
g axisX noDecimal; title: 'Generation'.
^ g
```

We bridge the GAEngine class with the GTInspector framework to render the visualization:

```
GAEngine>>gtInspectorViewIn: composite
    <gtInspectorPresentationOrder: -10>
    composite roassal2
        title: 'View';
        initializeView: [ self visualize ]
```

The gtInspectorViewIn: method configures the Pharo inspector to display a visualization when an engine is inspected. Consider the following script:

```
g := GAEngine new.
g populationSize: 1000.
g numberOfGenes: 4.
g createGeneBlock: [ :rand :index :ind | ($a to: $z) atRandom: rand ].
g fitnessBlock: [ :genes |
    (#($g $a $t $o) with: genes collect: [ :a :b | a = b
        ifTrue: [ 1 ] ifFalse: [ 0 ] ]) sum ].
g run.
```

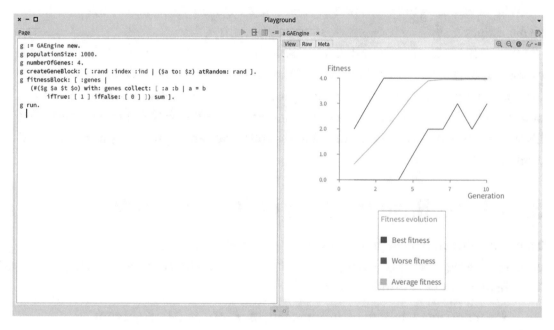

Figure 8-3. *Example of fitness evolution*

This script executes a genetic algorithm to find the word gato (*cat* in Spanish). It is configured as follows:

- The population is composed of 1,000 individuals.

- Each individual has four genes.

- Each gene is a random letter, ranging from the letter a and z.

- The fitness is a one-argument block that takes the genes of an individual as an argument. It returns the number of the matching letter with the word to find.

Figure 8-3 illustrates the historical evolution of the fitness score. Such a graph is used as a means to interpret how the algorithm execution went.

We can also easily give the list of log objects:

```
GAEngine>>gtInspectorLogsIn: composite
    <gtInspectorPresentationOrder: -5>
    composite list
        title: 'Logs';
        display: [ self logs ]
```

When inspecting the result of the execution, a Logs tab accompanies the visualization.

If we step back, we can see that we produced an efficient algorithm. At the beginning of the chapter, we had to produce 100,000 random three-letter words (*cat*) to find four instances of the correct words. Using genetic algorithm, only 4,000 individuals had to be created to find many instances of a four-letter word (*gato*). This is a simple scenario that illustrates how well-designed recombination operations are significantly more powerful than brute-force searches.

8.13 What Have We Seen in This Chapter?

That was a long chapter. It provided a full implementation of a genetic algorithm. In addition, the algorithm is open to new operations, as we will see in the next chapters. This chapter covered the following topics:

- It presented the complete implementation of a genetic algorithm.

- It presented a very simple, but representative, example of finding a word.

The following chapter will build on this chapter by showing some more interesting problems to solve using a genetic algorithm.

CHAPTER 9

Genetic Algorithms in Action

This chapter illustrates the use of genetic algorithms by solving a number of difficult algorithmic problems. Most of the problems presented in this chapter involve some arithmetic operations and therefore have a mathematical flavor.

9.1 Fundamental Theorem of Arithmetic

A prime number is a whole number greater than 1 whose only factors are 1 and itself. For example, 7 is a prime because it can only be divided by 7 and 1. The number 10 is not a prime because it can be divided by 2 and 5—two prime numbers.

In number theory, there is a theorem called *the fundamental theorem of arithmetic*, which states "any integer greater than 1 is either a prime number itself, or can be written as a unique product of prime numbers." Note that this representation is unique, except for the order of the factors. For example, the number 345 is a multiplication of factors 3*5*23. Finding this list of factors is computationally expensive. We will use genetic algorithms to identify the prime factors of any given number. As such, a gene will represent a prime number factor.

It is relevant to note that the number of factors depends on the number to be factored out. For example, the number 345 has three factors (3, 5, and 23), whereas the number $788,389$ has four factors since $788,389 = 7 * 41 * 41 * 67$. In the genetic algorithm we presented in the previous chapter, all the individuals have the exact same number of genes. How do we represent an arbitrary number of genes then? One way that fits well with our situation is to consider 1 as a possible factor. Assuming each individual has 10 genes, the factors of 345 can be encoded with the values 3, 5, 23, and seven times the factor 1. The solution will then be the factors contained in an individual for which we ignore the value 1.

© Alexandre Bergel 2020
A. Bergel, *Agile Artificial Intelligence in Pharo*, https://doi.org/10.1007/978-1-4842-5384-7_9

The fitness function is simply the absolute difference between the multiplication of the prime factors and the number we are interested in looking for the factors. If the fitness is equal to 0, then we found the solution.

Consider the following script:

```
numberOfIdentifyFactors := 345.
primeNumbers := #(2 3 5 7 11 13 17 19 23 29 31 37 41 43 47 53 59 61 67
    71 73 79 83 89 97 101 103 107 109 113 127 131 137 139 149 151 157
    163 167 173 179 181 191 193 197 199).
candidateFactors := #(1), primeNumbers.
g := GAEngine new.
g endIfNoImprovementFor: 10.
g populationSize: 10000.
g numberOfGenes: 10.
g createGeneBlock:
    [ :rand :index :ind | candidateFactors atRandom: rand ].
g minimizeComparator.
g
    fitnessBlock: [ :genes |
        ((genes inject: 1 into: [ :r :v | r * v ]) -
            numberOfIdentifyFactors) abs ].
g run.
```

We provided 46 prime numbers from which the algorithm has to pick the relevant ones. The fitness function contains the genes `inject: 1 into: [ :r :v | r * v ]` expression, which returns the multiplication of the numbers contained in the genes temporary variable. For example, `#(3 5 23)inject: 1 into: [ :r :v | r * v ]` evaluates to 345.

After the execution of the script, we can verify how it went with this expression:

```
...
g logs last bestFitness.
```

If the value is 0, we find the exact prime factors. If we did not find it, we could increase the population size or increase the argument of `endIfNoImprovementFor:`.

The prime factors may be obtained using the following expression:

```
...
g result copyWithout: 1.
```

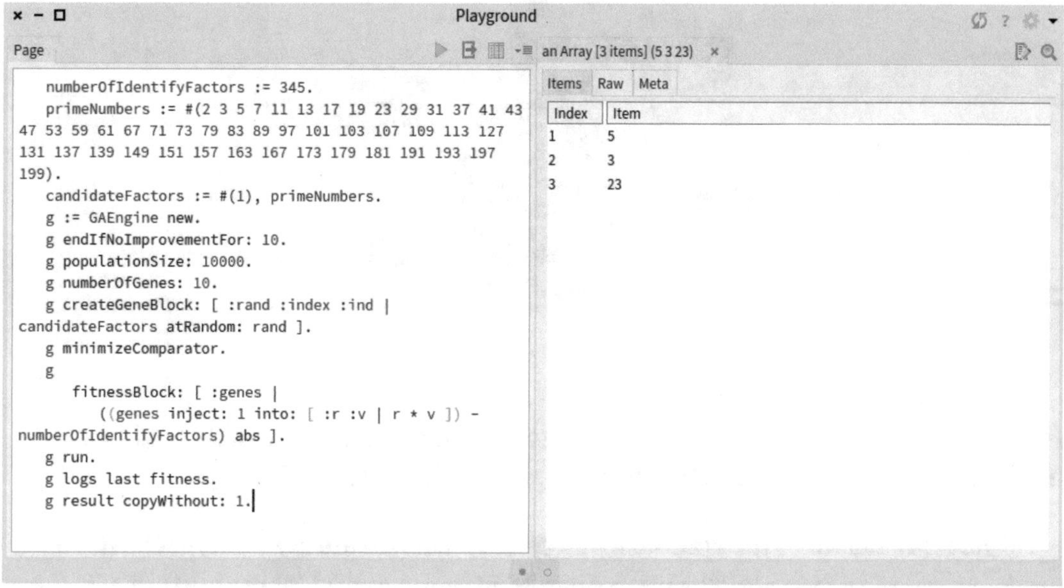

Figure 9-1. *Identification of prime factors of 345*

Figure 9-1 gives the results of executing the whole script.

For any non-prime number, the sequence of the prime factor is unique. This means that the number 345 can only be broken into the group of prime factors—3, 5, and 23. There is no other combination of prime factors that produce 345. The prime factors therefore constitute an "identity" of the 345 composite number. The fundamental theorem of arithmetic has a well chosen name. This theorem has many applications, and one of them is cryptography. If cryptography is as important as it is today, it is essentially due to this theorem. In cryptography, a prime factor represents a private key, and if the composite number is large enough, it takes an incredible amount of time to actually find the prime factors.

9.2 The Knapsack Problem

The knapsack problem is a well-known problem in combinatorial optimization. It can be summarized as follows: given a set of items, each having a value and a weight, determine the number of each item to include in a collection, such that (i) the total weight is less than or equal a given limit and (ii) the total value is as large as possible.

We will consider two variants of this problem—the unbounded knapsack problem and the 0-1 knapsack problem.

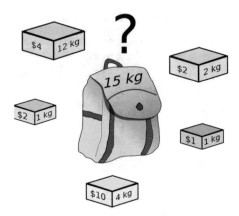

Figure 9-2. *The knapsack problem (obtained from Wikipedia, authored by Dake, under Creative Commons Attribution, Share Alike 2.5 Generic)*

Figure 9-2 illustrates the knapsack problem. Five boxes are available, each with a particular value and weight. The bag cannot hold more than 15 kilograms (kg). If we consider the unbounded variant of the problem, then the solution is three boxes of $10 and three boxes of $2. If we consider the 0-1 variant, the solution is all the boxes except the $4 one.

9.2.1 The Unbounded Knapsack Problem Variant

In this variant, a box may be used multiple times. We use the genetic algorithm to search for the optimal solution. The fitness function reflects the value of a given set of boxes (the sum of the value) minus a penalty. This penalty is the difference between the total weight with the knapsack's capacity. Consider the following script:

```
knapsackMaxWeight := 15.
"a box = (value, weight)"
boxes := #(#(4 12) #(2 1) #(2 2) #(1 1) #(10 4) #(0 0)).

g := GAEngine new.
g endIfNoImprovementFor: 10.
g populationSize: 20000.
g numberOfGenes: 15.
g createGeneBlock: [ :rand :index :ind | boxes atRandom: rand ].
g maximizeComparator.
g
```

```
fitnessBlock: [ :genes |
    | totalWeight totalValue penalty |
    totalValue := (genes collect: #first) sum.
    totalWeight := (genes collect: #second) sum.
    knapsackMaxWeight < totalWeight
        ifTrue: [ penalty := (knapsackMaxWeight - totalWeight) abs
            * 50 ]
        ifFalse: [ penalty := 0 ].
    totalValue - penalty
    ].
g run.
g result copyWithout: #(0 0)
```

The knapsackMaxWeight variable refers to the knapsack's capacity. The boxes variable contains all the available boxes. Each box is represented as a tuple (value, weight).

The capacity of the bag is 15kg and the lightest box weighs 1kg, as illustrated in Figure 9-2. The fact that the lightest box weighs 1kg sets the number of genes of our algorithm: each individual does not need to have more than 15 genes. A greater number of genes would not be meaningful since the sum of 16 or more boxes will weigh more than 15kg. Conversely, having fewer than 15 genes may exclude some solutions. For example, if the optimal solution is 15 boxes of 1kg, our algorithm should be able to find it. To conclude, it seems that each individual should have 15 genes.

However, if we tune our algorithm with 15 genes per individual, how can we represent a solution with fewer than 15 boxes? In particular, the solution of the unbounded knapsack problem has six boxes—three boxes of $10 and three boxes of $2— with a total weight of 15kg. This is not quite what our algorithm will produce since it will look for solutions made of *exactly* 15 boxes. As such, enforcing a solution to be made of 15 boxes will make our algorithm miss the solution. We therefore need a way to relax the fact that a solution must have 15 boxes. In this particular case, simply adding an empty box with no value to our algorithm, #(0 0), will do the job well: the algorithm can pick the six boxes (the true solution of the problem) and fill the nine remainder slots of the individual carrying the solution with empty boxes.

The fitness function contains three variables. The totalValue variable sums the value of the set of boxes contained in the genes variable. The totalWeight variable is the boxes' weight. We defined a penalty variable, which is the absolute difference between the bag capacity and the totalWeight. We use the 50 factor to make sure that the value does not take over the penalty.

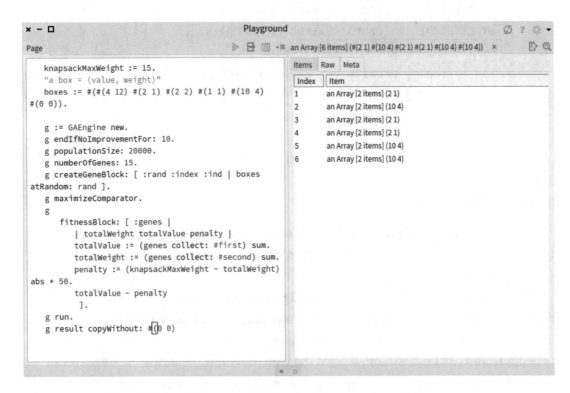

Figure 9-3. *Genetic algorithm applied to the Knapsack problem*

Figure 9-3 illustrates the execution of the script.

9.2.2 The 0-1 Knapsack Problem Variant

In this variant, each available box appears at most once. We treat this problem in a similar way as the previous one; however, the encoding and decoding of the genes has to reflect the fact that each box can appear at most once in each individual.

The key aspect to consider when solving this variant of the problem is to realize that this problem is similar to searching for a number written in binary (i.e., made of 0s and 1s). Assuming that the set of boxes is fixed and ordered, as we have specified so far, then we can assign the value 0 to a box to indicate that the box is *absent* from the solution represented by an individual. Similarly, the value 1 indicates that the box is *present*.

Consider the following script:

```
knapsackMaxWeight := 15.
"a box = (value, weight)"
boxes := #(#(4 12) #(2 1) #(2 2) #(1 1) #(10 4) ).
g := GAEngine new.
g endIfNoImprovementFor: 10.
g populationSize: 20000.
g numberOfGenes: boxes size.
g createGeneBlock: [ :rand :index :ind | #(0 1) atRandom: rand ].
g maximizeComparator.
g fitnessBlock: [ :genes |
        | totalWeight totalValue penalty |
        decodeToBoxes := OrderedCollection new.
        genes doWithIndex: [ :b :ind | b = 1 ifTrue: [ decodeToBoxes
           add: (boxes at: ind) ] ].
        decodeToBoxes
           ifEmpty: [ totalValue := 0. totalWeight := 0 ]
           ifNotEmpty: [
               totalValue := (decodeToBoxes collect: #first) sum.
               totalWeight := (decodeToBoxes collect: #second) sum ].
        knapsackMaxWeight < totalWeight
           ifTrue: [ penalty := (knapsackMaxWeight - totalWeight) abs
               * 50 ]
           ifFalse: [ penalty := 0 ].

        totalValue - penalty ].
g run.

"We now retrieve the solution"
decodeToBoxes := OrderedCollection new.
g result doWithIndex: [ :b :ind |
           b = 1 ifTrue: [ decodeToBoxes add: (boxes at: ind) ] ].
decodeToBoxes
```

Boxes selected by the algorithm are #(2 1)#(2 2)#(1 1)#(10 4). We will now detail the script. A gene is either a value 0 or 1. The fitness function first selects the boxes indicated by the set of 0 and 1 contained in the genes variable. Boxes that are part of the current solution are kept in the decodeToBoxes variable. We need to verify whether decodeToBoxes is empty or not. It may be empty if the genes variable is only made up of 0s. Once we have the total value and the total weight indicated by the genes variable, we need to set the penalty to the difference between knapsackMaxWeight and totalWeight, as we previously did.

9.2.3 Coding and Encoding

Conceptually, the two variants of the knapsack problem differ in the range of occurrences each box may appear. As we have seen, this may have an impact on how to encode a possible solution. In the unbounded variant we have a set of boxes, while in the 0-1 variant we have a set of 0 and 1 as a solution.

Finding adequate encoding is crucial, as we have to reduce the burden of the algorithm to meet different objectives and constraints. In particular, in the unbounded version, we have two objectives: maximizing the value of the bag and making sure that the overall weight of the bag does not exceed the limit. We solved this problem using a penalty, which is a sufficient approach for the formulation of this problem (with few boxes and a low weight limit). In the 0-1 version, we have a third objective, which is that boxes should not repeat themselves. We could have added a second penalty to express this constraint. However, the algorithm will be suboptimal because it will have to solve some trade-off involving the three objectives. To alleviate the search, we use an encoding for the 0-1 variant that implicitly avoids box repetition.

The knapsack problem is an example of a *multi-objective problem* because the overall objective may be broken down into smaller sub-objectives. There are multiple ways to solve multi-objective problems, which are out of the scope of this chapter.

9.3 Meeting Room Scheduling Problem

Meeting room scheduling is a classical problem that consists of assigning meetings to different rooms. Meetings should not overlap but we should still use the minimum number of different rooms. To illustrate this problem, we consider a meeting as a tuple (start time, end time). The two meetings #(#(1 3)(2 3)) do overlap, so as a consequence, we need to have each meeting in a different room. Conversely, the two meetings #(#(1 3)(4 5)) can be held in the same room. Consider the following meetings: #(#(1 3)#(2 3)#(5 6)#(7 9)#(4 7)). Two rooms are necessary since the meetings #(2 3) and #(4 7) can be held in a room, and #(1 3),#(5 6), and #(7 9) in another room.

We can use a genetic algorithm to identify the minimum number of rooms necessary to hold a set of provided meetings. Consider this script:

```
"We assume that each meeting is correctly defined"
"a meeting = (start time, end time)"
meetings := #(#(1 3) #(2 3) #(5 6) #(7 9) #(4 7)).
numberOfMeetings := meetings size.

g := GAEngine new.
g endIfNoImprovementFor: 10.
g populationSize: 20000.
g numberOfGenes: numberOfMeetings.
g createGeneBlock: [ :rand :index :ind | (1 to: numberOfMeetings)
    atRandom: rand ].
g minimizeComparator.
g
    fitnessBlock: [ :genes |
        | distribution |
        distribution := OrderedCollection new.
        numberOfMeetings timesRepeat: [ distribution add:
          OrderedCollection new ].
        genes doWithIndex: [ :roomNumber :index | (distribution at:
          roomNumber) add: (meetings at: index) ].

        numberOfOverlap := 0.
        distribution do: [ :aSetOfMeetings |
            table := OrderedCollection new: 10 withAll: 0.
            aSetOfMeetings do: [ :meet |
                meet first to: meet second do: [ :v | table at: v put:
                  (table at: v) + 1 ]
            ].
            numberOfOverlap := numberOfOverlap + (table select: [ :v |
              v >= 2 ]) size.
        ].
```

```
        (distribution select: #notEmpty) size + numberOfOverlap.
    ].
g run.
g result asSet size
```

The meetings variable contains the list of meetings. We are assuming that each meeting is correctly defined (e.g., the end time is greater than the start time). The numberOfMeetings variable contains the number of meetings we have.

We consider a gene as a room assignation for a particular meeting. If we consider the set of meetings #(#(1 3)#(2 3)#(5 6)#(7 9)#(4 7)), then a possible solution is #(1 5 1 1 5), which means that the meetings #(1 3), #(5 6), and #(7 9) are held in room 1, while meetings #(2 3) and #(4 7) are held in room 5. The solution is therefore two rooms.

Since we wish to minimize the number of rooms and the number of overlaps, the genetic algorithm will look for room assignments that minimize the fitness function. The fitness function computes the number of different rooms and the number of overlaps. Finally, the number of different rooms is given by the gresultasSetsize expression.

9.4 Mini Sodoku

Consider the following set of numbers: 8 4 6 2 10 12 14 16 18. How would you put these numbers in a 3×3 grid in such a way that each horizontal, vertical, and diagonal lines equal 30?

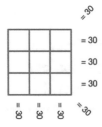

Figure 9-4. *Mini Sudoku*

Figure 9-4 shows the grid to which the numbers should be located. Check out the following script:

```
"The number of locate in the grid"
list := #(2 4 6 8 10 12 14 16 18).

"The different combinations to sum.
E.g., the three first cells could be summed (#(1 2 3))
     the diagonal top-left to bottom-right (#1 5 9))"
sums := {
    "Horizontal sums"
    #(1 2 3).
    #(4 5 6).
    #(7 8 9).

    "Diagonal sums"
    #(1 5 9).
    #(7 5 3).

    "Vertical sums"
    #(1 4 7).
    #(2 5 8).
    #(3 6 9) }.
g := GAEngine new.
g populationSize: 400.
g endIfFitnessIsAbove: 9.
g mutationRate: 0.01.
g numberOfGenes: 9.
g createGeneBlock: [ :rand :index | list atRandom: rand. ].
g fitnessBlock: [ :genes |
    | score penalty |
    score := (sums collect: [ :arr |
            (arr collect: [ :index | genes at: index]) sum ])
                inject: 0 into: [ :a :b | a + (b - 30) abs ].
    penalty := (genes size - genes asSet size) * 3.
    9 - (score + penalty) ].
g run.
```

```
"Visualize the grid"
v := RTView new.
label := RTLabel new.
elements := label elementsOn: g result.
v addAll: elements.
RTGridLayout on: elements.
v
```

The block provided to the `fitnessBlock:` method iterates over each combination contained in the `sums` variable and adds 1 if the sum is 30, or 0 otherwise. The maximum we can have is 9, so the algorithm ends when it reaches a fitness above 8.

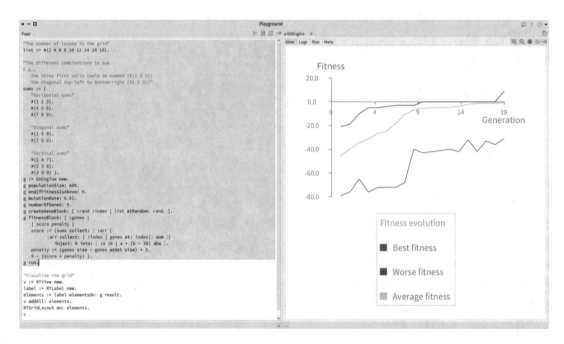

Figure 9-5. *Evolution of the fitness*

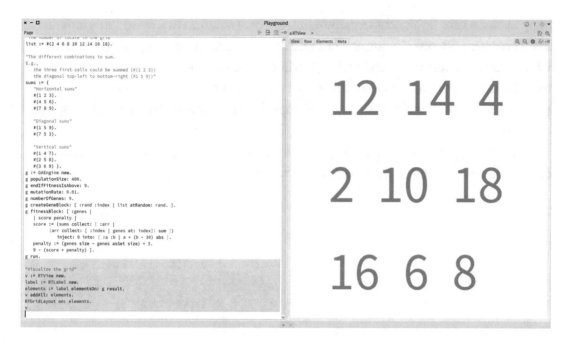

Figure 9-6. *The result of the mini Sudoku*

Figure 9-5 shows the evolution of the fitness and Figure 9-6 shows the result. We want to thank Milton Mamani for producing this example.

9.5 What Have We Seen in This Chapter?

The chapter presents three examples of how genetic algorithms can be efficiently employed to find a solution to apparently complex problems:

- The fundamental theorem of arithmetic finds, for a given number N, a set of prime numbers that when multiplied together, equal N.

- Two variants of the knapsack problem, namely the unbounded and 0-1 variants, select boxes without passing an overall limit while maximizing the value of the selected set.

- The room scheduling problem, which assigns meeting to rooms while avoiding overlapping.

The genetic algorithm is a simple and efficient way to solve these problems. However, it does not guarantee that the result is the optimal solution. The algorithm can find a candidate solution, for which we blindly take it as a convenient solution. It may happen that a genetic algorithm cannot find the best solution in a reasonable amount of time. In the previous chapter, we used a genetic algorithm to search for the word cat, which is three-letters long. Asking the algorithm to search for a word with 1000 letters would take so long that the algorithm would not seem to converge. When such a case happens, it is wise to specialize the genetic operations, as we will do in the coming chapters.

The next chapter covers a larger example using a genetic algorithm. It will also discuss a limitation of the genetic operators we have used so far.

CHAPTER 10

The Traveling Salesman Problem

The Traveling Salesman Problem (TSP) is a classical algorithm problem. It consists of identifying the shortest possible route between several connected cities. Not only is the problem relevant from an algorithmic point of view, but it also has many concrete applications, like microchip manufacturing, as you will shorty see.

The chapter incrementally builds a non-trivial solution to the problem using a genetic algorithm. The chapter begins with a naive approach to a robust, practical way of solving it.

10.1 Illustration of the Problem

Figure 10-1. *Setup of the Traveling Salesman Problem*

Consider the example given in Figure 10-1. The figure shows four cities located in a horizontal diamond. Each city has a 2D coordinate and is therefore located in a two-dimensional plane. Assuming the traveler begins their journey at City A, many paths are possible to visit all the cities.

© Alexandre Bergel 2020
A. Bergel, *Agile Artificial Intelligence in Pharo*, https://doi.org/10.1007/978-1-4842-5384-7_10

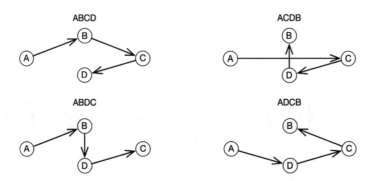

Figure 10-2. *Illustration of the Traveling Salesman Problem*

As illustrated in Figure 10-2, different paths are possible, including ABCD, ACDB, ABDC, and ADCB. What is the shortest path to visit all the cites? The four cities are located as a horizontal diamond. As such, City B and City D are closest to each other. The shortest path to visit all the cities should necessarily contain the segment BD (or DB), and then favor the segment of the external edge of the diamond. Segment AC (or CA) cannot belong to the shortest path.

10.2 Relevance of the Traveling Salesman Problem

The Traveling Salesman Problem (TSP) is a relevant problem to focus on, both from theoretical and practical points of view. The TSP was formulated in the early 1930s and is among the most studied algorithmic problems. Applications of the TSP are numerous, ranging from combinatorial optimization (i.e., finding an optimal object from a finite set of objects) to resource planning, DNA sequencing, and electronic circuit manufacturing. For example, when building an electronic board, a thin drill has to make holes in the board. Using the shortest route between the holes may have a significant impact on the time it takes to produce a board. Even though this problem has been studied for a long time, no general solution has been discovered yet.

The TSP is apparently a simple problem: you simply connect the cities in an optimal way. However, the TSP is a very difficult problem and is considered *NP-hard*. Being NP-hard means that, for two given candidate solutions, it is very easy to pick the best one (e.g., given two paths, it is easy to pick which one is shortest), but there is no efficient way to solve the problem itself. If someone, one day, finds an analytic solution to the TSP, the world would be profoundly impacted. Analytically solving an NP-hard problem (e.g., analytically finding the shortest path) means that any NP-complete problem can also be analytically solved. Have you heard about P vs. NP problems? This is one of the most challenging questions that mathematicians and theoretician computer scientists are facing today. The Clay Mathematics Institute will award a millennium prize of 1,000,000 USD to the person or group who solves a NP-hard problem analytically.

In this chapter we do not pretend to analytically solve this problem. However, using a genetic algorithm is a pretty solid technique for finding a good path, although it may not be the optimal path.

10.3 Naive Approach

How do we encode a path to make it exploitable by a genetic algorithm? For this problem, computing the fitness is trivial: it is simply the sum of the segment lengths. We can try the following script:

```
"We encode distances"
d := { ($A -> $B) -> 10 . ($A -> $D) -> 10 . ($B -> $C) -> 10 . ($C ->
    $D) -> 10 . ($A -> $C) -> 20 . ($B -> $D) -> 8 } asDictionary.
g := GAEngine new.
g endIfNoImprovementFor: 10.
g populationSize: 100.
g numberOfGenes: 4.
g createGeneBlock: [ :rand :index :ind | 'ABCD' atRandom: rand ].
g minimizeComparator.
g fitnessBlock: [ :genes |
    | currentCity length |
    currentCity := genes first.
    length := 0.
    genes allButFirst do: [ :nextCity |
        length := length + (d at: (currentCity -> nextCity) ifAbsent: [
            d at: (nextCity -> currentCity) ifAbsent: [ 0 ] ]).
        currentCity := nextCity ].
    length
    ].
g run
```

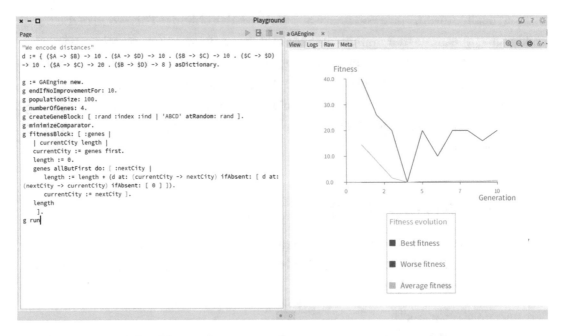

Figure 10-3. *Result of the naive approach*

We encode the map into a dictionary kept in the variable d. Each entry of the dictionary is a path between two cities. The gene is simply a city from the four possible cities. Since there are four different cities, and our algorithm has to go through these four cities, each individual has four genes. The fitness is computed as the length of the routes joining these four cities. We have two temporary variables—currentCity and length. For each city contained in the genes, the fitness function retrieves its distance from the current city. The segment to compute is given by the entry d at: (currentCity ->nextCity) or the opposite direction d at: (nextCity->currentCity).

Figure 10-3 shows the result of the run. The best fitness is 0, which is clearly not what we expect. A route that visits the four cities cannot have a length of 0. Clicking the Logs tab reveals that all the individuals are ($B $B $B $B). The genetic algorithm is telling us that the smallest amount of traveled distance is to not travel at all!

How can we force the algorithm to avoid visiting the same cities? A path, in order to be valid, should pass through all the cities only once. The easiest way to enforce this is to incur a penalty when this happens, in a similar fashion that we did in the previous chapter. Consider this revised version of the script:

```
"We encode distances"
d := { ($A -> $B) -> 10 . ($A -> $D) -> 10 . ($B -> $C) -> 10 . ($C ->
    $D) -> 10 . ($A -> $C) -> 20 . ($B -> $D) -> 8 } asDictionary.
```

```
g := GAEngine new.
g endIfNoImprovementFor: 10.
g populationSize: 1000.
g numberOfGenes: 4.
g createGeneBlock: [ :rand :index :ind | 'ABCD' atRandom: rand ].
g minimizeComparator.
g fitnessBlock: [ :genes |
    | currentCity length |
    currentCity := genes first.
    length := 0.
    genes allButFirst do: [ :nextCity |
        length := length + (d at: (currentCity -> nextCity) ifAbsent: [
            d at: (nextCity -> currentCity) ifAbsent: [ 0 ] ]).
        currentCity := nextCity ].
    length + ((4 - genes asSet size) * 100)
    ].
g run.
```

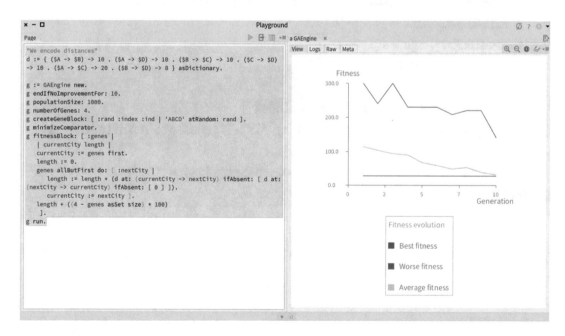

Figure 10-4. *Improving the naive approach*

Figure 10-4 now presents an acceptable result. The best path has a fitness of 28. The blue curve did not evolve over time, which means that the algorithm found the solution from the very beginning. Clicking the Logs tab reveals the solutions. For example, we see that ABDC and ABCD are solutions, which can be easily verified. At a first glance, it seems that our penalty seems to do its job. Well... not quite, as we will see.

Let's pick a more complex example. The following script replaces our list of cities with a list of points:

```
"We encode distances"
points := {(100@160). (20@40). (60@20). (180@100). (200@40). (60@200).
    (80@180). (40@120). (140@180). (140@140). (20@160). (200@160). (180
    @60). (100@120). (120@80). (100@40). (20@20). (60@80). (180@200).
    (160@20)}.

g := GAEngine new.
g endIfNoImprovementFor: 60.
g populationSize: 1000.
g numberOfGenes: points size.
g createGeneBlock: [ :rand :index :ind | points atRandom: rand ].
g minimizeComparator.
g fitnessBlock: [ :genes |
        | distance d |
        distance := 0.
        2 to: genes size do: [ :pointIndex |
            d := (genes at: pointIndex) dist: (genes at: pointIndex - 1).
            distance := distance + d ].
        distance + ((points size - genes asSet size) * 1000) ].
g run.
```

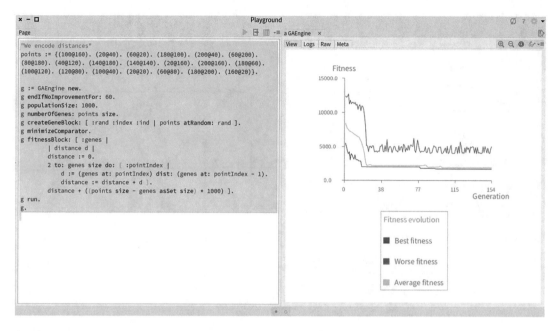

Figure 10-5. *Improving the naive approach*

The distance is computed using the dist: method, defined in the Point class. The result of the script is shown in Figure 10-5. It seems that the algorithm found a compelling solution since it reaches a plateau. We can append the following script to the previous script:

```
...
result := g result.
v := RTView new.
elements := RTEllipse new size: 10; color: Color red trans; elementsOn:
    result.
elements @ RTPopup.
v addAll: elements.
elements do: [ :e | e translateTo: e model ].
2 to: result size do: [ :index |
    | l |
    l := RTArrowedLine new color: Color blue; headOffset: 0.8.
    v add: (l edgeFrom: (v elementFromModel: (result at: index - 1)) to
        : (v elementFromModel: (result at: index))) ].
v
```

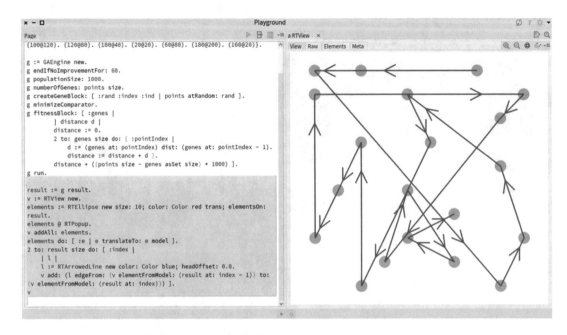

Figure 10-6. *Visualizing the result of the naive approach*

Figure 10-6 shows the result of the algorithm. Obviously, the blue arrowed line does not indicate the shortest path that connects all the cities. For example, there are two very close cities in the top-left portion of the figure that are not connected. An optimal solution should surely contain a segment between these two cities, but the result of the algorithm does not take advantage of this. So, the result given by our algorithm is likely to be very far from the optimal solution.

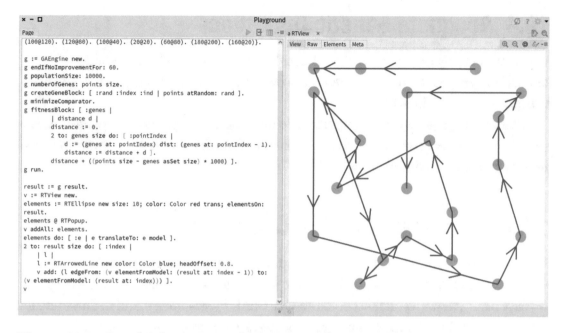

Figure 10-7.   *Result of a 10K population using the naive approach*

What if we increase the population size? Figure 10-7 shows the result of the same algorithm with a population of 10,000 individuals. The result is now apparently closer to the solution.

Such a problem should be easy to solve. So, why does the genetic algorithm struggling to solve it? The reason is that the algorithm is fighting hard to avoid redundant cities. Instead of exploring the set of possible valid candidates, the algorithm is struggling at identifying the valid candidates. This is why we label our solution as *naive*. Introducing a penalty as a way to guide the algorithm has a very negative side effect, which is that it looks for individuals that do not suffer from this penalty, thus leaving little room for exploring valid paths.

The moral of the story is that we should use the algorithm to explore valid paths, and not use it to struggle looking for any valid path. Remember Murphy's Law? If the algorithm generates random paths, it will surely have to deal with the randomly-generated mess. Instead of using a penalty for an invalid path, we should tune the algorithm in such a way that only valid paths can be generated, both in the initial population and as a result of the genetic operations.

10.4 Adequate Genetic Operations

Using our four-city example, consider the paths ABCD and DCBA. Any genetic operation, either a crossover between these two paths or a genetic mutation of any of it, will generate an invalid path.

Can we design genetic operations that do not produce an invalid path? The answer is yes. The remainder of the chapter will present two-the *swap mutation operation* and the *ordered crossover operation*.

10.5 The Swap Mutation Operation

Instead of replacing a gene value with any another one, as implemented by the GAMutationOperation class, we will *swap* two gene values in an individual. For example, if we have ABCD, a swap mutation could produce CBAD by swapping A and C. This mutation could never produce AACD, as that cannot be the result of swapping two elements.

Luckily, we prepared the ground to implement a new mutation operation. We can define the GASwapMutationOperation class:

```
GAAbstractMutationOperation subclass: #GASwapMutationOperation
    instanceVariableNames: ''
    classVariableNames: ''
    package: 'GeneticAlgorithm-Core'
```

We can override the doMutate: method to swap genes, as follows:

```
GASwapMutationOperation>>doMutate: individual
    "Mutate genes of the argument by swapping two gene values"

    | i2 tmp |
    self checkForRandomNumber.
    1 to: individual genes size do: [ :i1 |
        self randomNumber <= mutationRate
            ifTrue: [
                i2 := random nextInt: individual genes size.
                tmp := individual genes at: i1.
                individual genes at: i1 put: (individual genes at: i2).
                individual genes at: i2 put: tmp ] ]
```

The method randomly picks two gene indexes and swaps their values. This new GASwapMutationOperation operator ensures that a mutation does not produce an invalid result (i.e., a path with repeated cities).

10.6 The Ordered Crossover Operation

The ordered crossover operation is slightly more complex. It combines two paths and ensures that the resulting combination does not have repeated cities.

We will use a simple example to illustrate it. Consider the paths iA = ABCDE and iB = AEDBC. The new operation will consider a swath of genes, delimited by two indexes, 3 and 4, for example. The iC children will have the genes obtained from iA from index 3 to index 4. We have iC = **CD*. The three missing gene values (marked with *) will have to be obtained from iB. The C and D cities are removed from the gene values of iB because they are already obtained from iA. As a result, we have iC = AECDB.

We create the GAOrderedCrossoverOperation class, as follows:

```
GAAbstractCrossoverOperation subclass: #GAOrderedCrossoverOperation
    instanceVariableNames: ''
    classVariableNames: ''
    package: 'GeneticAlgorithm-Core'
```

The crossover randomly chooses the two extremities of the swath, as follows:

```
GAOrderedCrossoverOperation>>crossover: individualA with: individualB
    "Return a new child, which is the result of mixing the two
        individuals"
    | i1 i2 |
    i1 := self pickCutPointFor: individualA.
    i2 := self pickCutPointFor: individualA.

    "Make sure that i1 is smaller than i2"
    (i1 > i2) ifTrue: [ | t | t := i1. i1 := i2. i2 := t ].
    ^ self crossover: individualA with: individualB from: i1 to: i2
```

The core of the ordered crossover operation is this method:

```
GAOrderedCrossoverOperation>>crossover: individualA with: individualB
    from: i1 to: i2
    "Return a new child, which is the result of mixing myself the two
        individuals. The method assumes that i1 <= i2."

    | child crossOverGenes runningIndex swath |
    child := GAIndividual new.
    child random: random.

    swath := individualA genes copyFrom: i1 to: i2.
    crossOverGenes := Array new: individualA genes size.
    crossOverGenes := crossOverGenes copyReplaceFrom: i1 to: i2 with:
        swath.

    runningIndex := 1.
    (individualB genes copyWithoutAll: swath)
        do: [ :v | (crossOverGenes includes: v) ifFalse: [
                [(crossOverGenes at: runningIndex) notNil] whileTrue: [
                    runningIndex := runningIndex + 1 ].
                crossOverGenes at: runningIndex put: v ] ].

    child genes: crossOverGenes.
    ^ child
```

We then use the following utility method:

```
GAOrderedCrossoverOperation>>pickCutPointFor: partner
    "Simply return a random number between 1 and the number of genes of
        the individual provided as argument"
    ^ random nextInt: partner genes size
```

And *voila*! We can now test the new operator:

```
TestCase subclass: #GAOrderedCrossoverOperationTest
    instanceVariableNames: 'i1 i2 op'
```

```
classVariableNames: ''
package: 'GeneticAlgorithm-Tests'
```

We define a setUp method as follows:

```
GAOrderedCrossoverOperationTest>>setUp
    super setUp.
    i1 := GAIndividual new genes: #(8 4 7 3 6 2 5 1 9 0).
    i2 := GAIndividual new genes: #(0 1 2 3 4 5 6 7 8 9).
    op := GAOrderedCrossoverOperation new.
```

A first test could be the following:

```
GAOrderedCrossoverOperationTest>>testCrossover1
    | i3 |
    i3 := op crossover: i1 with: i2 from: 4 to: 8.
    self assert: i3 genes equals: #(0 4 7 3 6 2 5 1 8 9).
```

We take the first gene at an extremity:

```
GAOrderedCrossoverOperationTest>>testCrossover2
    | i3 |
    i3 := op crossover: i1 with: i2 from: 1 to: 4.
    self assert: i3 genes equals: #(8 4 7 3 0 1 2 5 6 9).
```

We consider the last two genes as the swath:

```
GAOrderedCrossoverOperationTest>>testCrossover3
    | i3 |
    i3 := op crossover: i1 with: i2 from: 9 to: 10.
    self assert: i3 genes equals: #(1 2 3 4 5 6 7 8 9 0).
```

This section concludes the implementation of a crossover operation that ensures that a produced path does not have repeated cities (i.e., gene values) in it. We have now implemented all the ingredients to run the algorithm on a larger example.

10.7 Revisiting Our Large Example

At the beginning of the chapter, we presented a configuration for which our naive approach could not find the shortest path. Now that we have defined our two new genetic operations, we can hook them up with the very same city map, as follows:

```
"We define the points"
points := {(100@160). (20@40). (60@20). (180@100). (200@40). (60@200).
    (80@180). (40@120). (140@180). (140@140). (20@160). (200@160). (180 @60).
    (100@120). (120@80). (100@40). (20@20). (60@80). (180@200).
    (160@20)}.
```

```
g := GAEngine new.
g endIfNoImprovementFor: 5.
g populationSize: 1000.
g numberOfGenes: points size.
g crossoverOperator: GAOrderedCrossoverOperation new.
g beforeCreatingInitialIndividual:
        [ :rand | points copy shuffleBy: rand ].
g mutationOperator: GASwapMutationOperation new.
g createGeneBlock: [ :rand :index :ind | points at: index ].

g minimizeComparator.
g fitnessBlock: [ :genes |
    | distance d |
    distance := 0.
    2 to: genes size do: [ :pointIndex |
        d := (genes at: pointIndex) dist: (genes at: pointIndex - 1).
        distance := distance + d ].
    distance ].
g run.
```

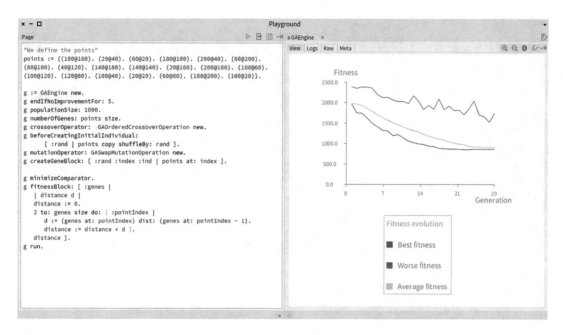

Figure 10-8. *The result of using the two new genetic operators*

Figure 10-8 illustrates the evolution of the fitness along the generations. We configured the algorithm to stop if it does not find an improvement in five generations, using the endIfNoImprovementFor: 5 message.

We can now visualize the result by appending the following code to the previous script:

```
...
result := g result.
v := RTView new.
elements := RTEllipse new size: 10; color: Color red trans; elementsOn:
    result.
elements @ RTPopup.
v addAll: elements.
elements do: [ :e | e translateTo: e model ].
2 to: result size do: [ :index |
    | l city1 city2 |
    l := RTArrowedLine new color: Color blue; headOffset: 0.8.
    city1 := v elementFromModel: (result at: index - 1).
    city2 := v elementFromModel: (result at: index).
    v add: (l edgeFrom: city1 to: city2) ].
v
```

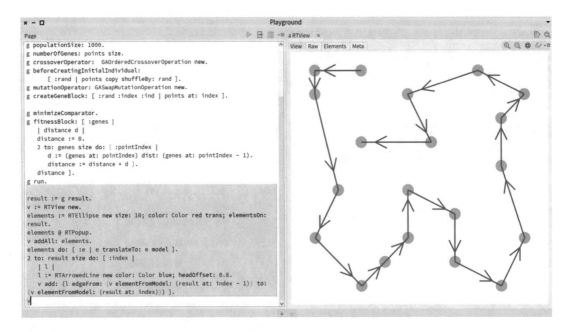

```
Page                                                      ▷  ⊟  ▥  -■  aRTView  ×
g populationSize: 1000.                                  View  Raw  Elements  Meta
g numberOfGenes: points size.
g crossoverOperator:  GAOrderedCrossoverOperation new.
g beforeCreatingInitialIndividual:
    [ :rand | points copy shuffleBy: rand ].
g mutationOperator: GASwapMutationOperation new.
g createGeneBlock: [ :rand :index :ind | points at: index ].

g minimizeComparator.
g fitnessBlock: [ :genes |
  | distance d |
  distance := 0.
  2 to: genes size do: [ :pointIndex |
      d := (genes at: pointIndex) dist: (genes at: pointIndex - 1).
      distance := distance + d ].
  distance ].
g run.

result := g result.
v := RTView new.
elements := RTEllipse new size: 10; color: Color red trans; elementsOn:
result.
elements @ RTPopup.
v addAll: elements.
elements do: [ :e | e translateTo: e model ].
2 to: result size do: [ :index |
    | l |
    l := RTArrowedLine new color: Color blue; headOffset: 0.8.
    v add: (l edgeFrom: (v elementFromModel: (result at: index - 1)) to:
(v elementFromModel: (result at: index))) ].
```

Figure 10-9. *The result of using the two new genetic operators*

Figure 10-9 shows the result of the algorithm. With only a population of 1,000 individuals, our algorithm was able to solve the TSP. Remember that with our first naive approach, we could not solve it with a population that was ten times larger! To address a complex problem, it can be relevant to consider adequate generation operators.

10.8 What Have We Seen in This Chapter?

This chapter presented a compelling way to solve a complex problem by using dedicated genetic operations. In particular, the chapter covered the following:

- The Traveling Salesman Problem, a classical algorithmic problem

- An illustration of the consequences of naively applying the genetic algorithm

- A motivation for introducing two new genetic operations—the *swap mutation operation* and the *ordered crossover operation*

The next chapter will leave the world of algorithms to focus on a robotic simulations.

CHAPTER 11

Exiting a Maze

Genetic algorithms are often presented as a way to solve a difficult algorithmic problem. This chapter applies a genetic algorithm to help a small robot find an exit. It formulates a simple situation (a robot looking for the exit) as an optimization problem (minimizing the distance between the robot and the exit). This chapter builds a small robot that lives in a randomly generated maze. The robot's objective is to exit the maze.

11.1 Encoding the Robot's Behavior

We will model the maze as a two-dimensional map, in which the maze entrance and exit are fixed positions. The entrance is located at the top-left corner of the map, and the exit at the bottom-right corner.

Our robot will follow a sequence of simple orders, and then can move one step to the north, south, west, or east. A path will be a linear sequence of orders.

Applied to our genetic algorithm, an individual will represent the path, beginning at the maze entrance. The fitness function will make (i) the robot follows the orders encoded in the genes, and subsequently (ii) return the distance of the robot from the exit. The genetic algorithm should therefore reduce the fitness, indicating that the robot is getting closer to the exit.

11.2 Robot Definition

The very first step is to model a robot. For that purpose, we define a GARobot class that knows its position and the map our robot lives in:

```
Object subclass: #GARobot
    instanceVariableNames: 'position map'
    classVariableNames: ''
    package: 'Robot'
```

© Alexandre Bergel 2020
A. Bergel, *Agile Artificial Intelligence in Pharo*, https://doi.org/10.1007/978-1-4842-5384-7_11

The position of the robot may be set using this method:

```
GARobot>>position: aPoint
    "Set the position of the robot"
    position := aPoint
```

The position of the robot may be obtained using:

```
GARobot>>position
    "Return the position of the robot"
    ^ position
```

Knowing the position is useful in the fitness function we will later implement. The initialization of the map is performed using this method:

```
GARobot>>map: aMap
    "Set the map where the robot lives in"
    map := aMap
```

A map is an instance of the GARobotMap class, which we will see later. A map will also encode the initial position of the robot.

A robot has the ability to follow a set of step orders, given as a collection of characters $N, $S, $W, and $E. The robot will move accordingly, if no wall prevents it. Our robot cannot go through a wall. The followOrders: method is defined as follows:

```
GARobot>>followOrders: orders
    "Make the robot follow the orders.
    Return the path taken by the robot"
    | delta possiblePosition path |
    delta := { $N -> (0 @ -1) . $S -> (0 @ 1) .
        $W -> (-1 @ 0) . $E -> (1 @ 0) } asDictionary.
    path := OrderedCollection new.
    path add: map initialPosition.
    self position: map initialPosition.
    orders
        do: [ :direction |
            possiblePosition := position + (delta at: direction).
```

```
"If we found the exit, then we return and
make no further progresses"
possiblePosition == map exitPosition ifTrue: [ ^ path ].

"If there is no wall, then we effectively do the move"
(map gridAt: possiblePosition) ~= #wall ifTrue: [
    position := possiblePosition.
    path add: position ] ].
^ path
```

The following section describes the map in which the robot can live.

11.3 Map Definition

The GARobotMap class is made of four variables:

- size represents the size of the map. A map is a squared space, and size is the number of units on a size.

- content is an array of arrays which contains the map itself.

- path contains the path taken by the robot after it follows some order.

- random, as always, is a random number generator.

The GARobotMap class is defined as follows:

```
Object subclass: #GARobotMap
    nstanceVariableNames: 'size content path random'
    classVariableNames: ''
    package: 'Robot'
```

The map is initialized with the following:

```
GARobotMap>>initialize
    super initialize.
    random := Random seed: 42.
    self size: 30.
```

The map has a default size of 30 units. Its content may be modified using the gridAt:put: method, defined as follows:

```
GARobotMap>>gridAt: aPoint put: value
    "Modify the map content.
    value is a symbol: #empty, #wall, #start, #exit, #robot"
    (self includesPoint: aPoint)
        ifFalse: [ ^ self ].
    ^ (content at: aPoint y) at: aPoint x put: value
```

Reading the content of a position is achieved with this method:

```
GARobotMap>>gridAt: aPoint
    "Return the content of a map at a given location.
    Everything outside the map is empty."
    (self includesPoint: aPoint) ifFalse: [ ^ #empty ].
    ^ (content at: aPoint y) at: aPoint x
```

Initialize the map with a given size. The map is filled with the #empty symbol. The size: method achieves this behavior:

```
GARobotMap>>size: aSize
    "Create a map of a given size and fills it with #empty"
    size := aSize.
    content := Array new: aSize.
    1 to: size do: [ :i |
        content at: i put: (Array new: aSize withAll: #empty) ].
    self fillEntranceAndExitPoints
```

We can fill the maze entrance point and then exit using a dedicated method:

```
GARobotMap>>fillEntranceAndExitPoints
    self gridAt: self initialPosition put: #start.
    self gridAt: self exitPosition put: #exit
```

A method that generates a random number is as follows:

```
GARobotMap>>rand: anInteger
    "Return a new random number"
    ^ random nextInt: anInteger
```

Another utility method checks whether a particular point is within the map:

```
GARobotMap>>includesPoint: aPoint
    "Answer whether a point is within the map"
    ^ (1 @ 1 extent: size @ size) containsPoint: aPoint
```

The exit is located at the bottom-right side of the map:

```
GARobotMap>>exitPosition
    "The exit position, as a fixed position,
    at the bottom right of the map"
    ^ (size - 1) @ (size - 1)
```

The initial position is located at the top-left side of the map:

```
GARobotMap>>initialPosition
    "The starting position is at the top left of the map"
    ^ 2 @ 2
```

Note that `initialPosition` and `exitPosition` consider the enclosing wall of the map, as such, the position `1@1` and `size@size` contain a wall. This is a simple way to ensure that the robot will not wander outside the physical map. Walls are added to the map using the `fillWithWalls:` method. This method takes an integer as a parameter, indicating the number of walls to be added. Each wall block is three units long, and a wall block is either horizontal or vertical. The `fillWithWalls:` method is as follows:

```
GARobotMap>>fillWithWalls: numberOfWalls
    "Fill the map with a given number of walls"
    | offsets |
    numberOfWalls timesRepeat: [
        | x y |
        x := self rand: size.
        y := self rand: size.

        offsets := (self rand: 2) = 1
            ifTrue: [ { 1 @ 0 . -1 @ 0 } ]
            ifFalse: [ { 0 @ -1 . 0 @ -1 } ].
        self gridAt: x @ y put: #wall.
        self gridAt: (x @ y) + offsets first put: #wall.
```

```
        self gridAt: (x @ y) + offsets second put: #wall.
    ].
    self fillEntranceAndExitPoints.

    "Fill the map border"
    1 to: size do: [ :i |
        self gridAt: i @ 1 put: #wall.
        self gridAt: 1 @ i put: #wall.
        self gridAt: size @ i put: #wall.
        self gridAt: i @ size put: #wall ]
```

Once a robot has found its way to the exit, it is convenient to draw the path taken by the robot. The following method achieves this:

```
GARobotMap>>drawRobotPath: aPath
    "Draw the robot path"
    path := aPath.
    aPath do: [ :pos | self gridAt: pos put: #robot ]
```

We are almost done. The last thing to implement is open, which is in charge of visually rendering the map. It uses Roassal to build the visual scene. Consider the open method:

```
GARobotMap>>open
    "Build and open the visual representation of the map"
    | v colors shape |
    colors := { #empty -> Color white . #wall -> Color brown .
        #start -> Color red . #exit -> Color green .
        #robot -> Color yellow } asDictionary.

    v := RTView new.
    shape := RTBox new size: 10; color: [ :c | colors at: c ].
    content do: [ :line |
        v addAll: (shape elementsOn: line) @ RTPopup
    ].
    RTGridLayout new gapSize: 0; lineItemsCount: size; on: v elements.
    v add: (RTLabel elementOn: path size asString, ' steps').
    TRConstraint move: v elements last below: v elements allButLast.
    ^ v open
```

The open method builds a visual map made of small color squares. The number of steps performed by the robot is indicated below the map. It is an indicator of how the search for the exit went.

11.4 Example

We are now ready to evolve our robot to find the exit. Consider the following script:

```
"We build a map with 80 wall blocks"
map := GARobotMap new fillWithWalls: 80.

"We build the robot"
robot := GARobot new.
"Make the robot lives in the map"
robot map: map.

g := GAEngine new.
g endIfNoImprovementFor: 5.
g numberOfGenes: 100.
g populationSize: 250.
"A gene value is a cardinal direction"
g createGeneBlock: [ :rand :index :ind | #($N $S $W $E) atRandom: rand].

"We want to minimize the distance between the robot and the exit"
g minimizeComparator.
g
    fitnessBlock: [ :genes |
        robot followOrders: genes.
        robot position dist: map exitPosition ].
g run.
```

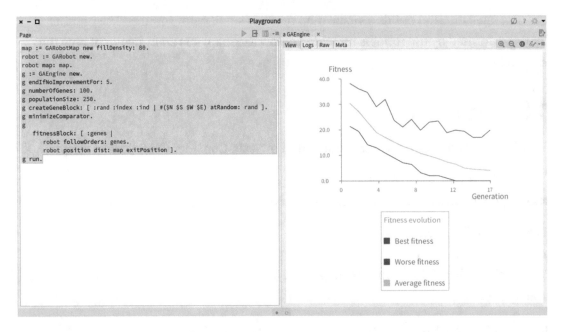

Figure 11-1. *Evolution of the robot fitness*

Figure 11-1 shows the evolution of the population along the generation. We can see the path by appending the following script:

```
...
map drawRobotPath: (robot followOrders: g result).
map open
```

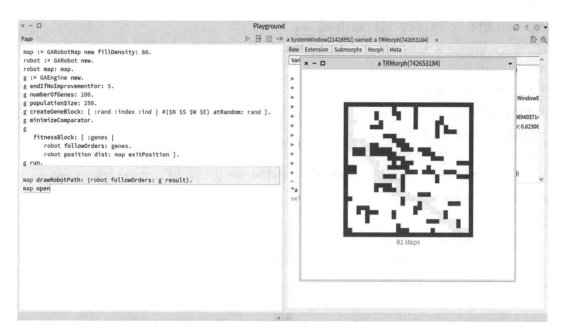

Figure 11-2. *Robot footprint*

Figure 11-2 shows the path taken by our robot. We see that the robot made 81 steps to reach the exit. This path, taken by our robot, is absolutely not the shortest. The robot made some unnecessary steps.

The situation could be improved by adding a penalty reflecting the path length. The penalty is a numerical value that is added to the distance between the robot and the exit. This penalty should be small for a short path, and high for a long path. How do we define this penalty? One way to define the penalty is to make the penalty equal to the path length. In such a case, the penalty is a value ranging from 56 to 100: 56 being the shortest path from `initialPosition` and `exitPosition`, and 100 being the number of genes an individual has. On the other hand, the distance between between the robot to the exit ranges from 0 to 39: 0 indicates that the robot has reached the exit and 39 is the result of the expression `map initialPosition dist: map exitPosition`. The distance and the penalty have different ranges of values, and as such, our penalty will always be greater than the distance. As a consequence, the penalty will have more relevance to the algorithm than the algorithm. If the penalty is equal to the path length, then the algorithm will try to minimize the distance path without caring much whether the robot has reached the exit. Consider the new revision of the script:

```
map := GARobotMap new fillWithWalls: 80.
robot := GARobot new.
robot map: map.
g := GAEngine new.
g endIfNoImprovementFor: 5.
g numberOfGenes: 100.
g populationSize: 250.
g createGeneBlock: [ :rand :index :ind | #($N $S $W $E) atRandom: rand ].
g minimizeComparator.
g
    fitnessBlock: [ :genes |
        | path penalty |
        path := robot followOrders: genes.
        penalty := path size / 2.
        (robot position dist: map exitPosition) + penalty ].
g run.
map drawRobotPath: (robot followOrders: g result).
map open
```

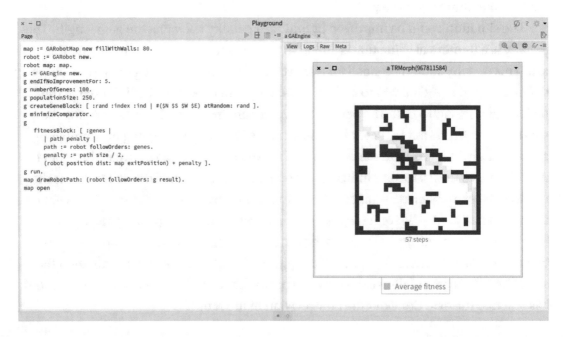

Figure 11-3. *Short robot footprint*

The `followOrders:` method, defined in the `GARobot` class, returns the path taken by the robots until it reaches the exit. We use this feature to compute the penalty.

Figure 11-3 gives the result of the new revision of the script and highlights a better path. Only 57 steps are necessary to reach the exit. Without the penalty, the path was 81 steps long.

We divide the path length by 2, an arbitrary value. Removing the division (`penalty := pathsize.`) would prevent the robot from looking for the exit. In this case, the reward for producing a short path is more attractive than reaching the exit. The value 2 is completely arbitrary. It is an ad hoc way to reduce the weight of the penalty compared to the distance. A proper solution would to have a *multi-objective fitness* function. However, this is out of the scope of this chapter.

11.5 What Have We Seen in This Chapter?

We have seen a compelling application of the genetic algorithm to help a robot to exit a maze. In particular, we covered:

- The robot and map modeling

- Modeling a robot path as a sequence of orders

- A simple way to significantly improve the solution by adding a small penalty

The robot scenario can be easily improved by adding new items in the map, such as a key, doors, and monsters. The algorithm can be employed to let the robot find the key, survive monsters, open doors, and find the exit.

CHAPTER 12

Building Zoomorphic Creatures

Genetic algorithms are often used to simulate aspects of how biological individuals behave. This chapter is about artificial life. It defines and creates what we call *zoomorphic creatures*. We refer to zoomorphic creatures as virtual beings that own particular traits of biological creatures. As such, a zoomorphic creature can be considered a small digital animal.

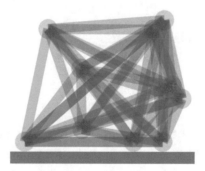

Figure 12-1. *Example of a creature*

Figure 12-1 shows the example of such a creature standing on a platform. A creature is made of join points and muscles. Each muscle has two extremities and each extremity is connected to a join point. Our creatures are boneless and join points connect muscles. A join point hosts the muscle extremities.

A muscle is a complex element in our model. Each muscle oscillates and has a strength, which makes it able to resist external forces (e.g., gravity or a reaction from a platform). Muscle oscillation is regulated by an internal clock, proper to each muscle. A creature is subject to (i) gravity and (ii) the reaction force from the platform on which the creature stands. Muscles have no weight, but a join point has a weight.

© Alexandre Bergel 2020
A. Bergel, *Agile Artificial Intelligence in Pharo*, https://doi.org/10.1007/978-1-4842-5384-7_12

A creature, at its inception, cannot do much. However, we will make it evolve to solve a particular task. The task we will consider is moving itself toward a direction. Watching any toddler helps us remember how complex walking can be and how difficult it is to learn.

The chapter lays out the infrastructure to model a complex simulation in which zoomorphic creatures will live. Note that this chapter is not directly related to genetic algorithms, as it only provides the necessary infrastructure to make creatures behave. n particular, it covers the implementation of a simple physics engine to simulate a physical environment. This chapter is about building zoomorphic creatures and the next chapter is about evolving such creatures so they can move around.

12.1 Modeling Join Points

Each element in our simulation has a visual representation. We will therefore define the CVisualElement class, which will be the root of the class hierarchy we will build in this chapter:

```
Object subclass: #CVisualElement
    instanceVariableNames: 'element'
    classVariableNames: ''
    package: 'Creature'
```

The CVisualElement class has a element variable, which will contain a Roassal visual element. The visual aspect of the creature and platform comes from dedicated Roassal elements. Each visual element will have to be created in subclasses of CVisualElement by overriding the createElement method, as follows:

```
CVisualElement>>createElement
    "Should be overridden in subclasses.
    The method initializes the element variable"
    self subclassResponsibility
```

The Roassal element may be accessed by using the following:

```
CVisualElement>>element
    "Return the Roassal element"
    ^ element
```

A join point is a point where several muscles are connected. Join points are represented as instances of the CNode class, which is defined as follows:

```
CVisualElement subclass: #CNode
    instanceVariableNames: 'speedVector force isOnPlatform'
    classVariableNames: ''
    package: 'Creature'
```

A node has three variables:

- force represents the sum of the external forces. This vector impacts the speed and therefore the movement of the node.

- speedVector represents the speed of the node. The speed is affected by the friction caused from the environment.

- isOnPlatform indicates whether a node is on a platform. Knowing this is important because it may introduce a friction with the platform.

The initialization of a node is defined as follows:

```
CNode>>initialize
    super initialize.
    isOnPlatform := false.
    self resetSpeed.
    self resetForce
```

When created, a node has no speed, is not on a platform, and has no external force exercised on it. The external force may be reset using this method:

```
CNode>>resetForce
    "Reset the force exercising on the node"
    force := 0 @ 0
```

Similarly, the speed is reset using this method:

```
CNode>>resetSpeed
    "Make the node stop by canceling its speed"
    speedVector := 0 @ 0
```

We decide to make a node visually represented by a small gray circle. We therefore override the createElement method defined in the CVisualElement class to give the visual aspect of a node:

```
CNode>>createElement
    element := RTEllipse new size: 10;
                color: Color gray trans; element.
    element @ RTDraggable
```

A node is subject to external forces. We define the addForce: method, which simply adds a force, expressed as a point, to the forces already exercising on the node. The method is as follows:

```
CNode>>addForce: aForceAsPoint
    "Make the node subject of an external force"
    force := force + aForceAsPoint
```

Overall, our simulation is driven by a beat, which is globally triggered, as we will later see when we model the physical world. A beat corresponds to a discrete unit of time and the beat method is defined as follows:

```
CNode>>beat
    "Make the node act according to the force and speed applied to the
    node"
    speedVector := (speedVector + self gravityForce + force) * 0.9.
    isOnPlatform ifTrue: [
        speedVector := speedVector x * 0.3 @ speedVector y ].
    self translateBy: speedVector
```

The beat method is at the heart of our physics engine. At each beat, the gravity and the external forces are summed to the speed. We arbitrarily set a friction, which is the effect of the air friction on the physical environment. This friction with the air, expressed with the value 0.9, is applied to each beat. If the node is in contact with a platform, the X component of speedVector is reduced by 70% (i.e., multiplied by 0.3). The beat method ends by translating the node by the computed amount of speedVector. Gravity is represented by an arbitrary point:

```
CNode>>gravityForce
    "A fixed force representing a gravity"
    ^ 0 @ 0.3
```

Creatures will live in a world made of platforms. A platform is an instance of the CPlatform class, which we will see later. However, a node has to respond to a collision with platforms. We define the checkForCollision: method on the CNode class as follows:

```
CNode>>checkForCollision: platforms
    "Verify if the node is on a platform. If it is the case,
    the variable isOnPlatform is set to true"
    isOnPlatform := false.
    platforms
        do: [ :p |
            (p collide: self)
                ifTrue: [
                    speedVector := speedVector x @ 0.
                    p adjustNodeIfNecessary: self.
                    isOnPlatform := true.
                    ^ self ] ]
```

First the isOnPlatform variable is set to **false**. If the node collides with at least one platform, then the Y component of the speed is set to 0 and the isOnPlatform variable is set to **true**. Due to some imprecisions of our model, we need to let the platform make some adjustments to the node. In particular, it ensures that a node is not located *inside* a platform as it may happen since the node movement is the result of a discrete increment and not a continuous one. The isOnPlatform variable may be accessed using the following accessor:

```
CNode>>isOnPlatform
    "Is the node on a platform?"
    ^ isOnPlatform
```

The position of the node is given by the position method. It simply asks the Roassal element for its position. A newly created node is at the position 0@0. Accessing the node position is simply defined as follows:

```
Node>>position
    "Return the position of the node"
    ^ element position
```

A node needs to be translated to reflect the effect of the environment. We define a method to translate the node by an incremental step, as follows:

```
CNode>>translateBy: aPoint
    "Translate the node by an incremental point"
    element translateBy: aPoint.
```

A new position may be set to a node using this method:

```
CNode>>translateTo: aPoint
    "Translate the node to a new position"
    element translateTo: aPoint.
```

This last method concludes the definition of a node. As you have seen, many operations, such as translation and maintaining the node position, are delegated to the Roassal visualization engine.

12.2 Modeling Platforms

In addition to the gravity that we have described previously, the environment may affect the nodes (and therefore the creatures) with platforms. We define the CPlatform class as a subclass of CVisualElement:

```
CVisualElement subclass: #CPlatform
    instanceVariableNames: 'width height'
    classVariableNames: ''
    package: 'Creature'
```

A platform is defined as a visual rectangle, having a width and height component. We initialize a platform with a default width of 100 pixels and a default height of 10 pixels:

```
CPlatform>>initialize
    super initialize.
    self width: 100.
    self height: 10
```

As usual, we need dedicated methods to change the values of these variables. The width of a platform is set using the following:

```
CPlatform>>width: aWidthAsNumber
    "Set the width of the platform"
    width := aWidthAsNumber
```

The height of a platform is set using the following:

```
CPlatform>>height: aHeightAsNumber
    "Set the height of the platform"
    height := aHeightAsNumber
```

A platform is visually represented as a gray rectangle. The createElement method has to be adequately defined:

```
CPlatform>>createElement
    "Create the visual representation of a platform"
    element ifNotNil: [ "already created" ^ self ].
    element := RTBox new width: width; height: height; color: Color gray;
    element.
```

A platform may be translated to a particular position using the following:

```
CPlatform>>translateTo: aPosition
    "Translate the platform to a particular position"
    self createElement.
    element translateTo: aPosition
```

Before carrying out the translation, the translateTo: method ensures that the visual element is created. The primitive that handles the effect of the platform is the collision detection. We define the collide: method, which tests whether a platform collides with a node:

```
CPlatform>>collide: node
    "Answer whether the platform collides with the node argument"
    ^ node element encompassingRectangle intersects: self element
    encompassingRectangle
```

Note that the encompassingRectangle call refers to methods provided by Roassal. An encompassing rectangle is an instance of the Rectangle class, provided by Pharo, that encompasses the visual element. The collide: method returns **true** or **false**, indicating whether the provided node is above a platform. The collision is identified if the two encompassing rectangles overlap. If a collision happens, it is important to adjust the position of a node if necessary:

```
CPlatform>>adjustNodeIfNecessary: node
    "Answer whether the platform collides with the node"
    | bottomNode topPlatform |
    bottomNode := node element encompassingRectangle bottomCenter y.
    topPlatform := self element encompassingRectangle topCenter y.

    topPlatform < bottomNode
        ifTrue: [ node translateBy: 0 @ (topPlatform - bottomNode) ]
```

Such an adjustment is necessary because the node translation is discrete and not continuous. As a consequence, a falling node could be within a platform and should therefore be translated to be above it.

12.3 Defining Muscles

A muscle, which is at the core of this simulation, is a complex data structure. A muscle is an oscillating edge with a strength. It connects two join points (i.e., nodes). We will first define the CConnection class to represent the connection between the two nodes. We define the CConnection class as follows:

```
CVisualElement subclass: #CConnection
    instanceVariableNames: 'node1 node2'
    classVariableNames: ''
    package: 'Creature'
```

We define node1 and node2 as the two extremities represented by an instance of the CNode class. The first extremity is obtained using the following:

```
CConnection>>node1
    ^ node1
```

The first extremity is set using this method:

```
CConnection>>node1: aNode
    node1 := aNode
```

The second extremity is obtained with this method:

```
CConnection>>node2
    ^ node2
```

It is set using the following:

```
CConnection>>node2: aNode
    node2 := aNode
```

A muscle has an internal timer that drives the oscillation. We define the CMuscle class as follows:

```
CConnection subclass: #CMuscle
    instanceVariableNames: 'time time1 time2 length1 length2 strength
    color'
    classVariableNames: ''
    package: 'Creature'
```

The CMuscle class has the following variables:

- An internal clock represented by the variable time.

- time1 and time2 are two thresholds used by the internal clock to determine the length of the muscle.

- The length of a muscle oscillates between two values—length1 and length2.

- The strength represents how much resistance a muscle has when it is subject to external forces, such as the weights of the connected join points.

- The color variable indicates the muscle's color.

A muscle length oscillates along its internal clock. The way the oscillation is modeled is simply by making the beat method increase the variable time by 1:

```
CMuscle>>beat
    "Beating a muscle increases its timer"
    time := time + 1.
    time = self maxTime ifTrue: [ time := 0 ].
```

If the time reaches a maximum, it is reset to 0. The internal timer is therefore cyclic. When a muscle is created, it has a timer set to 0. We initialize a muscle as follows:

```
CMuscle>>initialize
    super initialize.
    time := 0.
    color := Color red.
```

The visual representation of a muscle is given by the createElement method. A muscle is a straight line joining node1 and node2. The createElement method is defined as follows:

```
CMuscle>>createElement
    "A muscle is a transparent line between the two nodes"
    element := RTLine new color: (color alpha: 0.3); width: 5;
    edgeFrom: node1 element to: node2 element
```

The color of a muscle is set by the following:

```
CMuscle>>color: aColor
    "Set the color of the muscle"
    color := aColor
```

Note that the createElement method makes the color translucent. This is useful, as muscles do overlap. Having translucent muscles makes a creature, made up of many muscles, pleasant to see.

A muscle has a variable length. The actual length of a muscle is either length1 or length2. If the muscle timer is below a lower threshold (i.e., has a value of self minTime), then the muscle length is length1; otherwise, it is length2. We define the length method as follows:

```
CMuscle>>length
    "Maybe rename it to ideal length"
    ^ time < self minTime
        ifTrue: [ length1 ]
        ifFalse: [ length2 ]
```

If the time variable has a value lower than the lower threshold, then we say we are at the beginning of a cycle. We refer to the end of the muscle cycle if time is greater than `self minTime`. We define some accessing methods for the `length1` and `length2` variables:

```
CMuscle>>length1
    "Length of a muscle at the beginning of a cycle"
    ^ length1
```

The value is set using the following:

```
CMuscle>>length1: aLengthAsInteger
    "Set the muscle length at the beginning of a cycle"
    length1 := aLengthAsInteger
```

Similarly, `length2` is accessed using the following:

```
CMuscle>>length2
    "Length of a muscle at the end of a cycle"
    ^ length2
```

The second length is set using the following:

```
CMuscle>>length2: aLengthAsInteger
    "Set the muscle length at the end of a cycle"
    length2 := aLengthAsInteger
```

The cycle length is given by the value of `maxTime`, which is defined as the maximum value between `time1` and `time2`:

```
CMuscle>>maxTime
    "Return the cycle length"
    ^ time1 max: time2
```

Similarly, the threshold is given by the `minTime` method:

```
CMuscle>>minTime
    "Return the timer threshold between to switch between length1 and
    length2"
    ^ time1 min: time2
```

A muscle has a strength, which is accessible using the following:

```
CMuscle>>strength
    "Return the strength of the muscle"
    ^ strength
```

The strength of a muscle is used to compute the forces that will be applied to the extremity's nodes by the muscle. The strength is set using the following:

```
CMuscle>>strength: strengthAsFloat
    "Set the strength that is applied to the extremities"
    strength := strengthAsFloat
```

The muscle's internal timer is increased at each beat, as defined. The first timer threshold is set using the following:

```
CMuscle>>time1: anInteger
    time1 := anInteger
```

The time1 value is obtained with:

```
CMuscle>>time1
    ^ time1
```

As we will later see, muscle attributes have to be serialized in order to be encoded and decoded from individuals in the genetic algorithm. We therefore need to access these values. The second time threshold is set using the following:

```
CMuscle>>time2: anInteger
    time2 := anInteger
```

It is accessed using the following:

```
CMuscle>>time2
    ^ time2
```

Each creature is randomly generated. Generating a creature is not trivial since a well-formed creature must have all the nodes connected to some muscles, and two nodes cannot have more than one muscle. As a consequence, we will have to monitor how nodes are used by the muscles during the generation process. A simple method will be useful to test whether a muscle connects two indicated nodes:

```
CMuscle>>usesNodes: twoNodes
    "The method accepts an array of two nodes as an argument.
    Return true if the muscle connects the two nodes."
    ^ (node1 == twoNodes first and: [ node2 == twoNodes second ]) or:
        [ node1 == twoNodes second and: [ node2 == twoNodes first ] ]
```

The definition of a muscle is now complete. Our creature will be randomly generated, which means that the muscle will also be randomly generated. The next section defines a generator of muscles as a way to encapsulate the complexity of generating muscles.

12.4 Generating Muscles

When a muscle is randomly generated, attributes defining the muscle (i.e., time1, time2, length1, length2, and strength) also have to be randomly generated. The CMuscleGenerator class has the responsibility of generating random muscles. A muscle generator is parameterized with a value range for each attribute, expressed with a minimum value and a delta value. We define the CMuscleGenerator class as follows:

```
Object subclass: #CMuscleGenerator
    instanceVariableNames: 'random minStrength deltaStrength minLength
    deltaLength minTime deltaTime'
    classVariableNames: ''
    package: 'Creature'
```

The initialization of a generator is made by assigning some values that are convenient in most of the examples we will later see:

```
CMuscleGenerator>>initialize
    super initialize.
    self resetSeed.
    minLength := 10.
    deltaLength := 30.
    minTime := 4.
    deltaTime := 200.
    minStrength := 1.
    deltaStrength := 3
```

The random number generator is created using resetSeed:

```
CMuscleGenerator>>resetSeed
    random := Random seed: 42.
```

The delta of a value corresponds to an interval from which values will be randomly picked. The delta length is set using the following:

```
CMuscleGenerator>>deltaLength: anInteger
    deltaLength := anInteger
```

The delta strength is set using the following:

```
CMuscleGenerator>>deltaStrength: anInteger
    deltaStrength := anInteger
```

The delta time is set using the following:

```
CMuscleGenerator>>deltaTime: anInteger
    deltaTime := anInteger
```

The minimum value a length can have is set using the following:

```
CMuscleGenerator>>minLength: anInteger
    "Set the minimum value a muscle length may have"
    minLength := anInteger
```

Similarly, the minimum strength is set using the following:

```
CMuscleGenerator>>minStrength: anInteger
    "Set the minimum value a muscle strength can have"
    minStrength := anInteger
```

The minimum time threshold is set using the following:

```
CMuscleGenerator>>minTime: anInteger
    "Set the minimum value a muscle time threshold can be"
    minTime := anInteger
```

A length is generated using a dedicated method:

```
CMuscleGenerator>>generateLength
    "Return a length within the specified range"
    ^ minLength + (random nextInt: deltaLength)
```

Similarly, the strength is generated with the following:

```
CMuscleGenerator>>generateStrength
    "Return a strength within the specified range"
    ^ random next * deltaStrength + minStrength
```

A time threshold is generated with the following:

```
CMuscleGenerator>>generateTime
    "Return a time within the specified range"
    ^ (random nextInt: deltaTime) + minTime
```

A central method of the generator is `createMuscleFrom:to:`. This method is used to produce a muscle between two nodes, as follows:

```
CMuscleGenerator>>createMuscleFrom: aNode to: anotherNode
    "Return a new muscle connecting two nodes"
    | m |
    m := CMuscle new.
    m node1: aNode.
    m node2: anotherNode.
    m length1: self generateLength.
    m length2: self generateLength.
    m time1: self generateTime.
    m time2: self generateTime.
    m strength: self generateStrength.
    ^ m
```

A central aspect of applying a genetic algorithm to search for the optimal muscle configuration is to adequately manage the mapping between a set of values and a muscle definition. A muscle can be *serialized* into a set of values, and a set of values can be *materialized* into a muscle. These operations are necessary to produce a creature from a given individual in our genetic algorithm.

```
CMuscleGenerator>>serializeMuscle: aMuscle
    "Return an array describing the muscle provided as an argument"
    ^ Array
    with: aMuscle length1
    with: aMuscle length2
```

```
with: aMuscle strength
with: aMuscle time1
with: aMuscle time2
```

The materialization configures a muscle with an array of values:

```
CMuscleGenerator>>materialize: values inMuscle: aMuscle
    "Configure the provided muscle with some values"
    aMuscle length1: values first.
    aMuscle length2: values second.
    aMuscle strength: values third.
    aMuscle time1: values fourth.
    aMuscle time2: values fifth
```

An individual within our genetic algorithm contains the attributes of all the muscles within a creature. The genetic algorithm needs to produce a gene, and as such, we need a way to produce a particular value for a given gene position in the individual genetic information. The following method addresses this requirement:

```
CMuscleGenerator>>valueForIndex: anIndex
    "Produce a value for a given index of an individual chromosome.
    This method is used to generate a gene in the genetic algorithm"
    | i |
    i := (anIndex - 1) % 5. "% refers to modulo"
    i = 0 ifTrue: [ ^ self generateLength ].
    i = 1 ifTrue: [ ^ self generateLength ].
    i = 2 ifTrue: [ ^ self generateStrength ].
    i = 3 ifTrue: [ ^ self generateTime ].
    i = 4 ifTrue: [ ^ self generateTime ].
    self error: 'Should not be here'
```

It is important to note that the three methods—serializeMuscle:, materialize:inMuscle:, and valueForIndex:—heavily rely on the order of the attributes. If you want to add new attributes related to muscles weight, delay to act on the muscle), then these three methods must be modified accordingly. Our muscle generator is now complete. We are now able to model a zoomorphic creature.

12.5 Defining the Creature

We define a creature as an instance of the CCreature class, as follows:

```
Object subclass: #CCreature
    instanceVariableNames: 'nodes muscles random muscleGenerator color'
    classVariableNames: ''
    package: 'Creature'
```

A creature is essentially made of a set of nodes and a set of muscles, kept in the nodes and muscles variables, respectively. We will run our genetic algorithm to optimize the configuration of the muscles. The initial configuration of our muscle is random, which is why we need a random number generator. A muscle is a complex structure. As such, a creature requires a particular and dedicated object to create muscles, kept in the muscleGenerator variable. Each creature also has a color, which is useful to distinguish creatures when more than one are present onscreen.

A creature is initialized as follows:

```
CCreature>>initialize
    super initialize.
    nodes := OrderedCollection new.
    muscles := OrderedCollection new.
    random := Random seed: 42.
    muscleGenerator := CMuscleGenerator new.
    color := Color red.
```

A muscle is red per default. Its color may be changed with this method:

```
CCreature>>color: aColor
    "Set the color of the creature"
    color := aColor
```

A muscle can be generated and added to a creature using this method:

```
CCreature>>addMuscleFrom: aNode to: anotherNode
    "Generate and add a muscle between two nodes"
    muscles add: (muscleGenerator createMuscleFrom: aNode to: anotherNode)
```

To run the genetic algorithm, it is relevant to know the number of muscles a creature has. The number of muscles is obtained with the following:

```
CCreature>>numberOfMuscles
    "Return the number of muscles defining the creature"
    ^ muscles size
```

Each beat on a creature triggers a beat for each node and each muscle. Afterward, the physics rules have to be applied between the muscles and the nodes. The beat method is defined as follows:

```
CCreature>>beat
    "Execute a unit of behavior"
    nodes do: #beat.
    muscles do: #beat.
    self reachStable
```

The reachStable method, which we will describe later, acts on the creature by using the physics rules for a given unit of time. Whether a collision happens between a creature and the platforms is determined using the checkForCollision: method, defined as follows:

```
CCreature>>checkForCollision: platforms
    "Check if a creature is on a platform.
    If this is the case, then the variable isOnPlatform of each node
    is set to true"
    nodes do: [ :n | n checkForCollision: platforms ].
    self simulateNoise.
```

The physics engine we are implementing is minimal and is far from complete. We need to add some noise in the way that the physics is simulated. For example, random noise, which is an important property of a real physical world, also has to be modeled. This noise is necessary to avoid singular situations, for example, when all the nodes are exactly at the same X or Y coordinates. We simply add some noise by moving a node randomly:

```
CCreature>>simulateNoise
    "Produce noise in our simulation"
    | direction |
```

```
direction := ((random nextInt: 3) - 2) @ ((random nextInt: 3) - 2).
(nodes atRandom: random) translateBy: direction
```

All the necessary code to model the creature is now in place. The next section focuses on creating the creature.

12.6 Creating Creatures

Even if we will produce creatures with simple shapes, manually creating creatures is tedious. We can define some dedicated methods. Adding nodes to a creature is achieved with the configureNodes: method, which is defined as follows:

```
CCreature>>configureNodes: nbNodes
    "Add a number of nodes in our creature"
    nbNodes timesRepeat: [ nodes add: CNode new createElement ]
```

A ball-like shape is created using the following:

```
CCreature>>configureBall: numberOfNodes
    "Produce a ball-like creature"
    | existingMuscles |
    muscleGenerator := CMuscleGenerator new
        minStrength: 0.01;
        deltaStrength: 0.5;
        minLength: 10;
        deltaLength: 80;
        deltaTime: 200;
        minTime: 20.

    "Add some nodes"
    self configureNodes: numberOfNodes.

    "Connect each node with all the other nodes"
    existingMuscles := OrderedCollection new.
    nodes do: [ :n1 |
        (nodes copyWithout: n1) do: [ :n2 |
            (existingMuscles includes: n1 -> n2) ifFalse: [
            self addMuscleFrom: n1 to: n2.
            existingMuscles add: n1 -> n2; add: n2 -> n1 ] ] ].
```

```
"Create the visual elements"
self createElements.
self randomlyLocateNodes
```

configureBall: takes as an argument the number of nodes that will compose the ball. All the nodes are connected to all the other nodes. As a consequence, a ball creature will contain many muscles, which means that muscles should have a low strength to have a stable system. We use the existingMuscles variable to keep track of the muscles we create in our algorithm. This is necessary to prevent two muscles from being added between two nodes.

The graphical elements are created using the createElements method:

```
CCreature>>createElements
    "Force the creation of all graphical elements for nodes and muscles"
    nodes do: #createElement.
    muscles do: [ :m | m color: color ].
    muscles do: #createElement.
```

Nodes and muscles are subject to Newtonian physical laws, which are defined using this method:

```
CCreature>>reachStable
    "Apply the physical law on a creature"
    | n1 n2 delta actualLength unit force |
    nodes do: #resetForce.
    muscles do: [ :m |
        n1 := m node1.
        n2 := m node2.
        delta := n2 position - n1 position.
        actualLength := delta r max: 1.
        unit := delta / actualLength.
        force := 0.1 * m strength * (actualLength - m length) * unit.
        n1 addForce: force.
        n2 addForce: force negated ].
```

External forces on nodes are first canceled. We then compute the force from the strength of a muscle. Note that this force is applied to a node, and the opposite force is applied to the second extremity node.

The core of our physics engine and a model for the creature have now both been defined. We need to hook all the components together and prepare the model to be processed by the genetic algorithm.

12.6.1 Serialization and Materialization of a Creature

When we hook our genetic algorithm, it is crucial to transform the individual genetic information into an array of numbers. These numbers will represent the attributes of the creature's muscles. A creature is serialized using the following method:

```
CCreature>>serialize
    "Serialize the creature into an array of numbers"
    ^ (muscles
        flatCollect: [ :m |
            muscleGenerator serializeMuscle: m ]) asArray
```

The opposite operation, the materialization of a creature from a set of numerical values, is carried out by this method:

```
CCreature>>materialize: anArrayOfValues
    "Materialize a array of numbers into a creature"
    | valuesPerMuscles |
    valuesPerMuscles :=
        anArrayOfValues groupsOf: 5 atATimeCollect: [ :v | v ].
    muscles with: valuesPerMuscles do: [ :m :values |
        muscleGenerator materialize: values inMuscle: m ]
```

As we have seen, each muscle is defined with five attributes. For this reason, the materialize: method groups values given in anArrayOfValues into array of size 5.

12.6.2 Accessors and Utility Methods

The largest part of the creature's definition has already been presented. The muscles of a creature are accessed using the following:

```
CCreature>>muscles
    "The muscles composing the creature"
    ^ muscles
```

The nodes composing a creature are accessed using the following:

```
CCreature>>nodes
    "The nodes composing the creature"
    ^ nodes
```

The position of the creature is computed as the average position of the nodes composing the creature.

Knowing the position of the creature is necessary when we apply the genetic algorithm, since the fitness will be based on the distance walked by the creature. The position method is defined as follows:

```
Creature>>position
    "Return the position of the creature, as the average position of the
    nodes"
    ^ (self nodes collect: #position) sum / self nodes size
```

At the beginning of a simulation, the creature has to be located above the main platform, at position 0@0:

```
CCreature>>resetPosition
    "Locate the creature at the initial position"
    self translateTo: 0 @ 0
```

Before applying the physical rules, it is important that the nodes are not all at the same position. We randomly assign a position to each node using randomlyLocateNodes:

```
CCreature>>randomlyLocateNodes
    "Assign each node to a random position"
    nodes
        do: [ :n | n translateBy: (random nextInt: 50) @ (random
            nextInt: 50) ]
```

Translating the creature to a given position is achieved using this method:

```
CCreature>>translateTo: aPoint
    "Translate a creature to a specified position"
    | averageCenter delta |
    averageCenter := self position.
    delta := aPoint - averageCenter.
    self nodes do: [ :n | n translateBy: delta ]
```

This section concludes the definition of the creature. Creatures will have to live in a world, so we define one in the coming section.

12.7 Defining the World

A world is defined as a set of creatures, a set of platforms, and a global timer. A world, in our case, is defined as a host of a race. We define the CWorld class as follows:

```
CVisualElement subclass: #CWorld
    instanceVariableNames: 'creatures time platforms'
    classVariableNames: ''
    package: 'Creature'
```

When created, a world is initialized as empty. The initialize method is defined as follows:

```
CWorld>>initialize
    super initialize.
    creatures := OrderedCollection new.
    platforms := OrderedCollection new.
    time := 0.
    self createElement.
    self addGround
```

A world is associated with a Roassal view, as defined in:

```
CWorld>>createElement
    "The visual representation of a world is a Roassal view"
    element := RTView new.
```

259

The ground is represented as a large platform:

```
World>>addGround
    "Define the ground of the world"
    | platform |
    platform := CPlatform new width: self groundLength + 500.
    "We give an extra distance of 500 to make sure there is no issue with
    the border"
    self addPlatform: platform.
    "The platform is located below where creatures will be initially
    located"
    platform translateTo: self groundLength / 2 @ 100
```

The length of the ground is set by the groundLength method:

```
CWorld>>groundLength
    "Set the length of the ground platform"
    ^ 5000
```

Adding a creature to a world is achieved using this method:

```
CWorld>>addCreature: aCreature
    "Add a creature to the world"
    creatures add: aCreature.

    "Add all the graphical elements of the creature in the view"
    element addAll: (aCreature nodes collect: #element).
    element addAll: (aCreature muscles collect: #element).

    "Move the creature at the initial position"
    aCreature resetPosition.
```

When a creature is added to the world, all the graphical elements stemming from muscles and nodes are added to the view. Similarly, a platform is added to a world using the following:

```
CWorld>>addPlatform: aPlatform
    "Add a platform to the world"
    platforms add: aPlatform.
    aPlatform createElement.
    element add: aPlatform element.
```

A world has a global timer. The timer increases at each beat, occurring at each window refresh, dictated by the operating system. The beat method is defined as follows:

```
CWorld>>beat
    "Trigger a global beat"
    time := time + 1.
    creatures do: [ :c | c beat; checkForCollision: platforms ]
```

At each beat, physics rules must be applied on each creature. Note that creatures cannot interact with each other.

Decoration is important in order to make the world appealing. We add some pylons to a world using the following method:

```
CWorld>>addPylons
    "Add pylons to the world as decorating elements"
    (0 to: self groundLength by: 100)
        do: [ :flagPosition |
            | pylon |
            pylon := RTBox new
                color: Color green darker;
                width: 3;
                height: 100;
                elementOn: flagPosition.
            element add: pylon.
            pylon @ RTLabeled.
            pylon translateTo: flagPosition @ 50.
            pylon pushBack ]
```

The open method creates the visual representation of the world, adds some decorations (label for the timer and the pylons), triggers the animation, and opens the window:

```
CWorld>>open
    "Build the visual representation of the world"
    | lbl animation |
    creatures do: #resetPosition.
    lbl := (RTLabel new elementOn: time) setAsFixed; yourself.
    element add: lbl.
```

```
lbl translateBy: 80 @ 30.
animation := RTActiveAnimation new
    intervalInMilliseconds: 10;
    blockToExecute: [ | p |
        self beat.
        lbl trachelShape text: time asString.
        p := creatures first position x @ 0.
        element canvas camera translateTo: p.
        element signalUpdate.
        p x > self groundLength
            ifTrue: [ element removeAnimation: animation ] ].
element addAnimation: animation.
self addPylons.
element canvas camera scale: 2.2.
^ element open
```

The world may have more than one creature. The progress of the first creature is
monitored during the simulation. The animation ends if the first creature reaches the
end of the ground platform.

12.8 Cold Run

We have now defined all the relevant components to make a creature "live." We can now
open a world and add a creature to it (see Figure 12-2):

```
creature := CCreature new configureBall: 10.
c := CWorld new.
c addCreature: creature.
c open
```

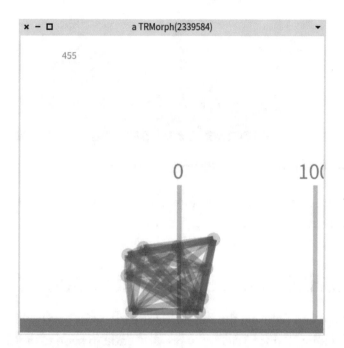

Figure 12-2. *Untrained creature*

Figure 12-3 shows the result of the script. Several creatures may be added to a world, each having a particular location, number of nodes, and color:

```
redCreature := CCreature new configureBall: 7.
blueCreature := CCreature new color: Color blue; configureBall: 10.
yellowCreature := CCreature new color: Color yellow; configureBall: 15.

c := CWorld new.
c addCreature: redCreature.
c addCreature: blueCreature.
c addCreature: yellowCreature.
c open.
blueCreature translateTo: 100 @ -50.
yellowCreature translateTo: 200 @ -50.
```

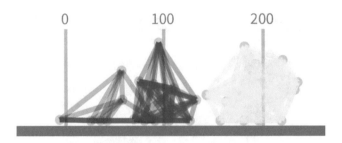

Figure 12-3. *Several untrained creatures*

At this stage, the creatures move without a particular objective. The next chapter covers how to make a creature evolve.

12.9 What Have We Seen in This Chapter?

This chapter focused on defining the infrastructure to model and build zoomorphic creatures. It was a long chapter. We had to provide enough code to build up an interesting codebase with which we can experiment in the next chapter.

The chapter covered:

- A simple physical engine, supporting muscles and nodes.

- The definition of a creature and a world in which it can live.

Note that we could have added bones when we modeled the creature. Once we have the notion of a bone, we could build skeletons. Although it's appealing, it would have significantly increased the amount of source code, which is the reason we left it out.

CHAPTER 13

Evolving Zoomorphic Creatures

The previous chapter presented the infrastructure that models and builds zoomorphic creatures. However, so far, the creature cannot do much: it stands where it was originally located, and we are lucky when it does not fall on its side. This chapter makes the creatures evolve to accomplish a displacement task, such as moving toward a particular direction or passing through some obstacles.

13.1 Interrupting a Process

Before jumping in and running the genetic algorithm, it is important to highlight an aspect of the Pharo programming language and environment.

Making creatures evolve is a very costly operation. Depending on your hardware configuration, you may have to let your computer evolve the creatures for hours. As such, most of the scripts in this chapter require a long time to complete. You should be familiar with the way that Pharo can be interrupted by pressing the Cmd and . (period) keys on MacOSX. On Windows or Linux, you use the Alt and . keys.

Interrupting Pharo opens up a Pharo debugger. When this happens, the execution has been interrupted. You may then do either of the following:

- Evaluate the code (e.g., to accurately monitor the computation progresses), which would happen in the debugger itself or in the playground

- Simply resume the computation by clicking Proceed

Closing a debugger will end the ongoing computation. Keeping the debugger open means you can always resume the execution you interrupted by clicking Proceed.

© Alexandre Bergel 2020
A. Bergel, *Agile Artificial Intelligence in Pharo*, https://doi.org/10.1007/978-1-4842-5384-7_13

Being able to interrupt Pharo means you have control over what is being executed. We also recommend that you regularly save your image. The top menu of Pharo provides relevant menu items for saving the environment.

13.2 Monitoring the Execution Time

Running a genetic algorithm on the creature is time consuming. We will extend our framework to keep track of the passing time. Elapsed time will be kept in a log entry, as modeled by the GALog class. So, we add a new variable to this class, as follows:

```
Object subclass: #GALog
    instanceVariableNames: 'generationNumber timeToProduceGeneration
        fittestIndividual worseFitness averageFitness time'
    classVariableNames: ''
    package: 'GeneticAlgorithm-Core'
```

Note that the GALog class was defined in a previous chapter. We revised its definition by adding a way to log time. The new variable, time, is set in a constructor:

```
GALog>>initialize
    super initialize.
    time := DateAndTime now
```

The DateAndTime class represents a point in time. When a log object is created, we keep the creation time in the time variable:

```
GALog>>time
    "Return the time the log was created"
    ^ time
```

We can now exploit this to determine the whole computation time. We define the timeTaken method:

```
GAEngine>>timeTaken
    "Return the time taken to compute all the generations"
    | lastLog |
    lastLog := self logs last.
    ^ lastLog time - self logs first time
```

We will illustrate the use of timeTaken later in this chapter.

13.3 The Competing Conventions Problem

The previous chapters presented two crossover operations:

- GACrossoverOperation performs a simple crossover, without enforcing any characteristics

- GAOrderedCrossoverOperation prevents repetitions of particular genes

These operations have proven to be useful in addressing various problems, as we have seen. However, they will be of little help in making our creature evolve, because of the *competing conventions problem*. This problem is associated with using default and standard genetic operations. To understand why exactly this is a problem, consider the robot example we saw in a previous chapter. The robot follows a list of orders, and each order is a step toward a direction. We used the genetic algorithm to find the sequence of orders to reach a particular point in the map. Figure 13-1 illustrates the competing conventions problem.

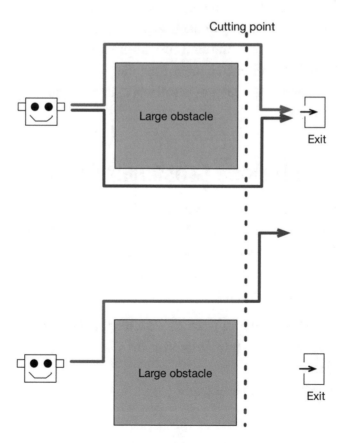

Figure 13-1. *Competing conventions problem*

We are assuming that the genetic information encodes a path, as we saw in the chapter about exiting a maze. The top part of the figure shows two relatively good paths, colored in green and blue. These two paths are different, but both lead the robot to a position very close to the exit. We can reasonably assume that a selection algorithm can designate these two paths to be combined, as they are very good. Once selected, these two paths have to be combined using the genetic algorithm. In the way we saw it, a random index is designated as the cutting point. The dashed red line indicates a possible cutting point.

The bottom part of the figure shows one result of the recombination. The new path leads the robot far from the exit. This small example illustrates the following situation: *two relatively good individuals are combined into a poorly-performing individual.* This situation is named the competing conventions problem and it is often considered a serious obstacle to evolving a non-trivial data structure.

If we blindly apply the GACrossoverOperation operation to evolve our creatures, we will immediately bump into the competing conventions problem, essentially because combining two good muscles is very unlikely to produce a better muscle. There is no general way to address the competing conventions problem. However, the way it is usually tackled is to define particular genetic operations that consider the structure to be recombined. This is exactly the strategy we will use in this chapter and in the part of the book about neuroevolution.

13.4 The Constrained Crossover Operation

One way to avoid the competing conventions problem is to restrict the crossover to happen at any point. Instead, we will permit a crossover to happen only at a muscle extremity. As such, a crossover cannot "cut" the genetic information of a muscle. We now define a new operator for that purpose, called GAConstrainedCrossoverOperation:

```
GAAbstractCrossoverOperation subclass: #GAConstrainedCrossoverOperation
    instanceVariableNames: 'possibleCutpoints'
    classVariableNames: ''
    package: 'GeneticAlgorithm-Core'
```

This new crossover operator considers a set of possible cutpoints with the variable possibleCutpoints. This variable contains a set of possible indices where a crossover can occur. The variable is set by using the following:

```
GAConstrainedCrossoverOperation>>possibleCutpoints: indexes
    "Set the possible pointcuts considered by the operator"
    possibleCutpoints := indexes
```

We also add a utility method that hooks it into our framework, as follows:

```
GAConstrainedCrossoverOperation>>pickCutPointFor: partnerA
    "Return a cutpoint"
    self assert: [ possibleCutpoints notNil ] description:
        'Need to provide the possible cut points, using #
            possibleCutpoints:'.
    ^ possibleCutpoints at: (random nextInt: possibleCutpoints size)
```

This new operator is the only increment we need to make to our framework and evolve the zoomorphic creatures.

13.5 Moving Forward

We will consider the task of moving to the right. Remember that evolving creatures take a significant amount of time. The following script takes approximately 31 minutes to run on an Intel Core i5, 3.7GHz:

```
numberOfNodes := 10.
numberOfMuscles := (CCreature new configureBall: numberOfNodes)
    numberOfMuscles.
mg := CMuscleGenerator new
        minStrength: 0.01;
        deltaStrength: 1;
        minLength: 10;
        deltaLength: 80;
        deltaTime: 200;
        minTime: 20.
```

```
g := GAEngine new.
g crossoverOperator: (GAConstrainedCrossoverOperation new
    possibleCutpoints: (1 to: numberOfMuscles*5 by: 5)).
g selection: (GATournamentSelection new).
g mutationRate: 0.02.
g endForMaxNumberOfGeneration: 128.
g populationSize: 100.
g numberOfGenes: numberOfMuscles * 5.
g createGeneBlock: [ :r :index | mg valueForIndex: index ].
g fitnessBlock: [ :genes |
    creature := CCreature new configureBall: numberOfNodes.
    creature materialize: genes.
    c := CWorld new.
    c addCreature: creature.
    3000 timesRepeat: [ c beat ].
    creature position x
].
g run.
```

The script considers a creature made of ten nodes, as indicated by the
numberOfNodes variable. The physics engine will locate these nodes in a circular fashion
as a result of the physical rules. The number of muscles is obtained by evaluating the
(CCreature new configureBall: numberOfNodes) numberOfMuscles expression. It
simply creates a dummy creature and counts the number of muscles. A ball creature
made of ten nodes has 45 muscles. We then define a muscle generator useful for building
the initial population and mutating a creature.

Each muscle is defined by five attributes. A crossover operation may happen
only at the extremity of a muscle definition in the linear genetic information. The
fitness function simulates the behavior of the creature in a new world. We took an
arbitrary number of beats, 3000, to simulate the behavior. After these 3000 beats, the
X coordinate of the creature is the result of the fitness function. Consequently, a fit
creature will move forward to the right. The evolution happens over 128 generations
(an arbitrary value).

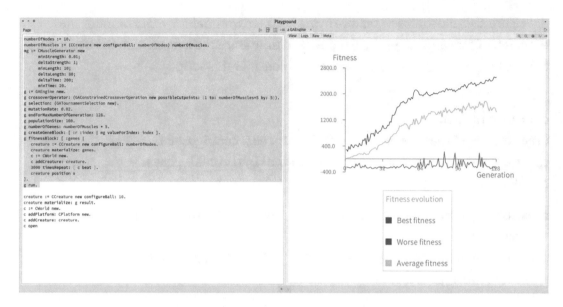

Figure 13-2. *Evolving a creature with 45 muscles*

Figure 13-2 shows the fitness evolution. The fitness indicates that the creature is able to move.

We can see the result using the script by appending the following instruction to the previous script:

```
...
creature := CCreature new configureBall: 10.
creature materialize: g result.
c := CWorld new.
c addCreature: creature.
c open
```

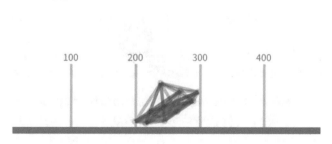

Figure 13-3. *A creature in its environment*

Figure 13-3 illustrates a creature living in its environment. We can monitor the evolution of a creature at particular points in time since the logs contain the historical information (see Figure 13-4). For example, consider this script:

```
...
c := CWorld new.
creature := CCreature new color: Color red; configureBall: 10.
creature materialize: g logs last fittestIndividual genes.
c addCreature: creature.

creature := CCreature new color: Color yellow darker darker;
    configureBall: 10.
creature materialize: (g logs at: 50) fittestIndividual genes.
c addCreature: creature.

creature := CCreature new color: Color blue darker darker;
    configureBall: 10.
creature materialize: (g logs at: 100) fittestIndividual genes.
c addCreature: creature.

creature := CCreature new color: Color green darker darker;
    configureBall: 10.
creature materialize: (g logs at: 120) fittestIndividual genes.
c addCreature: creature.

c open
```

2243

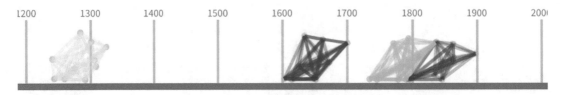

Figure 13-4. *Creature at different stages of its evolution (yellow = generation 50, blue = generation 100, green = generation 120, red = generation 128)*

If you watch these competing creatures, it is interesting to see that the red creature is not always in the first position. The green creature overtakes the red one multiple times. Ultimately, the red one reaches the final pylon.

13.6 Serializing the Muscle Attributes

The g result expression returns a large array containing the attributes of the muscles used in the creature. You can keep the computed result in case you do not want to run the genetic algorithm all the time. It would indeed be cumbersome to have to run the whole algorithm each time you want to see a creature moving! For example, if you evaluate the g result expression, you obtain the following:

```
creature := CCreature new configureBall: 10.
creature materialize: #(24 34 0.46040109215788594 216 145 75 50
    0.522318108469396 127 33 33 39 0.9105445367193523 70 93 30 88
    0.5458242390378492 55 104 32 78 0.9326984656055917 36 74 20 38
    0.23007194683890417 169 77 25 31 0.6407352956527543 219 147 28 14
    0.5132012814205146 70 67 41 32 0.4101663086936652 116 21 30 53
    0.4132064962215752 140 69 26 16 0.67239310366213 174 81 90 40
    0.9493843137376868 77 82 90 24 0.9472498080773512 72 76 77 15
    0.8207815849644977 51 46 63 21 0.23135899086546108 29 170 33 24
    0.8508932494190025 70 94 34 32 0.85425589900662 192 99 83 84
    0.8219266167338596 153 144 74 57 0.18008196523882541 38 136 76 82
    0.4098378945513805 108 122 73 25 0.13200707016606214 72 102 11 24
    0.525760215705149 60 33 34 53 0.47843877270279395 207 167 53 53
    0.06064744597796698 47 203 90 90 0.3480303188869871 101 204 77 42
    0.05166656036007524 143 155 67 89 0.5535930274164271 146 23 35 39
    0.8390450097196945 136 143 78 87 0.955747404799679 153 71 15 84
    0.9765097738460218 34 26 36 14 0.13894161191253998 78 51 38 41
    0.1316714140594338 114 205 74 74 0.7760572821116342 191 32 67 61
    0.08824125377379416 219 149 18 70 0.1469941007052521 169 175 39 43
    0.2866080141424239 133 71 90 42 0.8735930218098653 90 85 53 21
    0.18471918099313936 39 146 60 44 0.3135163908747567 120 38 57 43
    0.32777994628892276 187 148 34 23 0.3158802803540045 35 102 75 42
```

```
    0.1347404502354285 109 125 28 76 0.12238997760805766 64 23 68 70
    0.9608936917180632 179 175 28 24 0.06067319378753807 116 196 ).
c := CWorld new.
c addCreature: creature.
c open
```

This long array of numbers constitutes the "DNA" of the creature. The objective of the genetic algorithm is to evolve the DNA to make the creature move to the right as much as possible.

13.7 Passing Obstacles

So far, our creature has evolved to move right. It is easy to model a new environment, in particular with some obstacles. The script used previously can be adapted with obstacles (see Figure 13-5). This revision takes about 48 minutes to run (more than 60% slower):

```
numberOfNodes := 10.
numberOfMuscles := (CCreature new configureBall: numberOfNodes)
    numberOfMuscles.
mg := CMuscleGenerator new
        minStrength: 0.01;
        deltaStrength: 1;
        minLength: 10;
        deltaLength: 80;
        deltaTime: 200;
        minTime: 20.
g := GAEngine new.
g crossoverOperator: (GAConstrainedCrossoverOperation new
    possibleCutpoints: (1 to: numberOfMuscles * 5 by: 5)).
g selection: (GATournamentSelection new).
g mutationRate: 0.02.
g endForMaxNumberOfGeneration: 128.
g populationSize: 100.
g numberOfGenes: numberOfMuscles * 5.
g createGeneBlock: [ :r :index | mg valueForIndex: index ].
```

```
g fitnessBlock: [ :genes |
    creature := CCreature new configureBall: numberOfNodes.
    creature materialize: genes.
    creature resetPosition.
    c := CWorld new.
    c addPlatform:
        (CPlatform new height: 20; width: 80; translateTo: 100 @ 90).
    c addPlatform:
        (CPlatform new height: 20; width: 80; translateTo: 400 @ 90).
    c addPlatform:
        (CPlatform new height: 20; width: 80; translateTo: 700 @ 90).
    c addPlatform:
        (CPlatform new height: 20; width: 80; translateTo: 1000 @ 90).
    c addCreature: creature.
    3000 timesRepeat: [ c beat ].
    creature position x
].
g run.
```

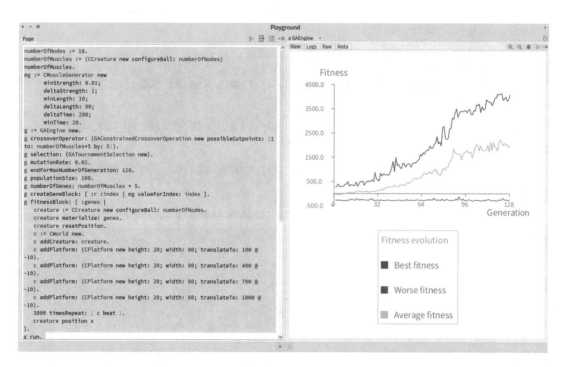

Figure 13-5. *Evolving a zoomorphic creature in the presence of obstacles*

The result can be rendered using the following script:

```
...
c := CWorld new.
creature := CCreature new color: Color red; configureBall: 10.
creature materialize: g logs last fittestIndividual genes.
c addCreature: creature.

creature := CCreature new color: Color yellow darker darker;
    configureBall: 10.
creature materialize: (g logs at: 50) fittestIndividual genes.
c addCreature: creature.

creature := CCreature new color: Color blue darker darker;
    configureBall: 10.
creature materialize: (g logs at: 100) fittestIndividual genes.
c addCreature: creature.

creature := CCreature new color: Color green darker darker;
    configureBall: 10.
creature materialize: (g logs at: 90) fittestIndividual genes.
c addCreature: creature.

c addPlatform:
    (CPlatform new height: 20; width: 80; translateTo: 100 @ 90).
c addPlatform:
    (CPlatform new height: 20; width: 80; translateTo: 400 @ 90).
c addPlatform:
    (CPlatform new height: 20; width: 80; translateTo: 700 @ 90).
c addPlatform:
    (CPlatform new height: 20; width: 80; translateTo: 1000 @ 90).
c open
```

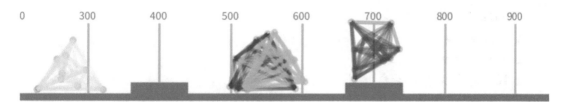

Figure 13-6. *Different stages of the evolution*

Figure 13-6 illustrates different stages of an evolved creature.

13.8 Climbing Stairs

The creature can also evolve to climb stairs. Consider this script, which takes around six hours to run:

```
numberOfNodes := 10.
numberOfMuscles := (CCreature new configureBall: numberOfNodes)
    numberOfMuscles.
mg := CMuscleGenerator new
        minStrength: 0.01;
        deltaStrength: 1;
        minLength: 10;
        deltaLength: 80;
        deltaTime: 200;
        minTime: 20.
g := GAEngine new.
g crossoverOperator: (GAConstrainedCrossoverOperation new
    possibleCutpoints: (1 to: numberOfMuscles*5 by: 5)).
g selection: (GATournamentSelection new).
g mutationRate: 0.02.
g endForMaxNumberOfGeneration: 128.
g populationSize: 100.
g numberOfGenes: numberOfMuscles * 5.
g createGeneBlock: [ :r :index | mg valueForIndex: index ].
g fitnessBlock: [ :genes |
    creature := CCreature new configureBall: numberOfNodes.
    creature materialize: genes.
```

```
creature resetPosition.
c := CWorld new.
c addCreature: creature.
1 to: 25 by: 3 do: [ :x |
    c addPlatform: (CPlatform new height: 20; width: 80;
        translateTo: x * 100 @ 90).
    c addPlatform: (CPlatform new height: 20; width: 80;
        translateTo: x * 100 + 50 @ 70).
    c addPlatform: (CPlatform new height: 20; width: 80;
        translateTo: x * 100 + 100 @ 50).
    c addPlatform: (CPlatform new height: 20; width: 80;
        translateTo: x * 100 + 150 @ 30).
].
c addCreature: creature.
3000 timesRepeat: [ c beat ].
creature position x
].
g run.
```

This script is very similar to the previous ones. The difference is in the way the fitness function is evaluated. This script adds platforms, considered obstacles, along the creature's way. This new script is slower than the previous one. The presence of these platforms significantly affects how the creature evolves. The script checks for collisions between the nodes and the platforms, which is time-consuming. At each movement of a node, the node encompassing box is intersected with the encompassing box of each platform. We implemented the minimum needed to support this simulation. A more robust implementation would probably use a more sophisticated technique to determine collisions between elements (e.g., quadtree).

This script simply uses some well-positioned platforms to form the stairs. The following script shows the results (see Figure 13-7):

```
...
creature := CCreature new configureBall: 10.
creature materialize: g result.
c := CWorld new.
"We build couple of stairs"
```

```
1 to: 25 by: 3 do: [ :x |
    c addPlatform: (CPlatform new height: 20; width: 80; translateTo:
        * 100 @ 90).
    c addPlatform: (CPlatform new height: 20; width: 80; translateTo:
        x * 100 + 50 @ 70).
    c addPlatform: (CPlatform new height: 20; width: 80; translateTo:
        x * 100 + 100 @ 50).
    c addPlatform: (CPlatform new height: 20; width: 80; translateTo:
        x * 100 + 150 @ 30).
].
c addCreature: creature.
c open
```

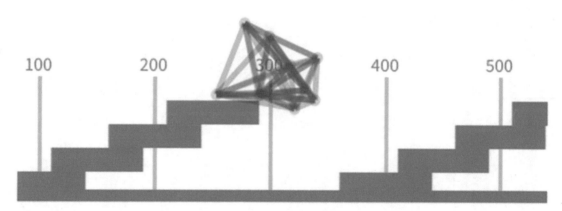

Figure 13-7. *Climbing the stairs*

A zoomorphic creature can indeed evolve to climb stairs.

13.9 What Have We Seen in This Chapter?

This chapter illustrated how creatures, which we call *zoomorphic* due to their organic way of moving, evolve to solve some walking tasks. In particular, the chapter covered the following:

- A basic technique to interrupt long-running processes. This is a central aspect of this chapter as the evolution we deal with takes several minutes, and being able to interrupt a running execution is important.

- The evolution of a creature in three different scenarios: without any obstacles, with some simple obstacles, and with stairs.

This chapter closes the second part of the book.

PART III

Neuroevolution

CHAPTER 14

Neuroevolution

This chapter covers the third and last part of the book. The book started with the topic of neural networks, which are computational metaphors for the biological brain. Subsequently, the book covered genetic algorithms, computational simulations of species evolution. After these two parts, the question that may naturally be asked is: Is it possible to evolve neural networks in a fashion similar to how our biological brains went through evolution over thousands of years? The answer is yes, and this evolution mechanism is the topic of this third and last part of the book. *Neuroevolution* is a form of artificial intelligence that combines neural networks and genetic algorithms.

After giving some theoretical background on different learning mechanisms, this chapter explores a simple neuroevolution mechanism, called *NeuroGenetic*.

14.1 Supervised, Unsupervised Learning, and Reinforcement Learning

When we discussed how a neural network operates, we learned that a neural network requires examples. In order for a neural network to learn classification patterns in a dataset (as with the Iris dataset), the dataset has to be labeled for the neural network to identify those patterns. In the case of the Iris dataset, each flower description accompanied the name of the flower. We referred to the flower name as the label of an example. Learning from a dataset that contains labels is called *supervised learning*: the machine learning algorithm learns patterns from labeled data. Supervised learning is characterized by operating on labeled data.

In many situations, obtaining a labeled dataset is not problematic. For example, Facebook has a large dataset of labeled pictures. Each time you label a friend in a picture, you provide an example that Facebook can use to improve its models. Supervised learning finds patterns in datasets for which we have the right answer, the label.

© Alexandre Bergel 2020
A. Bergel, *Agile Artificial Intelligence in Pharo*, https://doi.org/10.1007/978-1-4842-5384-7_14

Unsupervised learning is about finding patterns without having the right answers, the labels. Patterns are then extracted without telling the algorithm what these patterns are about. The machine learning scientific community produced numerous unsupervised learning techniques. Common techniques include *k-means* (clustering techniques based on element similarities) and *autoencoder* (particular architecture of a neural network to learn encoding of a set of data).

Reinforcement learning is a third form of learning in which software agents learn from the environment and make proper decisions. Neuroevolution is a technique that is associated with reinforcement learning in some ways. Autonomous vehicle, robots, and games are among the prominent domains for which having good quality examples is difficult. We use the term reinforcement learning in a broad sense here: this is an agent that is getting better by exploring a space and accumulating rewards. As such, neuroevolution may fall into this category since a population or a species may be considered an agent that is trying to maximize a fitness value, a kind of reward for its composing individuals.

The remainder of the chapter will explore this third way of learning with neuroevolution.

14.2 Neuroevolution

Neuroevolution consists of evolving a neural network. Along generations, the network becomes better at recognizing patterns. Wikipedia states that "Neuroevolution is a form of artificial intelligence that uses evolutionary algorithms to generate artificial neural networks."

Neuroevolution has many benefits over classical deep learning approaches. Since there is no training involved, there is no need to have examples. As such, neuroevolution is adequate for solving problems in which examples are either of a bad quality or difficult to obtain. A second benefit of neuroevolution is that it can evolve the architecture itself. In deep learning, the network architecture, defined in terms of layers, the layer size, and the activation functions all need to be specified. Neuroevolution frees the engineer from having to make arbitrary decisions.

14.3 Two Neuroevolution Techniques

This chapter and the following ones cover two neuroevolution techniques, *NeuroGenetic* and *NEAT*:

- *NeuroGenetic* is a direct application of a genetic algorithm to find weights and biases of a neural network. This technique was pioneered by Edmund Ronald and Marc Schoenauer in 1994. Note that with this technique, the architecture of the network is fixed, while the weights and biases are subject to the evolution.

- *NEAT* stands for *NeuroEvolution of Augmenting Topologies* and was proposed by Kenneth O. Stanley and Risto Miikkulainen in 2002. The key ingredients of NEAT is to make the neural network evolve, considering both the network's weights and its architecture.

The remainder of this chapter covers the NeuroGenetic approach, while NEAT is detailed in Chapter 15.

14.4 The NeuroGenetic Approach

In the NeuroGenetic technique, the number of layers, the number of neurons, and the activation functions are fixed and are therefore not subject to searching by the genetic algorithm. Instead, we only employ the genetic algorithm to find the weights and biases of each neuron.

When we discussed the zoomorphic creature, we presented the *competing convention problem*. This situation arises when two relatively good individuals are combined to form a poorly-performing individual. The child is worse than the parents. With the zoomorphic creature, we addressed this problem by making sure that a crossover operation considers a muscle as a whole. We will apply the very same technique here: the crossover operations will consider a neuron as a whole. As such, the operation cannot recombine two neurons to form a new one. Instead, crossover can recombine two sequences of neurons to form a new sequence made of neurons obtained from the parents.

14.5 Extending the Neural Network

Our implementation of the neural network needs a few extensions to be able to perform the constrained crossover operation. First, neurons from the network have to be accessible. This is necessary to be able to serialize a network into an individual chromosome. We define the neurons method as follows:

```
NNetwork>>neurons
    "Return the list of neurons contains in the network"
    ^ layers flatCollect: #neurons
```

To compute the size of the individual chromosome, we need to sum up the number of parameters of each neuron. We define the following method:

```
Neuron>>numberOfWeights
    "Return the number of weights contained in the neuron"
    ^ weights size
```

The number of parameters of a network is simply the sum of the number of weights of each neuron, added to the sum of the biases. Since each neuron has one bias, the number of biases in a network equals the number of neurons contained in the network. We therefore define this method:

```
NNetwork>>numberOfParameters
    "Return the number of weights and biases contained in the network"
    ^ (self neurons collect: #numberOfWeights) sum + self neurons size
```

As we saw with the zoomorphic creature, the constrained crossover operation has to be configured with a list of index cutpoints. We define the getPossibleCutpoints method to obtain the indexes corresponding to the limits of the neuron when parameters are linearly serialized:

```
NNetwork>>getPossibleCutpoints
    "Return the indexes of each neurons values.
    This method is useful when applying genetic algorithm to neural network"
    | result index |
    result := OrderedCollection new.
    index := 1.
```

```
self neurons do: [ :n |
    result add: index.
    index := index + n weights size + 1. ].
^ result asArray
```

During the evolution, we need to be able to reconstruct a network from a list of parameters. We therefore define the setWeightsAndBias: method, whose purpose is to fill a network with the provided weights and bias:

```
NNetwork>>setWeightsAndBias: weightsAndBias
    "Set the weights and bias of each neuron.
    This method is useful when applying genetic algorithm to neural network"
    | index |
    self assert: [ self numberOfParameters = weightsAndBias size ].
    self assert: [ weightsAndBias allSatisfy: #isNumber ].
    index := 1.
    self neurons do: [ :n |
        n weights: (weightsAndBias copyFrom: index to: n
            numberOfWeights + index - 1).
        index := index + n numberOfWeights.
        n bias: (weightsAndBias at: index).
        index := index + 1 ]
```

We now have all the pieces to try our first neuroevolution example.

14.6 NeuroGenetic by Example

A classical example of using neuroevolution is to produce a neural network that can express the XOR logical gate. Consider the following script:

```
data := {
    {0 . 0 . 0} .
    {0 . 1 . 1} .
    {1 . 0 . 1} .
    {1 . 1 . 0} }.

n := NNetwork new.
n configure: 2 hidden: 3 nbOfOutputs: 2.
```

```
g := GAEngine new.
g populationSize: 500.
g mutationRate: 0.01.
g endForMaxNumberOfGeneration: 30.
g crossoverOperator: (GAConstrainedCrossoverOperation new
    possibleCutpoints: n getPossibleCutpoints).

g numberOfGenes: n numberOfParameters.
g createGeneBlock: [ :rand :index :ind | rand next * 10 - 5 ].
g fitnessBlock: [ :genes |
    | r |
    n setWeightsAndBias: genes.
    r := (data collect: [ :row |
              (n predict: row allButLast) = row last ]) select: #
                  yourself.
    (r size / 4) round: 4.
    ].
g run.
```

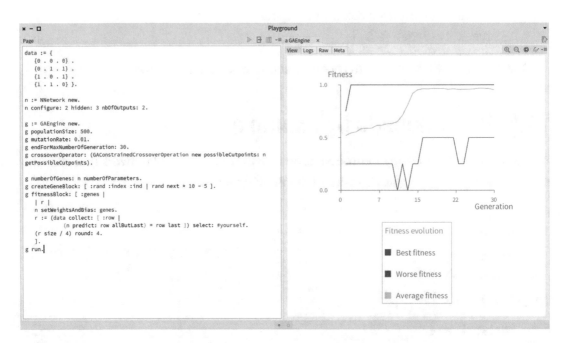

Figure 14-1. *Expressing the XOR logical gate using NeuroGenetic*

Executing the script produces the output given in Figure 14-1. The fitness is defined as the precision of the network on the small XOR dataset. As shown in the figure, the fitness quickly reaches 1.0, which means that the network can recognize the patterns contained in the dataset.

Similar to the scripts given in the first part of the book, the data variable contains the data we wish the algorithm to produce a neural network for. The n variable refers to a neural network made of two inputs, three hidden neurons, and two outputs, as defined by the variable n.

A genetic algorithm engine is defined with a population of 500 individuals and a mutation rate of 0.01. The algorithm has to run for 30 generations. The crossover is constrained to happen at any neuron indices provided by the result of the getPossibleCutpoints method. The number of genes is the number of parameters contained in the network. The value for a gene is simply a random number, ranging from -5 to 5.

As you can see in the code, there is no training of the network. The fitness is used to pick the best networks and combine them. As we saw in the chapter about genetic algorithms, the fitness block is computed for each individual of the population and takes as an argument the genes of that individual. We configure the network n with the parameters contained in the genes variable, using the setWeightsAndBias: method. The fitness then returns the number of predictions that are correct.

Figure 14-1 indicates that that best fitness across generations quickly reaches the value of 1, which means a perfect precision of the predictions. We can verify this by building a neural network, initializing it with the result of the genetic algorithm, and performing a prediction (see Figure 14-2):

```
...
n := NNetwork new.
n configure: 2 hidden: 3 nbOfOutputs: 2.
n setWeightsAndBias: g result.
n predict: #(1 0).
```

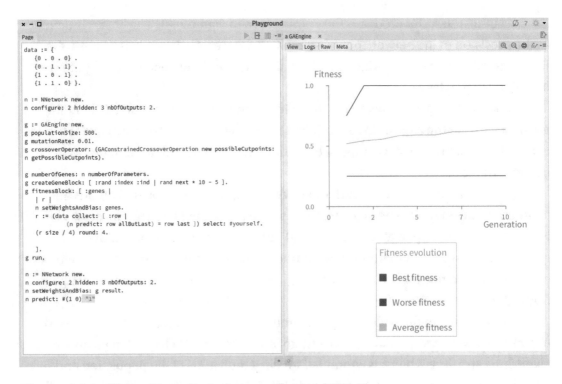

Figure 14-2. *Using NeuroGenetic to perform 1 XOR 0*

As expected, the script returns 1. In the same spirit, we can try a slightly more complex example. The following script builds a network that converts a binary number to its decimal representation:

```
data := {
        { 0 . 0 . 0 . 0 } .
        { 0 . 0 . 1 . 1 } .
        { 0 . 1 . 0 . 2 } .
        { 0 . 1 . 1 . 3 } .
        { 1 . 0 . 0 . 4 } .
        { 1 . 0 . 1 . 5 } .
        { 1 . 1 . 0 . 6 } .
        { 1 . 1 . 1 . 7 } }.
n := NNetwork new.
n configure: 3 hidden: 5 nbOfOutputs: 8.
```

```
g := GAEngine new.
g populationSize: 500.
g endForMaxNumberOfGeneration: 100.
g crossoverOperator: (GAConstrainedCrossoverOperation new
    possibleCutpoints: n getPossibleCutpoints).
g numberOfGenes: n numberOfParameters.
g createGeneBlock: [ :rand :index :ind | rand next * 10 - 5 ].
g fitnessBlock: [ :genes |
    | r |
    n setWeightsAndBias: genes.
    r := (data collect: [ :row |
            (n predict: row allButLast) = row last ]) select: #
                yourself.
    (r size / data size) round: 4.
    ].
g run.
```

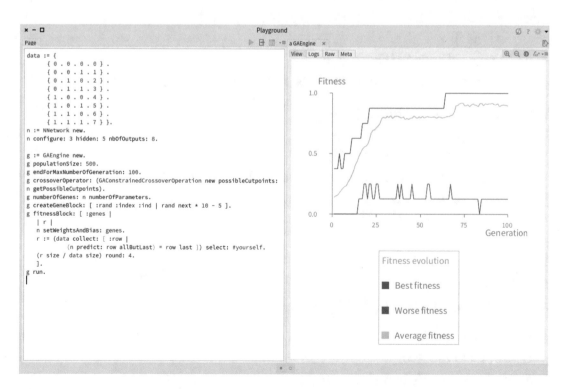

Figure 14-3. *Converting a number from binary to decimal*

Figure 14-3 shows the result of the script. The fitness reaches 1.0, which means that the perfect conversion is achieved. We can verify this with the following example:

```
...
n := NNetwork new.
n configure: 3 hidden: 5 nbOfOutputs: 8.
n setWeightsAndBias: g result.
n predict: #(1 1 0).
```

The result of converting the binary number 1 1 0 into decimal is 6.

14.7 The Iris Dataset

We can apply NeuroGenetic to process the Iris dataset introduced earlier. Consider this script:

```
irisCSV := (ZnEasy get: 'https://agileartificialintelligence.github.io/
    Datasets/iris.csv') contents.
lines := irisCSV lines allButFirst collect: [ :l |
        | ss |
        ss := l substrings: ','.
        (ss allButLast collect: [ :w | w asNumber ]), { ss last } ].

irisData := lines collect: [ :row |
        | l |
        row last = 'setosa' ifTrue: [ l := #( 0 ) ].
        row last = 'versicolor' ifTrue: [ l := #( 1 ) ].
        row last = 'virginica' ifTrue: [ l := #( 2 ) ].
        row allButLast, l ].

"The variable irisData contains the Iris dataset"

n := NNetwork new.
n configure: 4 hidden: 6 nbOfOutputs: 3.

g := GAEngine new.
g populationSize: 500.
g endForMaxNumberOfGeneration: 30.
```

```
g crossoverOperator: (GAConstrainedCrossoverOperation new
    possibleCutpoints: n getPossibleCutpoints).

g numberOfGenes: n numberOfParameters.
g createGeneBlock: [ :rand :index :ind | rand next * 10 - 5 ].
g fitnessBlock: [ :genes |
    | r |
    n setWeightsAndBias: genes.
    r := (irisData collect: [ :row |
            (n predict: row allButLast) = row last ]) select: #
                yourself.
    (r size / irisData size) asFloat round: 4 ].
g run.
```

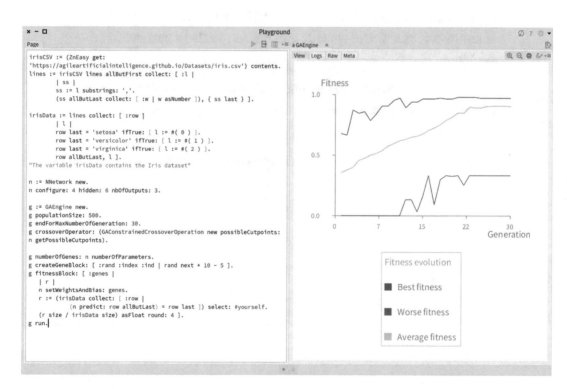

Figure 14-4. *NeuroGenetic and the Iris dataset*

Figure 14-4 indicates that the fitness reaches 97% in the last generations. This small example illustrates that the evolved neural network competes equally well with a trained neural network using backpropagation.

14.8 Further Reading About NeuroGenetic

NeuroGenetic, which is presented in this chapter, is the simplest way to use neuroevolution. The techniques only used weights and biases. It was first presented by Edmund Ronald and Marc Schoenauer in 1994, in their publication titled, "Genetic Lander: An Experiment in Accurate Neuro-Genetic Control." The article is available at `https://citeseerx.ist.psu.edu/viewdoc/summary?doi=10.1.1.56.3139`. It shows a small example of a lunar lander.

14.9 What Have We Seen in This Chapter?

This chapter combined the results of the first two parts of the book. In particular:

- It presented how genetic algorithms can be used to search for a relevant combination of weights and biases to solve a particular problem.

- It demonstrated that NeuroGenetic, a simple neuroevolution technique, can provide results similar to backpropagation on a simple dataset.

The next chapter covers NEAT, a sophisticated algorithm used with neuroevolution.

CHAPTER 15

Neuroevolution with NEAT

NEAT is an algorithm that builds neural networks following an incremental and evolutionary process. It uses a genetic algorithm to evolve networks. In the very early generations, neural networks are very simple, composed of a few nodes and connections. However, complexity is added in each generation. NEAT supports a number of mutations, and these mutations may add new nodes or new connections. As such, networks can only become more complex over time.

NEAT was proposed in 2002 by Kenneth O. Stanley and Risto Miikkulainen in their article titled, "Evolving Neural Networks Through Augmenting Topologies," published by MIT Press. Readers who wish to know more about the design decisions of the algorithm are welcome to read the article. The article is accessible, and it can be easily found on the web.

This chapter focuses on the implementation of the NEAT algorithm. NEAT builds neural networks made of nodes and connections. This chapter is self-contained. All the code provided in this chapter is meant to be kept in a package called NEAT and each class is prefixed with the two letters, NE.

Note that we slightly simplify the original NEAT algorithm to keep the chapter size under control. In particular, we use a simplified strategy to create species and evaluate similarities between individuals.

This chapter begins with some theoretical background before diving into the NEAT implementation.

15.1 Vocabulary

This chapter is about using a genetic algorithm to evolve neural networks. Although we have detailed these two concepts in previous chapters, the NEAT algorithm, as originally formulated by Kenneth and Risto in 2002, comes with its own terminology.

© Alexandre Bergel 2020
A. Bergel, *Agile Artificial Intelligence in Pharo*, https://doi.org/10.1007/978-1-4842-5384-7_15

We use it in this chapter to avoid a necessary gap between our implementation and the original description of the NEAT algorithm given by "Evolving Neural Networks Through Augmenting Topologies." In this chapter we use the following definitions:

- *Node*: A node is a representation of a neuron. A node may accept input values and produce output values.

- *Input node*: In NEAT, input values of a neural network are provided to an input node. The number of input nodes is fixed during the evolution since it depends on the problem the algorithm is trying to solve.

- *Output node*: Output nodes are nodes from which the network output are obtained.

- *Hidden node*: Hidden nodes are nodes that are neither input nor output. When values are provided to the input nodes, computed values are flown through hidden nodes in order to reach the output nodes.

- *Connection*: Nodes are connected via explicit connections. Each connection has a weight value.

- *Connection cache:* A node keeps the connections using a connection cache, which is simply a collection of associations.

- *Innovation number*: Each connection, when added to an individual, receives a historical marker, which we call the innovation number. This number is incremented by 1 at each new connection.

- *Individual*: An individual is a set of nodes and connections, a reference to the species in which it belongs to, and a connection cache.

- *Species*: Individuals who have similar structures are likely to belong to the same species. A species is a group of similar individuals.

- *Speciation*: The action of splitting a population into species is called speciation. Speciation occurs in each generation.

- *Log*: Monitoring the evolution of the NEAT algorithm is supported using log objects. Each log object contains relevant information.

15.2 The Node Class

A node represents a neuron in a network. We will use the word "node" over "neuron" because it is fairly distant to what we saw when we discussed neural networks. Nodes may be connected using connections that we will see later. We define the class as follows:

```
Object subclass: #NENode
        instanceVariableNames: 'id kind connectionsCache innovationNumber
            numberOfInputs zValue numberOfReceivedValues result'
        classVariableNames: ''
        package: 'NEAT'
```

The NENode class defines the following variables:

- id is a numerical identifier of each node. As we will later see, each connection is defined between two IDs. An ID uniquely refers to a node.

- kind represents the kind of node. The kind of the node may be #input, to represent a network in the input layer, #output, to represent a neuron located in the output layer, or #hidden, to represent a node that is neither input nor output.

- connectionsCache is used to cache the connections between nodes when a network is produced from an individual. The cache has to be reset when an individual is mutated.

- innovationNumber is a number that represents a historical marker. It is an identifier value of the performed mutation.

- numberOfInputs represents the number of inputs the node has.

- zValue represents the accumulated z value. As we have seen in the first part of the book, the z value is the sum of the weighted inputs. This value is used to compute the output of the node.

- numberOfReceivedValues is a counter indicating how many inputs have flown in the node. At each received input value, the zValue is adjusted and the numberOfReceivedValues variable is increased by 1. When numberOfReceivedValues equals numberOfInputs, then the node is read to produce an output value.

- `result` keeps the result of the node. This variable acts as a cache and it is useful to propagate the result of an evaluation to the connected nodes.

15.3 Different Kinds of Nodes

A neural network is composed of nodes. Each node, representing a neuron, may be an input node, an output node, or an hidden node. It is important to make the distinction between these kinds of nodes. We use the `kind` variable for that purpose. The variable may hold one of the following values: #input, #hidden, or #output.

We define `setAsInput` to set a node as an input node:

```
NENode>>setAsInput
        "Set the node as input"
        kind := #input
```

The `setAsOutput` method sets a node as output:

```
NENode>>setAsOutput
        "Set the node as output"
        kind := #output
```

Similarly, a hidden node is defined using `setAsHidden`:

```
NENode>>setAsHidden
        "Set the node as hidden, which means it is placed in the
            network between the input and output"
        kind := #hidden
```

The value of the `kind` variable may be checked using some testing methods. The `isInput` method returns `true` if the node is an input node:

```
NENode>>isInput
        "Return true if the node is an input node"
        ^ kind == #input
```

The isOutput method returns true if the node is an output node:

```
NENode>>isOutput
        "Return true if the node is an output node"
        ^ kind == #output
```

The kind method returns the kind of node:

```
NENode>>kind
            "Return the kind of node"
            ^ kind
```

The kind method is relevant to copying a node, as we will soon see. The kind: method assigns a value to the corresponding variable:

```
NENode>>kind: aSymbol
        "The argument aSymbol should be #input, #output, or #hidden"
        kind := aSymbol
```

Each node has a numerical identifier, which is kept in the variable id. This identifier corresponds to the index of the node in an individual.

```
NENode>>id
            "Return the numerical identifier of the node"
            ^ id
```

As we will later see, the bias node's identifier is always equal to 1. Similarly, the node identifier may be set using the following:

```
NENode>>id: anInteger
        "Set the node identifier, useful when an individual structure
                is modified"
        id := anInteger
```

To form a neural network, each input or hidden node may be connected to a number of other nodes. Establishing the connections will ordered by the NEIndividual class, when the network has to be built up. The connectionsCache variable will keep the connections within an appropriate data structure.

A connection between two nodes is set using the connect:weight: method, defined as follows:

```
NENode>>connect: anotherNode weight: aWeight
        "Establish a connection between two nodes (the receiver and
            the argument)
          The method is executed by NEIndividual>>buildNetwork"
        connectionsCache add: aWeight -> anotherNode
```

The list of the connected nodes may be obtained for a given node:

```
NENode>>connectedNodes
        "Return the nodes that are connected to the node receiver"
        ^ connectionsCache collect: #value as: Array
```

The weight between two connected nodes may be obtained using this method:

```
NENode>>weightOfConnectionWith: anotherNode
        "Return the weight of the connection with another node"
        ^ (connectionsCache detect: [ :assoc | assoc value == anotherNode
            ]) key
```

The weightOfConnectionWith: method is not essential to the logic of
NEAT. However, it will be used in the visualization by mapping a connection weight to a line width, as we will later see.

With the NEAT algorithm, the individuals on which the genetic operations are applied should not be modified. Instead, new individuals are produced, leaving the original ones intact. To obtained this preservation, it is central to be able to copy individuals. As a consequence, we should be able to copy a node. We define the copy method for this purpose:

```
NENode>>copy
        "Return a copy of the node"
        | newNode |
        newNode := NENode new.
        newNode id: self id.
        newNode kind: self kind.
        newNode innovationNumber: self innovationNumber.
        ^ newNode
```

During the evaluation of a neural network, values flow in a node. We define the evaluate: method to make values flow in. The evaluate: method on a node will be called when a network is being evaluated:

```
NENode>>evaluate: aValue
        "Provide an input value to the node and contribute to the
                intermediate zValue"

        "We just received a value. We add it to zValue."
        zValue := zValue + aValue.

        "We say we received a new value"
        numberOfReceivedValues := numberOfReceivedValues + 1.

        "If we received an adequate number of zValues,
          then we can compute the sigmoid and keep it."
        numberOfReceivedValues = numberOfInputs ifFalse: [ ^ self ].
        result := self isInput ifTrue: [ zValue ] ifFalse: [ self
        sigmoid: zValue ].

        "We go here only if not output"
        connectionsCache do: [ :assoc | assoc value evaluate: result *
                assoc key ]
```

NEAT favors an incremental process for building neural networks. During the evolution, networks get more complex in each generation. As such, new connections to hidden and outputs nodes are typically made. We therefore need a way to increase the number of inputs a node may take. We simply define the increaseNumberOfInputs method for that very purpose:

```
NENode>>increaseNumberOfInputs
        "Increase the number of input values the node accepts"
        numberOfInputs := numberOfInputs + 1
```

One purpose of the NEAT algorithm is to keep track of the individuals' histories. This is at the very root of the algorithm: by efficiently keeping track of the individual's history, individuals with a common history are likely to be structurally similar.

The global population is divided into species based on similarities between individuals. The innovation number is accessible from a node using the following:

```
NENode>>innovationNumber
        "Return the innovation number, the historical marker, an integer"
        ^ innovationNumber
```

The innovation number is set using the following:

```
NENode>>innovationNumber: anInteger
        "Set the node innovation number"
        innovationNumber := anInteger
```

When we visualize a neural network, we paint the bias node with a different color. We therefore need a way to discriminate among nodes:

```
NENode>>isBias
        "Return true if the node is the bias node,
           i.e., if its ID equals 1"
        ^ self isInput and: [ id = 1 ]
```

The number of inputs of a node is accessible using the following:

```
NENode>>numberOfInputs
        "Return the number of inputs the node accepts"
        ^ numberOfInputs
```

It is relevant to obtain a textual representation of a node. This is useful when visualizing the network. We define the printOn: method for that purpose:

```
NENode>>printOn: stream
        "Return a textual representation of a node. For example, a
               node may be printed
               a NENode<3,1,input>
           or
               a NENode<5,205167,hidden>
        The values 3 and 5 are the node id. 1 and 205167 are
               innovation number.
        The third component indicates the kind of node
        "
```

```
super printOn: stream.
stream nextPut: $<.
id ifNotNil: [ stream nextPutAll: id asString ].
stream nextPut: $,.
innovationNumber ifNotNil: [ stream nextPutAll: innovationNumber
    asString ].
stream nextPut: $,.
kind ifNotNil: [ stream nextPutAll: kind asString ].
stream nextPut: $>.
```

When an individual is modified by a genetic operation, the network associated with the individual needs to be invalidated. We therefore provide the resetConnections method, which removes all connections between the network nodes:

NENode>>resetConnections

```
"Remove connections associated with a node"
connectionsCache := OrderedCollection new.
zValue := 0.
numberOfInputs := 0.
numberOfReceivedValues := 0.
result := 0.
self isInput ifTrue: [ numberOfInputs := 1 ]
```

In our implementation of NEAT, each node evaluates its weighted inputs using the sigmoid activation function. We therefore define the sigmoid: function as follows:

NENode>>sigmoid: z

```
"Apply the sigmoid function to the argument"
^ 1 / (1 + z negated exp)
```

The result of the evaluation is kept in the result variable. We define an accessor for it:

NENode>>result

```
"Return the computed result"
^ result
```

As we will later see, the `result` method is executed to obtained the output values from a neural network evaluation. This last method concludes the definition of a node.

15.4 Connections

As we have seen, a neural network is an acyclic graph. Nodes need to be connected and each connection has a weight. In addition, NEAT encodes an activation state (a boolean value) and an innovation number. We define the following class:

```
Object subclass: #NEConnection
        instanceVariableNames: 'in out weight enabled innovationNumber'
        classVariableNames: ''
        package: 'NEAT'
```

The `NEConnection` class has the following variables:

- An individual, as we will later see, defines an ordered collection of nodes. The `in` variable represents the index of the node in the individual to be used as input. Values accepted by `in` are therefore positive integers.

- Similarly, `out` represents the index of the the node used as output.

- `weight` is the weight of the connection. This is typically a small positive or negative float value.

- `enabled` is a boolean flag indicating whether the connection is active or not.

- `innovationNumber` is the historical marker used by NEAT. The value of this variable is a positive integer.

  ```
  NEConnection>>in
          "Return the index of the input node in the individual"
          ^ in
  ```

The setter method of the input node is as follows:

```
NEConnection>>in: anInteger
        "Set the in node index"
        in := anInteger
```

Similar to the in method, the out method returns the index of the output node:

```
NEConnection>>out
        "Return the index of the output node in the individual"
        ^ out
```

The value for out is set using its corresponding method:

```
NEConnection>>out: anInteger
        "Set the out node index"
        out := anInteger
```

When a connection is created, it receives a historical maker (innovation number), which is set using the following:

```
NEConnection>>innovationNumber: anInteger
        "Set the innovation number"
        innovationNumber := anInteger
```

The innovation number is obtained using the following:

```
NEConnection>>innovationNumber
        "Return the historical marker of the connection, the innovation
                number"
        ^ innovationNumber
```

A connection may be enabled or disabled. A disable connection does not let the values flow. A connection is enabled using the following:

```
NEConnection>>makeEnabled
        "Enable the connection"
        enabled := true
```

A connection is disabled using the following:

```
NEConnection>>makeDisabled
        "Disable the connection"
        enabled := false
```

Only enabled connections are considered when the neural network is built. As such, a check method is necessary, as follows:

```
NEConnection>>isEnabled
        "Return true if the connection is enabled"
        ^ enabled
```

Connections let values flow through nodes. As we saw in the first part of the book, values are weighted when transmitted to nodes. The weight of a connection is set using the following:

```
NEConnection>>weight: aNumber
        "Set the weight for the connection"
        weight := aNumber
```

Conversely, the weight is obtained using the following:

```
NEConnection>>weight
        "Return the weight of the connection"
        ^ weight
```

15.5 The Individual Class

In NEAT, an individual is significantly more complex than in the standard genetic algorithm, as we have seen. In NEAT, an individual is not a simple, linear sequence of gene values. Instead, it is a complex abstraction. We define the NEIndividual class as follows:

```
Object subclass: #NEIndividual
        instanceVariableNames: 'nodes connections random fitness species'
        classVariableNames: ''
        package: 'NEAT'
```

We summarize its variables as follows:

- nodes is a collection of NENode objects. The collection is an instance of OrderedCollection. The nodes variable contains the neurons that are used to build a neural network.

- connections is a collection of NEConnection objects. These connections are used when the network has to be built.

- random is a random number generator that is used by the genetic operators.

- fitness is the fitness value of the individual. This value is computed during the population generation, as we will later see.

- species refers to the species to which the individual belongs.

The initialization of an individual is performed as follows:

```
NEIndividual>>initialize
        super initialize.
        nodes := OrderedCollection new.
        connections := OrderedCollection new.

        "This first node is the bias node"
        self addInputNode
```

Nodes may be added to an individual. We define the corresponding addNode: method as follows:

```
NEIndividual>>addNode: aNode
        "Add a node to the individual. Note that the connections must
                be invalided and are therefore reset."
        self resetNetwork.
        nodes add: aNode.
        aNode id: nodes size.
        ^ aNode
```

A hidden node is added using the following:

```
NEIndividual>>addHiddenNode
        "Add a hidden node"
        ^ self addNode: (NENode new setAsHidden)
```

An input node is added using the following:

```
NEIndividual>>addInputNode
        "Add an input node"
        self addNode: (NENode new setAsInput; innovationNumber: 1).
```

An output node is added as follows:

```
NEIndividual>>addOutputNode
        "Add an output node"
        self addNode: (NENode new setAsOutput; innovationNumber: 1).
```

Nodes must be accessible from an individual. We define the method as follows:

```
NEIndividual>>nodes
        "Return the nodes contained by the individual"
        ^ nodes
```

Nodes may be set, in particular when an individual is copied, as follows:

```
NEIndividual>>nodes: someNodes
        "Set the nodes"
        nodes := someNodes
```

The input nodes must be accessible from an individual as we will shortly see. We define the method as follows:

```
NEIndividual>>inputNodes
        "Return the input nodes"
        ^ nodes select: #isInput
```

Similarly, the output nodes are accessible using the following:

```
NEIndividual>>outputNodes
        "Return the output nodes"
        ^ nodes select: #isOutput
```

The number of input nodes is relevant to determine that the represented network is correctly built and determine when we visualize a neural network. We define the method as follows:

```
NEIndividual>>numberOfInputs
        "We substrate one for the bias"
        ^ self inputNodes size - 1
```

The total number of nodes may be obtained using this method:

```
NEIndividual>>numberOfNodesWithBias
        "Return the total number of nodes contained in the individual"
        ^ self nodes size
```

A connection is added using the following:

```
NEIndividual>>addConnection: aConnection
        "Add a connection to the individual"
        connections add: aConnection.
        self resetNetwork.
```

Similar to node addition, when we add a connection, the represented network and its associated caches must be reset and invalidated.

Each individual unambiguously refers to a neural network. This network is built using the following method:

```
NEIndividual>>buildNetwork
        "Build the neural network represented by the individual"
        self resetNetwork.
         (connections select: #isEnabled) do: [ :c |
                (nodes at: c in) connect: (nodes at: c out) weight: c
                weight.
                (nodes at: c out) increaseNumberOfInputs ]
```

The buildNetwork method first invalidates the network. Afterward, enabled connection objects are used to establish the connections between the nodes. For each connection between a node in and a node out, the number of inputs of out is increased.

```
NEIndividual>>computeFitness: oneArgBlock
        "Compute the fitness of an individual"
        "If already computed, then there is nothing to do"
        fitness ifNotNil: [ ^ self ].
        fitness := oneArgBlock value: self.
```

The fitness function is defined as a block with one argument. If the fitness has already been computed, then there is nothing to do.

The list of connections is available using the following:

```
NEIndividual>>connections
        "Return the list of connections"
        ^ connections
```

This list is necessary to compute the innovation number by the genetic operators. During the crossover, a new set of connections is determined, and it has to be set to a new individual. We therefore define this method:

```
NEIndividual>>connections: someConnections
        "Set some connections.
         This method is used when performing the crossover."
        connections := someConnections
```

An individual is copied using the following:

```
NEIndividual>>copy
        "Return a copy of the individual"
        | newInd |
        newInd := NEIndividual new.
        newInd random: self random.
        newInd nodes: (self nodes collect: #copy).
        newInd connections: (self connections collect: #copy).
        ^ newInd
```

The fitness will be set by the NEAT logic, so we define the following method:

```
NEIndividual>>fitness: aFitnessValue
        "Set the fitness value, useful when copying an individual"
        fitness := aFitnessValue
```

The neural network associated with an individual may be evaluated using the evaluate: method, which is defined as follows:

```
NEIndividual>>evaluate: anArray
        "Evaluate the network using some input values.
         The method returns the resulting outputs of the network"
```

```
    self assert: [ anArray size = self numberOfInputs ] description: '
        Wrong number of arguments'.

    self buildNetwork.

    "We provide 1 to the first node, which is considered the
            bias node"
    self inputNodes with: #(1), anArray do: [ :n :aValue | n evaluate:
        aValue ].
    ^ self outputNodes collect: [ :n | n result ] as: Array
```

The evaluate: method first checks whether the number of provided values corresponds with the number of input nodes. Since this is a common error when evaluating an individual, we provide an assertion to catch the error early.

After it's computed, the fitness of an individual may be returned using the following:

NEIndividual>>fitness

```
        "Return the fitness of the individual"
        self assert: [ fitness notNil ] description: 'Need to compute
            fitness first'.
        ^ fitness
```

Each connection has an innovation number. The sequence of innovation numbers may be used to determine the similarities between individuals. Later on, we will cover the way we define and identify species within a population. In the meantime, we need to obtain the sequence of innovation numbers in the same order as the connections. We define the following method:

NEIndividual>>innovationNumberSequence

```
        "Return the list of innovation number"
        self connections ifEmpty: [ ^ #(0) ].
        ^ self connections collect: #innovationNumber as: Array
```

At the beginning of the NEAT algorithm, individuals are created without any connections. NEAT evolves the simplest form of individuals, which are individuals with no connections and no hidden nodes. Although these extremely simple individuals have no connection, they still need to belong to a species. As such, if there is no connection, the innovation number sequence is simply #(0). The speciation algorithm will use this innovation number sequence.

When performing the crossover operation, it is important to know the number of connections an individual has:

```
NEIndividual>>numberOfConnections
        "Return the number of connections"
        ^ connections size
```

In the first part of the book, we defined the `predict:` method on the class describing a neural network. We will now define the same method on the `NEIndividual` class:

```
NEIndividual>>predict: inputs
        "Make a prediction. This method assumes that the number of
                outputs is the same as the number of different values
                the network can output"
        | outputs |
        outputs := self evaluate: inputs.
        "The index of a collection begins at 1 in Pharo"
        ^ (outputs indexOf: (outputs max)) - 1
```

The `predict:` method is used to make prediction for a given set of input values, exactly the same way as when we discussed neural networks.

An individual has a random number generator, which is used when genetic operations have to be performed. This generator is provided by the NEAT algorithm itself, as we will later see. The random is set using the following:

```
NEIndividual>>random: aRandomNumberGenerator
        "Set the random number used by the genetic operations"
        random := aRandomNumberGenerator
```

The random number is accessed using the following:

```
NEIndividual>>random
        "Return the random number used by the genetic operations"
        ^ random
```

When a genetic operation is applied to an individual, the fitness has to be invalidated. We define this method:

```
NEIndividual>>resetFitness
        "Invalidated the fitness"
        fitness := nil
```

If the structure of an individual is modified, the network has to be reset. We define this method:

```
NEIndividual>>resetNetwork
        "Reset the network, which invalidates the network and the
            fitness value"
        nodes do: #resetConnections
```

The resetNetwork method is called by addConnection:, addNode:, and buildNetwork.

Each individual belongs to a species. The association between individuals and species is made by a dedicated class, NESpeciation, which we will later see. An individual must be able to return the species it belongs to, which is what this method does:

```
NEIndividual>>species
        "Return the species to which the individual belongs"
        ^ species
```

The species may be set using the following:

```
NEIndividual>>species: aSpecies
        species := aSpecies
```

This last method concludes the definition of the NEIndividual class. We are halfway through the implementation of the NEAT algorithm.

15.6 Species

We now need to define what exactly a species is. In our implementation, a species is simply a group of individuals. The species has a numerical identifier, which is used to keep track of the evolution of the species.

We define the NESpecies class as follows:

```
Object subclass: #NESpecies
        instanceVariableNames: 'individuals id'
        classVariableNames: ''
        package: 'NEAT'
```

The class has two instance variables:

- `individuals` is a collection of individuals. These individuals are a fraction of the whole population. In NEAT and the standard genetic algorithm, the size of the population is fixed. A species therefore corresponds to part of the population. An individual belongs to only one species, which means that all the species are disjoint.

- `id` is a numerical identifier. As we saw with `NESpeciation>>process:`, this identifier is simply the innovation number used to discriminate individuals.

The identifier may be obtained from the following:

```
NESpecies>>id
        "Return the identifier of the species"
        ^ id
```

The species identifier is set by the `process:` method, as described earlier. The corresponding method is:

```
NESpecies>>id: anInteger
        "Set the species identifier"
        id := anInteger
```

The individuals of a species are accessed using the following:

```
NESpecies>>individuals
        "Return the individuals composing the species"
        ^ individuals
```

The species may be initialized with some individuals by the speciation object:

```
NESpecies>>individuals: someIndividuals
        "Set the individuals of the species"
        individuals := someIndividuals
```

It is important to have some metrics to characterize a particular species and compare species. We define three simple metrics—the average fitness, the maximum fitness, and the number of individuals.

The average fitness is given using the following:

```
NESpecies>>averageFitness
        "Return the average fitness of the species"
        ^ (self individuals collect: #fitness) average
```

The maximum (and therefore best) fitness of a species is given by this method:

```
NESpecies>>maxFitness
        "Return the max fitness of the species individuals"
        ^ (self individuals collect: #fitness) max
```

The number of individuals composing a species is accessed using this method:

```
NESpecies>>numberOfIndividuals
          "Return the size of the species"
          ^ individuals size
```

This last method concludes the definition of the species, and therefore completes the whole speciation mechanism of our implementation.

15.7 Speciation

So far, we have defined individuals, nodes, connections, and species. We define the notion of *speciation* as the action of dividing the population and groups of similar individuals into species. A species is made of individuals that are structurally similar. This is where the innovation number comes into place: if two individuals have two similar sequence of innovation numbers, then we conclude they are structurally similar.

Earlier we defined the innovationNumberSequence method, which returns the innovation number for all the individual's connections. We illustrate how our speciation algorithm operates. Consider three individuals—i1, i2, and i3—and their expressions:

- i1 innovationNumberSequence returns #(1 2 4 6),

- i2 innovationNumberSequence returns #(1 2 4 7),

- i3 innovationNumberSequence returns #(1 2 4 6 8 9)

Our algorithm will consider the earliest historical marker within a frame of size k. If we have k = 2, then the kth values before the end of individuals are: 4 for i1, 4 for i2, and 8 for i3. Given these three individuals and the value k = 2, we have two species. - i1 and i2 are the same species, while - i3 is a different species.

Note that the window frame size is a new hyperparameter that we need to consider when tuning the NEAT algorithm. We can now define the speciation algorithm with the NESpeciation class. The class is defined as follows:

```
Object subclass: #NESpeciation
        instanceVariableNames: 'frameSize groups'
        classVariableNames: ''
        package: 'NEAT'
```

The class defines two variables:

- frameSize is an integer representing the size of the window frame to pick the relevant innovation number.

- groups is a collection of instances of the NESpecies class. As we will see, the NESpecies class is a group of individuals.

Per the default, we pick a frame size of 3:

```
NESpeciation>>initialize
        super initialize.
        frameSize := 3.
```

The window frame size may be set using this method:

```
NESpeciation>>frameSize: anInteger
        "Set the window frame size hyperparameter"
        frameSize := anInteger
```

The process: method contains the algorithm used in the speciation. It implements the strategy just described and is defined as follows:

```
NESpeciation>>process: someIndividuals
        "Run the speciation algorithm for a given collection of
              individuals.
```

```
This method takes as an argument a collection of
        innovation numbers"
| g |
g := someIndividuals groupedBy: [ :individual |
        | seq |
        seq := individual innovationNumberSequence.
        seq size < 2
                ifTrue: [ seq first ]
                ifFalse: [ (seq last: (frameSize min:
                seq size - 1)) first
                        ] ].
```

```
"Bind each species to its corresponding individuals"
groups := g associations collect: [ :assoc | NESpecies new
        individuals: assoc value; id: assoc key ].
groups do: [ :aSpecies |
        aSpecies individuals do: [ :i | i species: aSpecies ] ]
```

The process: method initializes the groups variable with a collection of NESpecies objects. The groups are obtained using the following:

```
NESpeciation>>groups
        "Return the groups of species. Each group being an instance
            of NESpecies"
        ^ groups
```

Each speciation results in a number of species, which varies during evolution. Accessing the number of produced species is a good metric to track. Consider this method:

```
NESpeciation>>numberOfSpecies
        "Return the number of species produced by the speciation"
        ^ groups size
```

The end of this chapter covers the visualization of the evolution and we will use this metric.

15.8 The Crossover Operation

Due to the complex representation of individuals, NEAT employs a dedicated set of genetic operations. This section covers the crossover. The crossover operation is performed *between individuals that belong to the same species*. This is an important aspect of NEAT. We define the NECrossoverOperation class as follows:

```
Object subclass: #NECrossoverOperation
        instanceVariableNames: ''
        classVariableNames: ''
        package: 'NEAT'
```

The original publication about NEAT very informally describes the crossover operation. To keep this implementation simple, short, and easy to explain, we propose a crossover that deviates slightly from the original definition of the crossover.

The crossover algorithm we consider may be described as follows. Assume two individuals, i1 and i2. i1 has a better fitness level than i2. If i1 or i2 have no connection, which is likely to happen in a very early generation, then the child individual has the node of i1 and no connections. This seems to be a rather arbitrary decision, but in fact, it shows a conservative decision by preserving the genetic information from the fittest individual.

If i1 or i2 have at least one connection, then we iterate along the common sequence of historical markers. As mentioned earlier, individuals within the same species have a common sequence of markers. The children have connections that are randomly picked from either i1 or i2. Once we iterated over the common markers, we complete the connections for the child with the remainder connections of i1, which are the best individuals.

As we said, this algorithm is a simplified version of the original description of NEAT. Although it's simplified, it performs a good job.

We define the performOn:and: method as follows:

```
NECrossoverOperation>>performOn: i1 and: i2
            "Return a child individual that is the result of a crossover
                between individuals i1 and i2"
            "The method ASSUMES that the fitness of i1 is higher than
                the one of i2"
```

```
| newConnections indexI1 indexI2 shouldIterate newNodes |
"newNodes are the nodes of the child individual.
 It is simply a copy of the nodes of the best individual, i1."
newNodes := i1 nodes collect: #copy.

"newConnections are the connections of the child individual"
newConnections := OrderedCollection new.

"If any individuals has no connection, then we create a new
    individual with no connection"
(i1 connections notEmpty and: [ i2 connections notEmpty ])
    ifFalse: [ ^ NEIndividual new nodes: newNodes; connections:
        newConnections; random: i1 random ].

"We initialize some temporary variables"
indexI1 := 1.
indexI2 := 1.
shouldIterate := true.

"The iteration loop"
 [ shouldIterate ] whileTrue: [
        | c1 c2 |
        indexI1 := indexI1 min: i1 numberOfConnections.
        indexI2 := indexI2 min: i2 numberOfConnections.
        c1 := i1 connections at: indexI1.
        c2 := i2 connections at: indexI2.
        c1 innovationNumber = c2 innovationNumber
            ifTrue: [
                newConnections add: (i1 random next > 0.5
                ifTrue: [ c1
                        ] ifFalse: [ c2 ]) copy.
                indexI1 := indexI1 + 1.
                indexI2 := indexI2 + 1. ]
            ifFalse: [ shouldIterate := false ].
```

```
        (indexI1 >= i1 numberOfConnections and: [ indexI2 >= i2
            numberOfConnections ])
            ifTrue: [ shouldIterate := false ]
    ].
    "We consider the remainder connection from the best individual"
    newConnections addAll: ((i1 connections allButFirst: indexI1 - 1)
        collect: #copy).

    "A new individual is returned"
    ^ NEIndividual new nodes: newNodes; connections: newConnections;
        random: i1 random
```

Different variants of the crossover may be envisaged, and our implementation of NEAT may be easily extended with new ways to perform the crossover.

15.9 Abstract Definition of Mutation

Since several mutation operations will be implemented, we will define a class hierarchy in which the superclass will define the functionalities used by the subclasses.

The NEAbstractMutationOperation class is defined as follows:

```
Object subclass: #NEAbstractMutationOperation
        instanceVariableNames: 'random'
        classVariableNames: ''
        package: 'NEAT'
```

Mutation operations require generating random number. The NEAbstractMutationOperation class defines the random variable. The random number is set using the following method:

```
NEAbstractMutationOperation>>random: aRandomNumberGenerator
        random := aRandomNumberGenerator
```

We define the randomWeight method as a utility method that returns a random value that can be used as a connection weight. We define the method as follows:

```
NEAbstractMutationOperation>>randomWeight
        "Return a random number within -5 and 5"
        ^ random next * 10 - 5
```

The main entry method of a mutation operation is performOn:, defined as follows:

```
NEAbstractMutationOperation>>performOn: anIndividual
        "Public method that performs a mutation on the argument
        the method modifies an Individual"
        random := anIndividual random.
        anIndividual resetFitness.
        self on: anIndividual
```

The performOn: method takes an individual as an argument and modifies it. Before we call this method, it is important to make a copy of the individual. This is because, when building a new population, individuals should not be modified. The method invokes the on: method. The NEAbstractMutationOperation>>on: method is abstract, meaning that it must be overridden in subclasses. It is defined as follows:

```
NEAbstractMutationOperation>>on: anIndividual
        "Override this method to perform the mutation"
        self subclassResponsibility
```

15.10 Structural Mutation Operations

Our implementation of NEAT supports two mutation operations that modify the structure of an individual:

- NEAddConnectionMutationOperation adds a connection between two nodes.

- NEAddNodeMutationOperation adds a hidden node.

These two operations need to access a global counter, the innovation number. We define the NEAbstractStructuralMutationOperation class as follows:

```
NEAbstractMutationOperation subclass: #
        NEAbstractStructuralMutationOperation
        instanceVariableNames: ''
        classVariableNames: 'InnovationNumber'
        package: 'NEAT'
```

The NEAbstractStructuralMutationOperation class defines the class variable InnovationNumber. This variable is shared among all subclasses. Each time the operation is applied, the innovation number is increased by one. We therefore override the performOn: method as follows:

```
NEAbstractStructuralMutationOperation>>performOn: anIndividual
        InnovationNumber isNil ifTrue: [ InnovationNumber := 1 ].
        InnovationNumber := InnovationNumber + 1.
        super performOn: anIndividual.
```

The InnovationNumber variable is lazily initialized: it is set to 1 the first time performOn: is executed.

15.10.1 Adding a Connection

The NEAddConnectionMutationOperation class is defined as follows:

```
NEAbstractStructuralMutationOperation subclass: #
        NEAddConnectionMutationOperation
            instanceVariableNames: ''
            classVariableNames: ''
            package: 'NEAT'
```

The on: method is overridden to provide the behavior of adding a connection:

```
NEAddConnectionMutationOperation>>on: anIndividual
        "Add a connection between two nodes to an individual"
        | array |

        "Find two nodes in which we can add a connection. No more
         than 5 tries are made"
        array := self findMissingConnectionIn: anIndividual nbTry: 5.

        "We did not find a solution, so we merely exit. There is not
            much we can do"
        array ifNil: [ ^ self ].

        "Else, we add the connection"
        anIndividual
```

```
addConnection:
        (NEConnection new
                in: array first;
                out: array second;
                weight: self randomWeight;
                makeEnabled;
                innovationNumber: InnovationNumber)
```

The added connection has a random weight, it is enabled, and it has an innovation number. The `array` variable is the reference of two nodes, for which we can safely add a connection going from `arrayfirst` to `arraysecond`. By "safely," we mean that the connection does not add a cycle within the individual and there is no existing connection.

The `findMissingConnectionIn:nbTry:` method returns the nodes for which a connection may be added. The method is rather complex. It takes as an argument an individual and the number of tries the algorithm can do before giving up. It is defined as follows:

```
NEAddConnectionMutationOperation>>findMissingConnectionIn: anIndividual
        nbTry: nbTry
        "Return an array containing two nodes.
         Only a finite number of tries are made to find those nodes."
        | node1 node2 |
        "If we made our tries, then we return nil meaning that no
            connections can be made"
        nbTry = 0 ifTrue: [ ^ nil ].

        "The connection goes from node1 to node2. node1 cannot be
                an output node therefore"
        node1 := (anIndividual nodes reject: #isOutput) atRandom: random.

        "Similarly, node2 cannot be an input node."
        node2 := (anIndividual nodes reject: #isInput) atRandom: random.

        "Is there already a connection from node1 to node2?"
        (anIndividual connections anySatisfy: [ :c |
                (c in = node1 id and: [ c out = node2 id ]) ]) ifTrue: [
```

```
                    "If yes, then we iterate once more"
                    ^ self findMissingConnectionIn: anIndividual
                    nbTry: (nbTry - 1) ].

        "We check if there is no path going from node2 to node1.
          Adding a connection should not introduce a cycle"
        (self is: node1 accessibleFrom: node2 in: anIndividual)
                ifTrue: [ ^ self findMissingConnectionIn: anIndividual
                nbTry: (nbTry - 1) ].

        ^ { node1 id . node2 id }
```

If no connection is found when `nbTry` = 0, then it returns `nil`, leading to the mutation operator having no effect. The `is:accessibleFrom:in:` method verifies whether there is an existing path going from `node2` to `node1`. In such a case, adding a path going from `node1` to `node2` will introduce a cycle. We therefore forbid this. The result of the method is two node identifiers.

```
NEAddConnectionMutationOperation>>is: node1 accessibleFrom: node2 in:
        anIndividual
        "Is there a path going from node2 to node1?"
        anIndividual buildNetwork.
        ^ self privateIs: node1 accessibleFrom: node2
```

We use the following utility method to perform the recursion:

```
NEAddConnectionMutationOperation>>privateIs: node1 accessibleFrom:
        node2
        "Recursively look for a path from node2 to node1"
        node1 == node2 ifTrue: [ ^ true ].
        node2 connectedNodes do: [ :n |
                node1 == n ifTrue: [ ^ true ].
                (self privateIs: node1 accessibleFrom: n) ifTrue: [ ^ true ] ].
        ^ false
```

15.10.2 Adding a Node

The mutation operation that adds a node is defined with the NEAddNodeMutationOperation class:

```
NEAbstractStructuralMutationOperation subclass: #
        NEAddNodeMutationOperation
        instanceVariableNames: ''
        classVariableNames: ''
        package: 'NEAT'
```

The on: method defines the behavior of this mutation operation:

```
NEAddNodeMutationOperation>>on: anIndividual
        "Add a hidden node and two connections in the individual"
        | relevantConnections c |
        relevantConnections := anIndividual connections select: #isEnabled.
        relevantConnections ifEmpty: [ ^self ].

        "We pick a random connection and disable it"
        c := relevantConnections atRandom: anIndividual random.
        c makeDisabled.

        "We add a hidden node ..."
        anIndividual addHiddenNode innovationNumber: InnovationNumber.

        "... and two connections"
        anIndividual addConnection:
                (NEConnection new in: c in; out: anIndividual
                        numberOfNodesWithBias; weight: 1; makeEnabled;
                        innovationNumber: InnovationNumber).
        anIndividual addConnection:
                (NEConnection new in: anIndividual
                numberOfNodesWithBias; out:
                        c out; weight: c weight; makeEnabled;
                        innovationNumber:
                        InnovationNumber).
```

This last method concludes the definition of the operations that modify the individual structure.

15.11 Non-Structural Mutation Operation

We define the empty class NEAbstractNonStructuralMutationOperation as follows:

```
NEAbstractMutationOperation subclass: #
        NEAbstractNonStructuralMutationOperation
        instanceVariableNames: ''
        classVariableNames: ''
        package: 'NEAT'
```

The mutation operation that consists of modifying a connection weight is defined with NEConnectionWeightMutationOperation:

```
NEAbstractNonStructuralMutationOperation subclass: #
        NEConnectionWeightMutationOperation
        instanceVariableNames: ''
        classVariableNames: ''
        package: 'NEAT'
```

The core of the mutation is defined as follows:

```
NEConnectionWeightMutationOperation>>on: anIndividual
        "Modify the weight of a connection"
        | c |
        anIndividual connections ifEmpty: [ ^ self ].
        c := (anIndividual connections atRandom: random).
        c weight: self randomWeight + c weight
```

The on: method simply adds a random value to a connection weight. This operations close the genetic operation supported by our implementation of NEAT.

15.12 Logging

Being able to monitor the execution of the NEAT algorithm is an essential ability our implementation should support. Without it, we would not be able to measure whether we are converging toward a solution or not.

We will summarize the population at each generation in an instance of the NELog class. We define that class as follows:

```
Object subclass: #NELog
        instanceVariableNames: 'generation speciation minFitness maxFitness
            averageFitness bestIndividual'
        classVariableNames: ''
        package: 'NEAT'
```

NELog defines the following instance variables:

- generation is the number of the represented generation.

- speciation refers to the current speciation.

- minFitness is the minimum fitness of the population.

- maxFitness is the maximum fitness of the population.

- averageFitness is the average fitness of the population.

- bestIndividual refers to the best individual of the population.

There is one NELog object at each generation. Each log refers to the speciation object of the current generation. This is a useful way to analyze the generation at a fine grain. For example, we could monitor the evolution of each species along the algorithm execution.

The class has a number of accessor methods. The average population fitness is accessible using the following:

```
NELog>>averageFitness
        "Return the average population fitness"
        ^ averageFitness
```

The average fitness is set by the NEAT class, which we will present later. We define the method as follows:

```
NELog>>averageFitness: aNumber
        "Set the average population fitness"
        averageFitness := aNumber
```

The maximum fitness is accessible with the following:

```
NELog>>maxFitness
        "Return the maximum fitness"
        ^ maxFitness
```

The maximum fitness is set using the following:

```
NELog>>maxFitness: aNumber
        "Set the maximum fitness"
        maxFitness := aNumber
```

The minimum fitness is obtained using the following:

```
NELog>>minFitness
        "Return the minimum fitness"
        ^ minFitness
```

The minimum fitness is set using the following:

```
NELog>>minFitness: aNumber
        "Set the minimum fitness"
        minFitness := aNumber
```

The best individual of the population is accessed using the following:

```
NELog>>bestIndividual
        "Return the best individual of the population"
        ^ bestIndividual
```

The best individual is set using the following:

```
NELog>>bestIndividual: anIndividual
        "Set the best individual of the population"
        bestIndividual := anIndividual
```

The generation number is accessible using the following:

```
NELog>>generation
        "Return the generation number represented by the log"
        ^ generation
```

The generation number is set using the following:

```
NELog>>generation: anInteger
        "Set the generation number"
        generation := anInteger
```

The speciation is obtained from a log object using the following:

```
NELog>>speciation
        "Return the speciation of the generation represented by the log"
        ^ speciation
```

The speciation is set using the following:

```
NELog>>speciation: aSpeciation
        "Set the speciation"
        speciation := aSpeciation
```

The number of species in which the population is split may be accessed using the following:

```
NELog>>numberOfSpecies
        "Return the number of species in the speciation"
        speciation ifNil: [ ^ 0 ].
        ^ speciation numberOfSpecies
```

As we will see later, the number of species in a log is useful for visualizing the execution of the algorithm.

A log object refers to the speciation. Although convenient for looking at the algorithm execution, keeping a reference of the speciation could be very costly, especially with a large population over a large number of generations. The following method enables us to release the memory when necessary:

```
NELog>>release
        "Release the specification, and thus reduce the amount of
            consumed memory"
        speciation := nil.
        bestIndividual := nil
```

15.13 NEAT

We have defined all the relevant components of the NEAT algorithm. An essential step is to connect the different components. The NEAT class is the main entry point to use NEAT. We define the NEAT class as follows:

```
Object subclass: #NEAT
        instanceVariableNames: 'configuration populationSize population
            numberOfInputs numberOfOutputs logs fitness random speciation
            numberOfGenerations shouldUseElitism'
        classVariableNames: ''
        package: 'NEAT'
```

The NEAT class is long and contain many variables:

- configuration contains all the relevant information to configure the algorithm. In particular, it refers to a collection of a association following operation->probability, which represents the probability (a float between 0.0 and 1.0) of applying a genetic operation on an individual.

- populationSize represents the size of the population. As in a genetic algorithm, this size is constant over time.

- population is a collection of NEIndividual objects.

- numberOfInputs is the number of inputs each individual should have. This is a fixed constant, common to all individuals.

- numberOfOutputs is the number of outputs each individual has.

- logs is a collection of NELog, describing the execution of the algorithm.

- fitness is a one-argument block that computes the fitness. The block returns a numerical value for a provided individual.

- random is the random number used by the algorithm.

- speciation represents the current speciation. This variable points to a new speciation at each generation.

- `numberOfGenerations` is the maximum number of generations. This is the main mechanism to end the algorithm execution.

- `shouldUseElitism` is a boolean that determines whether we should use elitism or not. As explained later, elitism is a simple technique that ensures that the overall maximum fitness does not decrease over the generation.

The algorithm is initialized as follows:

```
NEAT>>initialize
        super initialize.
        self defaultConfiguration.

        "We have two inputs and one bias per default"
        numberOfInputs := 2.
        numberOfOutputs := 1.

        populationSize := 150.
        random := Random seed: 42.

        logs := OrderedCollection new.
        numberOfGenerations := 10.

        self doUseElitism
```

Per the default, the algorithm is tuned to produce individuals with two inputs and one output. The population size is 150, which is adequate in various situations. The algorithms ends after ten generations.

The NEAT class requires a number of method accessors to support the configuration and accessing information. The number of generations is set using the following:

```
NEAT>>numberOfGenerations: anInteger
        "Set the maximum number of generations to run before
                stopping the algorithm"
        numberOfGenerations := anInteger
```

The number of inputs each individual has is set using the following:

```
NEAT>>numberOfInputs: anInteger
        "Set the number of inputs each individual has"
        numberOfInputs := anInteger
```

The number of outputs is set using the following:

```
NEAT>>numberOfOutputs: anInteger
        "Set the number of outputs each individual has"
        numberOfOutputs := anInteger
```

The population size is set using the following:

```
NEAT>>populationSize: anInteger
        "Set the population size"
        populationSize := anInteger
```

The fitness function is set by providing a block accepting one argument, the individual for which the fitness is being computed:

```
NEAT>>fitness: aOneArgumentBlock
        "Set a one-argument block as the fitness function.
         The block must return a numerical value, higher the value,
                better the individual"
        fitness := aOneArgumentBlock
```

To keep our implementation of NEAT small, we only support one way to compare individuals: an individual is better than another if its fitness is higher. A high fitness therefore represents a good individual.

Elitism is a simple technique that consists of passing on the best element from the previous generation. When building a new population of size N, only N − 1 have to be created from the genetic operation since the best individual automatically survives through generations. One consequence of elitism is that we do not have decreasing maximum fitness values. Using Elitism, the fitness value can only go up or be constant. At a first glance, this is very appealing. However, it slightly reduces the possibility of creating a new individual, which could have been better than the best individual of the previous generation. In general, elitism gives very good results, which is the reason we enable it by default.

Elitism is enabled using the following:

```
NEAT>>doUseElitism
        "Use elitism when generating a new population"
        shouldUseElitism := true
```

Elitism can be disabled using the following:

```
NEAT>>doNotUseElitism
        "Do not use elitism when generating a new population"
        shouldUseElitism := false
```

In our implementation, a configuration is defined as a set of probabilities for each genetic operation. The configuration is reset using the following:

```
NEAT>>resetConfiguration
        "Reset the configuration of the algorithm"
        configuration := OrderedCollection new
```

The configuration variable contains all the parameters defining the configuration of the algorithm. It is a collection of associations, as we will shortly see. We define the defaultConfiguration method, invoked by the initialize method, as follows:

```
NEAT>>defaultConfiguration
        "Make the algorithm use a default configuration"
        self resetConfiguration.
        self for: NEConnectionWeightMutationOperation prob: 0.2.
        self for: NEAddConnectionMutationOperation prob: 0.2.
        self for: NEAddNodeMutationOperation prob: 0.01.
        self for: NECrossoverOperation prob: 0.2
```

So far, we defined four genetic operations. The defaultConfiguration method gives a probability for each of the operations. The value provided to the prob: keyword indicates the probability of an individual to be mutated or applied a crossover. As such, 20% of each generation (except the very first one) is made up of new individual obtained from crossover. These values are arbitrary and may be easily changed, using the following method:

```
NEAT>>for: anOperationClass prob: prob
        "Set the probability to apply a genetic operation"

        "Check if we have an existing configuration for the operation"
        configuration do: [ :assoc | (assoc key isKindOf:
        anOperationClass)
```

```
                                     ifTrue: [ assoc value: prob. ^ self ] ].

        "If no, then we simply add it"
        configuration add: anOperationClass new -> prob
```

The crossover between two individuals, ind1 and ind2, is performed using this method:

```
NEAT>>crossoverBetween: ind1 and: ind2
        "Perform a crossover between two individuals
         The method returns a new individual"

        ^ ind1 fitness > ind2 fitness
            ifTrue: [ NECrossoverOperation new performOn: ind1 and: ind2 ]
            ifFalse: [ NECrossoverOperation new performOn: ind2 and:
            ind1 ]
```

An individual is mutated using this method:

```
NEAT>>doMutate: individual
        "Perform a mutation on the individual.
         You provide a copy of an individual as an argument"
        configuration
            do: [ :cAssoc |
                (cAssoc key isKindOf: NEAbstractMutationOperation)
                ifTrue:
                    [
                    random next <= cAssoc value
                        ifTrue: [ cAssoc key random: random;
                        performOn:
                            individual ] ] ]
```

The doMutate: method takes an individual as an argument. This individual should be a copy of an existing individual since, when we're building a new generation, the previous generation must remain *unmodified*. The method simply performs the mutation as defined in defaultConfiguration or by the user with for:prob:.

We can now see the run method, which is used to run the NEAT algorithm. We define run as follows:

```
NEAT>>run
        "Run the algorithm"
        self buildInitialPopulation.
        self doSpeciation.
        self computeFitnesses.
        self doLog.
        self runFor: numberOfGenerations
```

The run method first builds the initial population. It then performs the speciation as seen earlier. The fitness is computed for each individual. A log is performed to describe the initial population. Iterations are then run using runFor:. We will sequentially explain each of these methods.

When starting the algorithm, the initial population is built before the evolution process. We define the buildInitialPopulation method, which initializes the very first population:

```
NEAT>>buildInitialPopulation
        "Randomly build the initial population"
        population := OrderedCollection new.
        populationSize timesRepeat: [
        | i |
        i := NEIndividual new.
        i random: random.
        numberOfInputs timesRepeat: [ i addInputNode ].
        numberOfOutputs timesRepeat: [ i addOutputNode ].
        population add: i ]
```

Each individual contained in population has some input and output nodes, which are preserved during the evolution. As we have seen, none of the genetic operations we defined modify them. The individuals are now ready to have their fitness computed. The fitness value for each individual is computed using computeFitnesses.

```
NEAT>>computeFitnesses
        "Compute the fitness value for each individual"
        population do: [ :i | i computeFitness: fitness ]
```

A log has to be created to describe the current generation. Logs created during the evolution process are kept in the logs variable. The doLog method creates a snapshot of the execution and is defined as follows:

```
NEAT>>doLog
        "Create a log object that summarizes the actual generation"
        | log |
        log := NELog new.
        log generation: logs size.
        log speciation: speciation.
        log minFitness: (population collect: #fitness) min.
        log maxFitness: (population collect: #fitness) max.
        log averageFitness: ((population collect: #fitness) average asFloat
                round: 3).
        log bestIndividual: self result.
        logs add: log.
```

The runFor: method executes the algorithm for a particular number of generations, which is provided as an argument:

```
NEAT>>runFor: nbOfGenerations
        "Run the algorithm for a given number of generations"
        'Running the NEAT algorithm'
        displayProgressFrom: 1 to: nbOfGenerations
        during: [:bar |
                1 to: nbOfGenerations do: [:x |
                bar value: x.
                self runOneGeneration. ] ].
```

The runFor: method uses a progress bar as a visual indicator to monitor the number of generations left to be run before obtaining a result. The NEAT algorithm is often time consuming, so having a progress bar is helpful.

The main logic of the algorithm is implemented in the runOneGeneration method. This method evolves a population into a new one:

```
NEAT>>runOneGeneration
        "Run the evolution algorithm for one generation"
        | newPopulation ind1 ind2 newInd numberOfIndividualToCreate |
        "Create the species"
        self doSpeciation.

        "We have an empty new population"
        newPopulation := OrderedCollection new.

        "The number of individual to create is populationSize, or
                populationSize - 1"
        numberOfIndividualToCreate :=
                (shouldUseElitism and: [ self currentGeneration > 1 ])
                                ifTrue: [
                                        eli best |
                                        best := self result.
                                        eli := best copy.
                                        eli fitness: best fitness.
                                        new Population add: eli.
                                        population Size - 1 ]
                                ifFalse: [ populationSize ].

        "The new population is built"
        numberOfIndividualToCreate
                timesRepeat: [
                        "Should we do a crossover or not?"
                        random next <= self crossoverRate
                                ifTrue: [
                                        s"If yes, two picked elements are combined"
                                        ind1 := self selectIndividual.
                                        ind2 := self selectIndividual: ind1 species
                                                        individuals.
                                        newInd := self crossoverBetween: ind1 and: ind2 ]
```

```
                        ifFalse: [
                                "If no, then we simply copy a selected
                                individual"
                                        newInd := self selectIndividual copy ].

        "We perform the mutation on the new individual"
        self doMutate: newInd.

        "Add it to the population"
        newPopulation add: newInd.

        "Compute its fitness value"
        newInd computeFitness: fitness ].

    "The old population is replaced by the new population"
    population := newPopulation.
    self doLog
```

The first step of runOneGeneration is to do the speciation of the population. This action helps perform a crossover between individuals since only individuals that belong to the same species can be combined. We define the doSpeciation method as follows:

NEAT>>doSpeciation

```
        "Perform the speciation algorithm"
        speciation := NESpeciation new.
        speciation process: population.
```

The crossover rate is obtained from the configuration variable:

NEAT>>crossoverRate

```
        "Return the crossover rate"
        | t |
        t := configuration detect: [ :assoc | assoc key isKindOf:
          NECrossoverOperation ] ifNone: [ ^ 0 ].
        ^ t value
```

The current generation is useful for checking whether we have passed the first generation or not in runOneGeneration. This is important since elitism cannot be done in the first generation. We can determine the current number of generations with the following:

```
NEAT>>currentGeneration
        "Return the current generation"
        ^ logs size
```

An individual can be selected from the population using the following:

```
NEAT>>selectIndividual
        "Select an individual from the population using the tournament
                selection algorithm"
        ^ self selectIndividual: population
```

The tournament selection algorithm is implemented in the selectIndividual: method, which is defined in NEAT. This method simply picks five individuals from the provided set of individuals and returns the one with the highest fitness value. The method is implemented as follows:

```
NEAT>>selectIndividual: someIndividuals
        "Use the tournament selection algorithm to pick the best
                individual "

        | i k winner |
        winner := someIndividuals atRandom: random.

        "We have already picked the winner, we need 4 more individuals"
        k := 4.
        k timesRepeat: [
            i := winner species individuals atRandom: random.
            winner fitness < i fitness ifTrue: [ winner := i ] ].

        "The winner of the tournament is returned"
        ^ winner
```

The NEAT algorithm may run for long period of times (e.g., minutes, hours, days, or even weeks). Being able to release unnecessary resources, such as memory, may be essential in some cases. We define the `releaseHistory` method, which helps reduce the amount of used memory:

```
NEAT>>releaseHistory
        "Release the memory kept in the historical logs"
        logs allButLast do: #release
```

This method may be invoked within the fitness block function. When doing so, the speciation of each log will be discarded, thus significantly reducing the memory consumption. When performing a non-trivial execution (as we will do with the platform game in the next chapter), it is important to monitor the memory consumption using a dedicated tool of the operating system. For example, on MacOS, the Activity Monitor system tool does an excellent job at estimating the memory consumed by Pharo.

Finally, the result of the algorithm may be obtained as the individual with the highest fitness value.

```
NEAT>>result
        "Return the result of the algorithm, i.e., the fittest neural
            network"
        | winner |
        winner := population first.
        population do: [ :i | winner fitness < i fitness ifTrue: [ winner
            := i ] ].
        ^ winner
```

The logic and structure of the NEAT algorithm is now complete, and it can be run. However, the implementation at this stage only produces a result, without telling us much about how the evolution went. So, there is one last step before seeing the first example, which is the visualization part.

15.14 Visualization

Being able to visualize the evolution of the execution is not essential to using it. However, it is a crucial source of relevant information that helps us decide whether one should stop or pursue the algorithm execution. As we did in some previous chapters, we will use

Roassal and GTInspector to visualize some objects. These two important tools are not described in this book. Instead, we recommend the reader search for additional sources of documentation (any web search engine will do a remarkable job).

Probably the most relevant piece of information to visualize are the fitness values. Understanding how the fitness has evolved over the generations is central to knowing whether the algorithm is converging toward what is expected to be a solution. We define the visualizeFitness method as follows:

```
NEAT>>visualizeFitness
        "Visualizing the max, min, and average fitness for each generation"
        | g d |
        g := RTGrapher new.

        "Min fitness"
        d := RTData new.
        d label: 'Minimum fitness'.
        d noDot; connectColor: Color red.
        d points: logs.
        d y: #minFitness.
        g add: d.

        "Max fitness"
        d := RTData new.
        d label: 'Maximum fitness'.
        d noDot; connectColor: Color blue.
        d points: logs.
        d y: #maxFitness.
        g add: d.

        "Average fitness"
        d := RTData new.
        d label: 'Average fitness'.
        d noDot; connectColor: Color green.
        d points: logs.
        d y: #averageFitness.
        g add: d.
```

```
g axisX noDecimal; title: 'Generation'.
g axisY title: 'Fitness'.
g legend addText: 'Fitness evolution'.
^ g
```

When visualizing the fitness, the red curves give the worst fitness (i.e., the smallest one) along the generation, the blue curves give the best fitness (i.e., the highest one), and the green curves represent the average fitness. The visualizeFitness method is hooked into the GTInspector framework using the following code:

```
NEAT>>gtInspectorViewIn: composite
        <gtInspectorPresentationOrder: -10>
        composite roassal2
                title: 'Fitness';
                initializeView: [ self visualizeFitness ]
```

By being hooked into GTInspector, one simply has to "inspect" the code to see its results in the Pharo playground tool.

Another great source of data is the evolution of species. For example, it helps to assess whether the population has enough diversity. Again, a diverse population has a better chance of converging toward a solution. But it should not be too diverse, because convergence is likely to slow down too much. The visualizeNumberOfSpecies method is defined as follows:

```
NEAT>>visualizeNumberOfSpecies
        "Visualize the evolution of the number of species"
        | g d |
        g := RTGrapher new.
        d := RTData new.
        d points: logs.
        d y: #numberOfSpecies.
        g add: d.
        g axisX title: 'Generation'; noDecimal.
        g axisY title: '# species'.
        ^ g
```

The method we just defined is hooked into the GTInspector as follows:

```
NEAT>>gtInspectorNumberOfSpeciesIn: composite
        <gtInspectorPresentationOrder: -10>
        composite roassal2
                title: '#Species';
                initializeView: [ self visualizeNumberOfSpecies ]
```

NEAT produces neural networks, and we need a way to visualize these networks. The speciation object has access to the whole population. Visualizing the speciation is therefore appealing in that respect. The species are visualized using the following method:

```
NESpeciation>>visualize
        "Visualize groups of individuals"
        | b legendBuilder |
        b := RTMondrian new.
        b shape box size: [ :s | s individuals size ].
        b nodes: (self groups reverseSortedAs: #maxFitness).
        b layout grid.
        b normalizer normalizeColor: #maxFitness.
        b build.

        legendBuilder := RTLegendBuilder new.
        legendBuilder view: b view.
        legendBuilder addText: 'Species visualization'.
        legendBuilder addText: 'Box size = Species size'.
        legendBuilder addColorFadingFrom: Color gray to: Color red text:
            'Max fitness'.
        legendBuilder build.
        ^ b view
```

This method is hooked into the GTInspector using this method:

```
NELog>>gtInspectorViewIn: composite
        <gtInspectorPresentationOrder: -10>
        composite roassal2
                title: 'View';
                initializeView: [ speciation visualize ]
```

The visualization of the species is accessible by clicking a dot within the #Species visualization that we defined earlier. When we click an individual species, the list of individuals composing the species is given:

```
NESpecies>>gtInspectorListOfIndividualIn: composite
        <gtInspectorPresentationOrder: -10>
        composite list
                title: 'Individuals';
                display: individuals
```

When selecting an individual, the neural network is visualized using this method:

```
NEIndividual>>visualize
        "Visualization of the associated neural network"
        | b legendBuilder |
        self buildNetwork.
        b := RTMondrian new.
        b shape label text: #id;
                color: Color gray;
                if: #isInput color: Color blue;
                if: #isOutput color: Color red;
                if: #isBias color: Color yellow.
        b nodes: self nodes.

        b shape line color: (Color gray alpha: 0.8).
        b edges connectToAll: #connectedNodes.
        b layout tree; ifNotConnectedThen: RTGridLayout new.

        "The line width reflects the weight of the connection"
        b normalizer
                normalizeLineWidth: [ :from :to | from
                weightOfConnectionWith:
                        to ] min: 0.5 max: 4.
        b build.
```

```
"Render a legend on demand, accessible from the ? top left icon"
legendBuilder := RTLegendBuilder new.
legendBuilder onDemand.
legendBuilder view: b view.
legendBuilder addText: 'Individual visualization'.
legendBuilder addColor: Color blue text: 'Input node'.
legendBuilder addColor: Color red text: 'Output node'.
legendBuilder addColor: Color yellow text: 'Bias node'.
legendBuilder addColor: Color gray text: 'Hidden node'.
legendBuilder build.
^ b view
```

The neural network is visualized as follows:

- Each node is represented by a number, indicating its identifier.

- Input nodes are blue numbers.

- Output nodes are red numbers.

- The bias node is yellow.

- Hidden nodes are gray.

- Connections between nodes are straight lines.

- Connection width indicates the connection weight, in which a thin line is a negative weight while a thick line is positive.

The method is hooked with GTInspector using the following:

```
NEIndividual>>gtInspectorViewIn: composite
        <gtInspectorPresentationOrder: -10>
        composite roassal2
                title: 'View';
                initializeView: [ self visualize ]
```

One could design more sophisticated visualizations, but this is a very good base to experiment with NEAT. Our implementation is now complete, and we can see the first example.

15.15 The XOR Example

In the chapter about neural networks, expressing the XOR logical gate was among the first examples we saw. We can also produce a neural network to model this logical gate using the following:

```
dataset := #( #(0 0 0) #(0 1 1) #(1 0 1) #(1 1 0) ).
```

```
neat := NEAT new.
neat numberOfInputs: 2.
neat numberOfOutputs: 1.
neat fitness: [ :ind |
            | score |
            score := 0.
            dataset do: [ :tuple |
                    diff := (ind evaluate: tuple allButLast) first - tuple
                    last.
                    score := score + (diff * diff) ].
              (score / -4) asFloat ].

        neat numberOfGenerations: 180.
        neat run.
```

First the script defines the dataset variable, which contains the behavior of the XOR gate. We use the same convention as before. The last value of each example is the expected value, while all the other values are input values.

We need a neural network with two inputs and one output to express the XOR gate. We therefore configure the NEAT algorithm accordingly.

The fitness function is expressed as a block, taking into account an individual. We compute the score of each individual by trying out each of the examples of the dataset. The score is divided by a negated value. This is important since our algorithm is only able to maximize the fitness value. If the fitness value reaches 0, then it means the evolution produced a perfect network. After the algorithm execution, we can obtain the result from the produced network using the following:

```
neat result evaluate: #(1 1).
```

This expression evaluates to #(0.007300764789699831), which is a value close to 0, which is the result of 1 XOR 1.

We next provide a number of visual interactions to explore the evolution process. The execution of this script is shown in Figure 15-1.

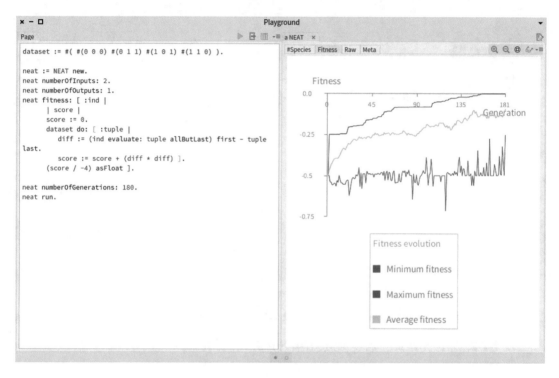

Figure 15-1. *Fitness evolution using NEAT*

The right side of the figure shows that the maximum fitness reaches 0, thus indicating that NEAT has produced a perfect neural network. The figure also shows that the average fitness is increasing, which is expected since overall, the population is getting better. The minimum fitness value is relatively low, which is also a good thing because it indicates that the population is diverse.

The #Species tab shows a representation of the number of different species during the execution, as shown in Figure 15-2.

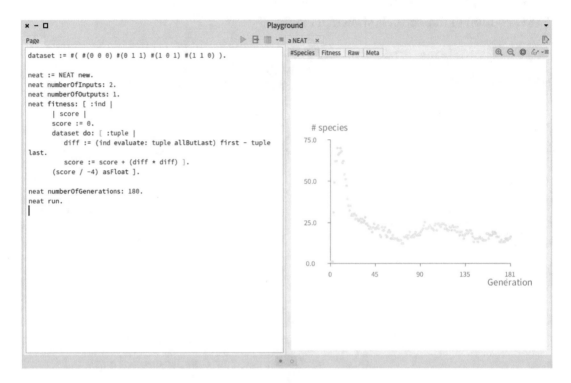

Figure 15-2. *The number of species during the evolution*

The graph indicates that the algorithm began its execution with only one species, which is not surprising since the algorithm generates connectionless individuals in the first generation, and as such, all these individuals are identical. All the individuals of the first generation belong to the same species. Quickly, we see that the number of species reaches 70, indicating that the population is getting diverse. Along the execution, the number of species falls to stay at a level of 16 different species. The right-most dot represents the population that contains the result of the algorithm. Clicking it reveals how the population is structured, as shown in Figure 15-3.

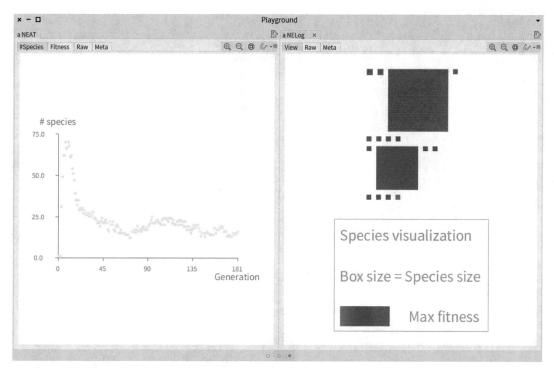

Figure 15-3. *Population structure*

Species are ordered along their maximum fitness. The species that has the maximum fitness are located in the top-left part of the figure. While the species with the lowest fitness is in the bottom right. Clicking the small top-left box reveals the individual with the best fitness, as shown in Figure 15-4.

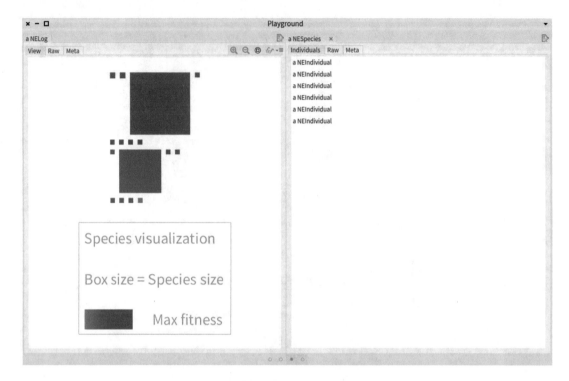

Figure 15-4. *Getting individuals from best performing species*

Clicking one individual from the list shows the visual representation of its neural network, as shown in Figure 15-5.

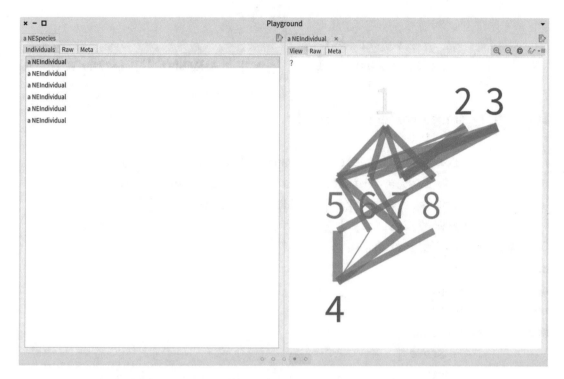

Figure 15-5. *Visualizing a neural network*

The visualization shows the input nodes in blue, the bias node in yellow, the output node in read, and the hidden nodes in gray. The width of the lines indicates the weight. A low negative weight is represented by a very thin line, while a high weight is represented as a thick line.

15.16 The Iris Example

In the chapter about neural networks, we used the Iris dataset to illustrate the backpropagation mechanism. We can easily adapt the Iris dataset script to use NEAT:

```
"We prepare the data"
irisCSV := (ZnEasy get: 'https://agileartificialintelligence.github.io/
   Datasets/iris.csv') contents.
lines := irisCSV lines.
lines := lines allButFirst.
tLines := lines collect: [ :l |
```

```
            | ss |
            ss := l substrings: ','.
             (ss allButLast collect: [ :w | w asNumber ]), (Array with: ss
                last) ].

irisData := tLines collect: [ :row |
            | l |
            row last = 'setosa' ifTrue: [ l := #( 0 ) ].
            row last = 'versicolor' ifTrue: [ l := #( 1 ) ].
            row last = 'virginica' ifTrue: [ l := #( 2 ) ].
            row allButLast, l ].
"We run the NEAT algorithm"
neat := NEAT new.
neat numberOfInputs: 4.
neat numberOfOutputs: 3.
neat fitness: [ :ind |
            | score |
            score := 0.
            irisData do: [ :tuple |
                diff := (ind predict: tuple allButLast) - tuple last.
                score := score + (diff * diff) ].
             (score / -4) asFloat ].

neat numberOfGenerations: 180.
neat run.
```

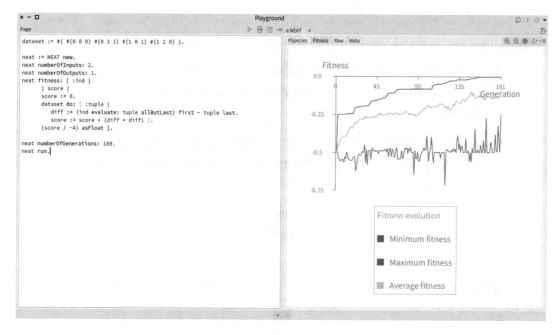

Figure 15-6. *NEAT and the Iris dataset*

The result of running the Iris example is given in Figure 15-6.

The fitness function clearly indicates that NEAT can produce, through evolution, a perfect neural network. In the chapter about neural networks, we trained the network to learn the patterns present in the dataset. Using NEAT, we evolve a network up to the point where it can correctly identify these patterns. Although the result is comparable in this case, obtaining the result is completely different—in the previous chapter we used backpropagation, whereas this chapter uses evolution.

15.17 What Have We Seen in This Chapter?

This chapter focused on the NEAT algorithm. The chapter provided a complete implementation of NEAT, which follows the original paper that describes NEAT (with some minor simplifications). The chapter covered:

- An incremental implementation of the NEAT algorithm.

- The implementation of a number of visualizations to explore the algorithm execution.

- Two small examples.

We provided a simplified version of the NEAT algorithm. In particular, for sake of keeping the chapter short, we took a number of convenient decisions:

- The activation function is not subject to the searching carried out by the genetic algorithm, i.e., our nodes only use the sigmoid function activation.

- We restrict our algorithm to increase the fitness only. One could easily adapt the implementation to offer the expressiveness we had with the genetic algorithm.

- We use a rather simple definition of species. One could easily come up with a more sophisticated definition.

Nevertheless, we provided a complete implementation of the algorithm. The next chapter implements a small Mario-like game and runs NEAT on it to produce an artificial player.

CHAPTER 16

The MiniMario Video Game

This chapter builds a small video game inspired by Nintendo's Mario Bros. Our version of the game is a simplification of the real Mario Bros game. The purpose of this chapter is to provide a solid and realistic base on which we can build an intelligent artificial player. The goal of this chapter is *not* to provide a wonderful gaming experience. Instead, the game is about providing a challenging scenario for exercising the NEAT algorithm covered in the previous chapter. Our game, which we call *MiniMario*, has the following characteristics:

- The game has one hero, *Mario*, located at the center of the screen.

- Mario can be controlled by using the keyboard or by an artificial player.

- Mario can move left, right, and jump.

- The map is composed of bricks and tubes, which Mario cannot go through.

- The map is populated by monsters and Mario must avoid them or the game ends.

- Monsters walk in one direction until they bump into a brick or a tube, in which case, the walking direction changes to the opposite.

- The goal of the game is to bring Mario to the right-most location of the map.

This game is driven by a global pulse, which we call a *beat*. A beat represents an indivisible time unit. At each beat, Mario and the monster may move by one cell. Note that for the sake of simplicity, a monster cannot jump.

© Alexandre Bergel 2020
A. Bergel, *Agile Artificial Intelligence in Pharo*, https://doi.org/10.1007/978-1-4842-5384-7_16

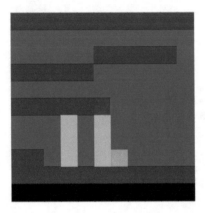

Figure 16-1. *The MiniMario game*

Figure 16-1 shows a screenshot of a game. The graphical aspect is reduced to its minimum, we simplified the goal of the game, and the physical engine is only briefly sketched. Mario is located at the center and is painted in red. Platforms are brown, the sky is blue, tubes are green, and monsters are orange. The figure shows Mario on top of a tube, next to a platform. A monster is at the bottom of the tube. The figure illustrates the drastic simplification we made to the visual aspect of the game.

16.1 Character Definition

We begin the implementation of our game by defining characters. Two kinds of characters are part of the MiniMario world: Mario and the monsters that Mario should avoid. Mario and the monsters have commonalities, expressed by the MNAbstractCharacter class:

```
Object subclass: #MNAbstractCharacter
        instanceVariableNames: 'position jumpNbSteps phase game isFalling
            isJumping'
        classVariableNames: ''
        package: 'MiniMario'
```

The MNAbstractCharacter class has the following variables:

- position refers to a point that indicates where in the map the character is located.

- jumpNbSteps counts the number of beats that occurred while the character was jumping. This is a necessary piece of information to express a jump without having a physical engine.

- phase indicates the phase of a jump. The phase can be #goingUp or #goingDown.

- game refers to the game, an instance of the MNWorld class, which we define later.

- isFalling is a boolean indicating whether the character is falling.

- isJumping is a boolean indicating whether the character is jumping.

When it's first created, a character is not jumping or falling and is set to the 0 @ 0 position. We therefore define the initialize method as follows:

MNAbstractCharacter>>initialize

```
        super initialize.
        isJumping := false.
        position := 0 @ 0.
        isFalling := true.
```

As mentioned, the MiniMario game is driven by a global beat. We define the beat method as follows:

MNAbstractCharacter>>beat

```
        "Execute a unit of behavior"
        isJumping ifTrue: [
                phase == #goingUp ifTrue: [ self translateBy: 0 @ -1 ].
                phase == #doingDown ifTrue: [ self translateBy: 0 @ 1 ].
                jumpNbSteps := jumpNbSteps + 1.
                jumpNbSteps = 5 ifTrue: [ phase := #doingDown ].
                jumpNbSteps = 10 ifTrue: [ isJumping := false ] ].

        isJumping ifFalse: [
                self isThereAPlatformBelowMe
                        ifTrue: [
                                self setAsFalling.
                                self translateBy: 0 @ 1 ]
                        ifFalse: [ self setAsNotFalling ] ].
```

The beat method executes a unit of behavior of the character. If the character is jumping, the phase indicates the direction of the vertical translation: the character goes up or down. The time of a jump is 10, and the direction changes at the fifth beat. If the character is not jumping, it is set as falling if it is not above a platform.

The isThereAPlatformBelowMe helper method is useful for checking if there is a platform below the character. This method is useful for deciding if the character must fall or not. It is defined as follows:

```
MNAbstractCharacter>>isThereAPlatformBelowMe
        "Return true if there is no platform below the character"
        ^ (game getCellAt: self position + (0 @ 1)) = 0
```

If there is no platform below the character and it is not jumping, it is marked as falling:

```
MNAbstractCharacter>>setAsFalling
        "Set the character as falling"
        isFalling := true
```

If there is a platform below the character, then it is not falling:

```
MNAbstractCharacter>>setAsNotFalling
        "Set the character as not falling"
        isFalling := false
```

A character lives in a world, which is set using the following:

```
MNAbstractCharacter>>game: aWorldGame
        "Set the world in which I live"
        game := aWorldGame
```

The action of jumping is defined using the following method:

```
MNAbstractCharacter>>jump
        "Make the character jump"
        "Do nothing if it is jumping or falling"
        isJumping ifTrue: [ ^ self ].
        isFalling ifTrue: [ ^ self ].
        isJumping := true.
        phase := #goingUp.
```

If the character is falling or already jumping, then there is nothing to do. When it's jumping, the phase is set to #goingUp and no jump step is recorded (jumpNbSteps:= 0).

We define the action of moving left as follows:

```
MNAbstractCharacter>>moveLeft
        "Make the character move left"
        self translateBy: -1 @ 0
```

Similarly, the action of moving right is defined as follows:

```
MNAbstractCharacter>>moveRight
        "Make the character move right"
        self translateBy: 1 @ 0
```

The position of the character is used by the game itself. We therefore define an accessor that will be used by the MNWorld class, which will define later:

```
MNAbstractCharacter>>position
        "Return the position of the character"
        ^ position
```

A character may be translated by a given distance, expressed as a point:

```
MNAbstractCharacter>>translateBy: aDeltaPosition
        "Translate the character by a delta, if possible"
        (self canGoToward: aDeltaPosition) ifFalse: [ ^ self ].
        position := position + aDeltaPosition
```

Note that the translation is done only if there is room in that direction.

The canGoToward: utility method is useful for checking if a character can move in a particular direction:

```
MNAbstractCharacter>>canGoToward: aDeltaPosition
        "Return true if the character can go toward a direction"
        ^ (game getCellAt: position + aDeltaPosition) = 0
```

When built, the world game sets the position of the character using the following method:

```
MNAbstractCharacter>>translateTo: aPosition
        "Set a position of the character"
        position := aPosition
```

We can now define some concrete character implementations.

16.2 Modeling Mario

We define the MNMario class as follows:

```
MNAbstractCharacter subclass: #MNMario
        instanceVariableNames: ''
        classVariableNames: ''
        package: 'MiniMario'
```

We override the beat method as follows:

```
MNMario>>beat
        super beat.
        "The game ends if Mario reaches the
        right-most position of the game"
        self position x = (game size x - 1) ifTrue: [ game gameOver ].

        "The game also ends if Mario bumps into a monster"
        game monsters do: [ :m |
                (m position = self position) ifTrue: [ game gameOver ] ]
```

There are two possible ways to end the game. Either (i) Mario reaches the right-most extremity of the map or (ii) Mario bumps into a monster. As you can see, the definition of Mario is relatively short since most of the logic is defined in MNAbstractCharacter.

16.3 Modeling an Artificial Mario Player

After defining the Mario player, which is meant to be controlled by a human, we can set up Mario to be steered by a neural network. We define the MNAIMario class as follows:

```
MNMario subclass: #MNAIMario
        instanceVariableNames: 'network'
        classVariableNames: ''
        package: 'MiniMario'
```

The unique variable defined by MNAIMario is network, which refers to a neural network, which acts as Mario's brain. This network is provided by the NEAT algorithm. The beat method should now adequately use the network:

```
MNAIMario>>beat
        | actionToPerform |
        super beat.
        actionToPerform := network predict: game whatMarioSees.
        actionToPerform = 0 ifTrue: [ self moveLeft ].
        actionToPerform = 1 ifTrue: [ self moveRight ].
        actionToPerform = 2 ifTrue: [ self jump ].
```

Mario has three possible actions: move left, move right, or jump. As such, the neural network must have three outputs. We use the predict: method seen in the previous chapter to determine the most appropriate action. The input of the network is a representation of what Mario sees.

A network may be provided to the artificial player using this:

```
MNAIMario>>network: aNeuralNetwork
        "Set the neural network meant to be used by Mario"
        network := aNeuralNetwork
```

16.4 Modeling Monsters

A monster is modeled as a character in our game. We define the MNMonster class as a subclass of MNAbstractCharacter:

```
MNAbstractCharacter subclass: #MNMonster
        instanceVariableNames: 'movingLeft pauseCounter'
        classVariableNames: ''
        package: 'MiniMario'
```

The class defines two variables:

- movingLeft indicates whether the monster moves to the left or to the right.

- pauseCounter slows down the behavior of a monster.

Based on the definition of these two variables, a monster is initialized as follows:

```
MNMonster>>initialize
        super initialize.
        movingLeft := true.
        pauseCounter := 0
```

When created, a monster moves to the left. When it bumps into a platform, then the monster turns in the opposite direction and moves to the right until it bumps into something again. This behavior is implemented in the MNMonster>>beat method:

```
MNMonster>>beat
        "A monster can go to the left or to the right"
        super beat.
        pauseCounter := pauseCounter + 1.
        pauseCounter < 10 ifTrue: [ ^ self ].
        pauseCounter := 0.

        movingLeft
                ifTrue: [ (self canGoToward: -1 @ 0) ifFalse: [
                movingLeft :=
                    false ] ]
                ifFalse: [ (self canGoToward: 1 @ 0) ifFalse: [
                movingLeft :=
                    true ] ].
        movingLeft ifTrue: [ self moveLeft ] ifFalse: [ self moveRight ].
```

We use the pauseCounter variable to slow down the execution of the monster behavior by a factor of ten. This factor helps make the MiniMario game playable by a human.

16.5 Modeling the MiniMario World

After having defined the characters, we now need to define the world. The `MNWorld` class is rather long, but it is also rather simple. We define the `MNWorld` class as follows:

```
Object subclass: #MNWorld
        instanceVariableNames: 'map mario view monsters isGameRunning
            random'
        classVariableNames: ''
        package: 'MiniMario'
```

The class defines these variables:

- `map` is a large 2D array that contains numerical values describing the map. In particular, the value 0 indicates an empty cell, 1 indicates a brick, and 2 indicates a tube.

- `mario` refers to the Mario object.

- `view` is the Roassal view in which elements will be added.

- `monsters` is the collection of monsters living in the game.

- `isGameRunning` is a boolean indicating whether the game is running or not.

- `random` is a random number generator, useful for generating the map.

The world is initialized using the following:

```
MNWorld>>initialize
        super initialize.
        self initializeMario.
        self seed: 42.
        self initializeMonsters.
        isGameRunning := true
```

The world is initialized by first initializing Mario, generating the map with the arbitrary seed of 42. Subsequently, monsters are initialized and the game is set as runnable. The map of the world is a long horizontal map, and its size is given by the following:

```
MNWorld>>size
        "Return the size of the map"
        ^ 300 @ 10
```

The size of the map is expressed in the number of cells. The random number generator is triggered with the seed: method, which is defined as follows:

```
MNWorld>>seed: aNumber
        "Create a random number generator with a particular seed"
        random := Random seed: aNumber.
        self generateMap.
```

The generateMap method generates a map for the world, as we will see later. Mario is created using the following:

```
MNWorld>>initializeMario
        "Create a Mario object"
        mario := MNMario new.
        mario translateTo: 2 @ 2.
        mario game: self.
```

The initial position of Mario is in the top-left corner, at the position 2 @ 2. The monsters are created as follows:

```
MNWorld>>initializeMonsters
        "Add a number of monsters"
        monsters := OrderedCollection new.
        10 timesRepeat: [
                | m |
                m := MNMonster new translateTo: (random nextInt:
                self size x) @ 2.
                self addMonster: m ]
```

Monsters are randomly located in the map. Mario and the monsters have an initial location with a Y component of 2. At the beginning of the game, the monsters will fall since they are initially located in the upper part of the map and the platforms are below. A monster is added to the world using the following:

```
MNWorld>>addMonster: aMonster
        "Add a monster to the world"
        monsters add: aMonster.
        aMonster game: self.
```

A brick is added to the world using this method:

```
MNWorld>>addBrick: position
        "Add a brick to a position"
        (self isInMap: position)
                ifTrue: [ self cellAt: position put: 1 ]
```

A platform is simply five bricks that are lined up. The addPlatform: method adds a platform located at a particular position to the world:

```
MNWorld>>addPlatform: position
        "A platform is horizontal and made of 5 bricks"
        -2 to: 2 do: [ :i |
            self addBrick: position + (i @ 0) ]
```

In Mario's world, bricks and tubes are the two kinds of elements that Mario cannot go through, forcing him to jump around them. We define a tube as follows:

```
MNWorld>>addTube: positionX
        "Add a tube at a given position in the map"
        | indexY |
        indexY := self size y - 1.
        3 timesRepeat: [
            self addTubeCell: positionX @ indexY.
            indexY := indexY - 1 ].
```

A tube cell is added using this method:

```
MNWorld>>addTubeCell: position
            "Add a cell representing a tube at a given position"
            (self isInMap: position)
                    ifTrue: [ self cellAt: position put: 2 ]
```

The overall map used in the world is defined using the generateMap method:

```
MNWorld>>generateMap
            "Randomly generate the map used in the world"
            map := Array2D rows: self size y columns: self size x
            element: 0.
            1 to: self size x do: [ :x | self addBrick: (x @ self size y);
                addBrick: (x @ 1) ].
            1 to: self size y do: [ :y | self addBrick: (1 @ y);
            addBrick: (
                self size x @ y) ].

            "The map has 80 platforms..."
            80 timesRepeat: [
                    self addPlatform: (random nextInt: self size x) @ (random
                        nextInt: self size y) ].

            "... and 30 tubes"
            30 timesRepeat: [ self addTube: (random nextInt: self size x) ]
```

The generateMap method relies on the random number generator. At each new generation, a new world is built. First, the map content is filled with the value 0, representing an empty cell. The map is surrounded by bricks to prevent Mario from reaching a place where the map is not defined. We then generate 80 platforms and 30 tubes. Note that this way of building a playable world is very simplistic. For example, the code does not verify whether the exit is reachable. In practice, it appears that only a few maps cannot be played until the end.

The value of a cell may be retrieved using the following method:

```
MNWorld>>getCellAt: aPoint
            "Return the value of a particular cell"
            ^ map at: aPoint y at: aPoint x
```

```
MNWorld>>cellAt: aPoint put: value
        "Set the value of a particular cell"
        ^ map at: aPoint y at: aPoint x put: value
```

This is relevant to whether a character should fall or not, depending on if it is standing on a platform. Determining whether a position is within the map is useful to prevent accessing a cell outside the map:

```
MNWorld>>isInMap: position
        "Return true if the position is within the map"
        ^ (1 @ 1 extent: self size) containsPoint: position
```

We can now focus on the logic of the game itself. The first aspect to focus on is the beat. The global beat of the game is defined as follows:

```
MNWorld>>beat
        "The world beat performs a beat on each monster and on Mario"
        isGameRunning ifFalse: [ ^ self ].
        monsters do: #beat.
        mario beat.
        self refreshView
```

The game is over if Mario reaches the right-most wall or if he bumps into a monster. The gameOver method displays a message and ends the game:

```
MNWorld>>gameOver
        "End the game"
        isGameRunning := false.
        view ifNil: [ ^ self ].
        view add: ((RTLabel new color: Color red; text: 'GAME OVER')
        element translateBy: 0 @ -100)
```

A new Mario character may be inserted in a world using the following:

```
MNWorld>>mario: aMario
        "Set Mario in the game"
        mario := aMario.
        mario game: self.
        mario translateTo: 2 @ 2
```

When added to the game, a Mario character is moved to the top-left corner of the map, at the coordinate 2@2. The Mario character is accessed from the world using this method:

```
MNWorld>>mario
            "Return the Mario character"
            ^ mario
```

As we will see, accessing Mario is useful in the fitness function, because we can obtain the position of Mario after having performed a particular number of beats.

Monsters must be accessible from the outside, because the Mario character needs to know when he bumps into a monster. Monsters are accessible using the following:

```
MNWorld>>monsters
            "Return the list of monsters living in the world"
            ^ monsters
```

This last method concludes the definition of the game model. We can now focus on the visual aspects of the game.

16.6 Building the Game's Visuals

The model of the game is now ready, and we "simply" need to hook it into Roassal to create a visual representation. The map is a long horizontal matrix containing cells. When presented to a human or an artificial player, only a small portion of the game is visible. The visible portion is a square portion of visible game cells. The size of this portion is determined by the following:

```
MNWorld>>windowSize
            "Number of pixels of a window frame side"
            ^ 11
```

As such, a square of 11 * 11 cells will be shown when playing. In total, 121 cells are visible. This number of cells is important when we tune the NEAT algorithm. The game's user interface is built using the generateUI method:

```
MNWorld>>generateUI
            "Build the game user interface"
            | e upperBounds lowerBounds cellSizeInPixel |
```

```
"Size of each cell"
cellSizeInPixel := 25.

"Create the visual representation of cells"
view := RTView new.
upperBounds := self windowSize // 2.
lowerBounds := upperBounds negated.
lowerBounds to: upperBounds do: [ :x |
lowerBounds to: upperBounds do: [ :y |
        e := RTBox new size: cellSizeInPixel + 1;
        elementOn: x @ y.
        view add: e.
        e translateTo: (x @ y) * cellSizeInPixel ] ].

"Define the actions to be taken when keys are pressed"
view when: TRKeyDown do: [ :evt |
      "Key D"
      evt keyValue = 100 ifTrue: [ mario moveRight ].

      "Key A"
      evt keyValue = 97 ifTrue: [ mario moveLeft ].

      "Key W"
      evt keyValue = 119 ifTrue: [ mario jump ] ].

"A beat is performed at each update of the UI"
view addAnimation: (RTActiveAnimation new intervalInMilliseconds:
        30; blockToExecute: [ self beat ]).
self refreshView.
```

The generateUI method begins with defining the cellSizeInPixel variable, which corresponds to the size of the visual representation of each cell. Reducing the cellSizeInPixel value has the effect of making the window smaller. A Roassal element is created for each cell of the visible map portion.

Three actions are bound to keystrokes made by pressing the D, A, and W keys. A beat of the game is performed every 30 milliseconds and is accompanied by updating the UI. The refreshView method implements this behavior:

```
MNWorld>>refreshView
            "Research the UI"
            | p t color |
            view isNil ifTrue: [ ^ self ].
            isGameRunning ifFalse: [ ^ self ].

            p := mario position.
            view elements doWithIndex: [ :e :index |
                    t := p + e model.
                    "Empty cells are blue
                    Platform cells are brown
                    Tube cells are green
                    Cells outside the map are black"
                    (self isInMap: t)
                            ifTrue: [
                                    (self getCellAt: t) = 0 ifTrue: [ color :=
                                    Color blue ].
                                    (self getCellAt: t) = 1 ifTrue: [ color :=
                                    Color brown ].
                                    (self getCellAt: t) = 2 ifTrue: [ color :=
                                    Color green ] ]
                            ifFalse: [ color := Color black ].

                "Mario is red"
                e model = (0 @ 0) ifTrue: [ color := Color red ].
                e trachelShape color: color ].

        monsters do: [ :m |
                    t := m position - p.
                    "Only monsters that are within the window frame are
                    rendered"
```

```
        t x abs < self windowSize ifTrue: [
            | cell |
            cell := view elements elementFromModel: t.
            "Monsters are orange"
            cell notNil ifTrue: [ cell trachelShape color:
            Color orange ] ].
    ].
    view signalUpdate.
```

The refreshView method defines the color encoding of the various graphical elements. The UI is open using this method:

MNWorld>>open

```
        "Open the UI"
        self inspect.
        self generateUI.
        ^ view open
```

The open method displays the UI of the game and opens an inspector on the game itself. This is convenient in order to tweak the game. The NEAT algorithm will need to provide some inputs to the neural work. These inputs correspond to the values of the visible cells. For that purpose, we define the following method:

MNWorld>>whatMarioSees

```
        "Return the values of the visible cells"
        | result p t upperBounds lowerBounds |
        result := OrderedCollection new.
        p := mario position.

        upperBounds := self windowSize // 2.
        lowerBounds := upperBounds negated.
        lowerBounds to: upperBounds do: [ :x |
            lowerBounds to: upperBounds do: [ :y |
                t := p + (x @ y).
                (self isInMap: t)
                ifTrue: [ result add: (self getCellAt: t) ]
                ifFalse: [ result add: 1 ] ] ].
        ^ result
```

The whatMarioSees method returns a collection of 0, 1, and 2, which corresponds to what Mario sees. These values will be fed into the neural network when we use NEAT.

We will now define a method to provide an overview of the game. Note that this method is not necessary to play the game or train an AI. Consider the following method:

```
MNWorld>>showCompleteMap
        "Show the complete map"
        | v cellSizeInPixel color e |
        v := RTView new.
        v @ RTDraggableView.
        cellSizeInPixel := 4.
        1 to: self size x do: [ :x |
            1 to: self size y do: [ :y |
                color := Color black.
                 (self getCellAt: x @ y) = 0 ifTrue:
                 [ color := Color blue ].
                 (self getCellAt: x @ y) = 1 ifTrue:
                 [ color := Color brown ].
                 (self getCellAt: x @ y) = 2 ifTrue:
                 [ color := Color green ].

                e := RTBox new size: cellSizeInPixel + 1;
                color: color;
                    elementOn: x @ y.
                v add: e.
                e translateTo: (x @ y) * cellSizeInPixel ] ].
        v open
```

The showCompleteMap method shows an overview of the level.

16.7 Running MiniMario

The game is now complete. A human can play it by simply executing this expression:

```
MNWorld new open
```

Mario is controlled using the A and D keys to move left and right, respectively. The W key makes Mario jump. Thanks to the way we generated the levels, you can easily create a new level using the seed: method. For example:

```
MNWorld new seed: 7; open
```

The number provided to seed: is associated with a particular level. The default map is shown using this expression:

```
MNWorld new showCompleteMap
```

When a seed is provided, the expression becomes:

```
MNWorld new seed: 7; showCompleteMap
```

The results of the two maps are shown in Figure 16-2.

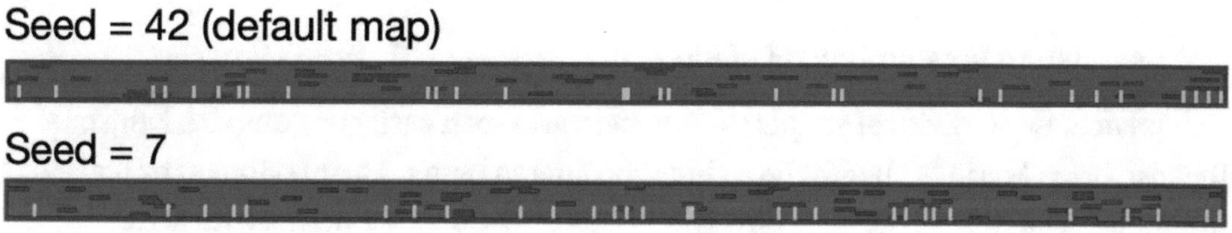

Seed = 42 (default map)

Seed = 7

Figure 16-2. *Example of generated maps for MiniMario*

16.8 NEAT and MiniMario

The UI of MiniMario is a squared portion of the map made of colored cells. As defined in the MNWorld>>windowSize method, each side of the visual frame has 11 cells. The number of displayed cells is 11 times 11, which is 121. Mario is controlled using three different commands—move left, move right, and jump. This information gives some hints to what the network should look like: 121 input neurons and three output neurons. Consider the following script:

```
neat := NEAT new.
        neat numberOfInputs: 121.
        neat numberOfOutputs: 3.
        neat populationSize: 200.

        neat fitness: [ :ind |
                w := MNWorld new.
```

```
        w mario: (MNAIMario new network: ind).
        450 timesRepeat: [ w beat. ].
        w mario position x ].

    neat numberOfGenerations: 160.
    neat run.
```

The algorithm maintains a population of 200 individuals, each representing a neural network. The fitness score is computed as the distance of Mario from the end of the level. The block provided to `fitness:` has the following sequence of instructions:

1. Create a MiniMario world.

2. Define Mario as a `MNAIMario` with the network represented by the individual.

3. Perform 450 world beats.

4. Return the x position of Mario.

As such, two individual scripts (neural networks) can easily be compared: the one that can bring Mario farther to the right is considered better. The previous script takes time: approximately 13 minutes on a Dual-Core Intel Core i5, 1.6GHz, with 8GB.

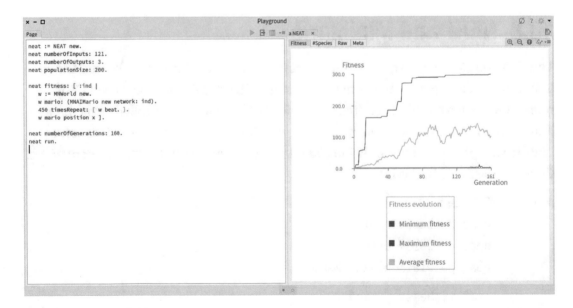

Figure 16-3. *MiniMario and NEAT*

Figure 16-3 shows the result of the evolution.

The neat result expression returns the best individual of the evolution, the one that can bring Mario farthest to the right of the map. MiniMario can be run using an artificial intelligence player, with this script:

```
...
w := MNWorld new.
w mario: (MNAIMario new network: neat result).
w open
```

As you can see, the AI we defined can lead Mario to the end of the level while avoiding the monsters. We have therefore built an artificial player!

16.9 What Have We Seen in This Chapter?

This chapter is not directly on the topic of artificial intelligence. However, it provides a small implementation of a simplified version of the famous Mario Bros game. In particular, the chapter covered:

- The design of a small game tuned to be plugged into the NEAT algorithm.

- A skeleton of an artificial player with the MNAIMario class.

- The application of NEAT on MiniMario.

NEAT can evolve a neural network to complete the MiniMario game. This therefore concludes this third and last part of the book.

AFTERWORD

Last Words

It has been a long journey through three long parts. The first part of the book presented neural networks and the way such networks can learn using backpropagation. The second part covered genetic algorithms and presented several applications of them. The third part combined the result of the first two parts to evolve neural networks. The result of this combination culminates by building an artificial player for a Mario Bros-like game.

The book provides a shallow overview of three fascinating topics. Most of the chapters could be expanded in many different ways. We truly hope the book contributed to awakening your interest in these topics. We invite you to make contributions and share them, which you can do in the following ways:

- Open an issue on the accompanying GitHub repository at `https://github.com/Apress/agile-ai-in-pharo`

- Send an email to the book's author at alexandre.bergel@me.com

- Send a tweet to `@AlexBergel`

Notifications about typos and code improvements are very welcome. If you feel the book can be improved in some way, please share your opinion.

Thank you.

© Alexandre Bergel 2020
A. Bergel, *Agile Artificial Intelligence in Pharo*, https://doi.org/10.1007/978-1-4842-5384-7

Index

© Alexandre Bergel 2020
A. Bergel, *Agile Artificial Intelligence in Pharo*, https://doi.org/10.1007/978-1-4842-5384-7

M

Z

Printed in the United States
By Bookmasters